D1124561

DATE DUE

NO 2 03			
MY - 2 '09			

DEMCO 38-296

THE UNFINISHED STRUGGLE

THE UNFINISHED STRUGGLE

Turning Points in American Labor, 1877–Present

STEVE BABSON

ROWMAN & LITTLEFIELD PUBLISHERS, INC.
Lanham • Boulder • New York • Oxford

Riverside Community College
Library
4800 Magnolia Avenue
Riverside, CA 92506

HD 8072 .B213 1999

Babson, Steve.

The unfinished struggle

ROWMAN & LITTLEFIELD PUBLISHERS, INC.

Published in the United States of America
by Rowman & Littlefield Publishers, Inc.
4720 Boston Way, Lanham, Maryland 20706
http://www.rowmanlittlefield.com

12 Hid's Copse Road
Cumnor Hill, Oxford OX2 9JJ, England

Copyright © 1999 by Rowman & Littlefield Publishers, Inc.

All rights reserved. No part of this publication may be reproduced, stored in a retrieval system, or transmitted in any form or by any means, electronic, mechanical, photocopying, recording, or otherwise, without the prior permission of the publisher.

British Library Cataloging in Publication Information Available

Library of Congress Cataloguing-in-Publication Data

Babson, Steve.
    The unfinished struggle : turning points in American labor, 1877–present / Steve Babson.
    p. cm.—(Critical issues in history)
    Includes index.
    ISBN 0-8476-8828-3 (alk. paper)
    ISBN 0-8476-8829-1 (alk. paper)
    1. Labor movement—United States—History. 2. Trade-unions—United States—History. 3. Strikes and lockouts—United States—History. 4.Labor movement—Illinois—Chicago—History. 5. Trade-unions—Illinois—Chicago—History. 6. Strikes and lockouts—Illinois—Chicago—History. I. Series.
    HD8072 .B213 1999
    331.88'0973—dc21

                                     99-35062
                                       CIP

Printed in the United States of America

∞™ The paper used in this publication meets the minimum requirements of American National Standard for Information Sciences—Permanence of Paper for Printed Library Materials, ANSI/NISO Z.39.48–1992.

Riverside Community College
Library
4800 Magnolia Avenue
Riverside, CA 92506

CONTENTS

Abbreviations   *vii*

Series Editor's Foreword   *ix*

Acknowledgments   *xi*

Introduction   *xiii*

1 The Great Uprising, 1877–1910   *1*

2 Rise and Fall, 1910–1929   *19*

3 Triumph and Containment, 1929–1941   *51*

4 Growth and Accommodation, 1941–1965   *113*

5 At the Crossroads   *155*

Suggested Reading   *179*

Notes   *183*

Index   *197*

About the Author   *205*

ABBREVIATIONS

AAFLN	American Association of Foreign Language Newspapers
ACW	Amalgamated Clothing Workers
AFL	American Federation of Labor
AFSCME	American Federation of State, County, and Municipal Employees
AIU	American Industrial Union
ALA	Alliance for Labor Action
ARU	American Railway Union
BSCP	Brotherhood of Sleeping Car Porters
CIO	Committee for Industrial Organization
CIO	Congress of Industrial Organizations
CP	Communist Party
ERP	Employee Representation Plan
FAA	Federal Aviation Administration
FAA	Foreman's Association of America
FTA	Food, Tobacco, and Agricultural Workers
HRE	Hotel and Restaurant Employees
HSM	Hart, Schaffner & Marx
HUAC	House Un-American Activities Committee
ILGWU	International Ladies Garment Workers Union
IUAW	Independent Union of All Workers
IUE	International Union of Electrical Workers
IWW	Industrial Workers of the World
KKK	Ku Klux Klan
LMRA	Labor Management Relations Act
LNPL	Labor's Non-Partisan League
MESA	Mechanics Educational Society of America

NAACP	National Association for the Advancement of Colored People
NCF	National Civic Federation
NLB	National Labor Board
NLRA	National Labor Relations Act
NLRB	National Labor Relations Board
NRA	National (Industrial) Recovery Act
NRA	National Recovery Administration
NWLB	National War Labor Board
PAC	Political Action Committee (CIO)
PATCO	Professional Air Traffic Controllers Organization
PWOC	Packinghouse Workers Organizing Committee
SEIU	Service Employees International Union
SP	Socialist Party
STFU	Southern Tenant Farmers' Union
SWOC	Steel Workers Organizing Committee
UAW	United Auto Workers
UE	United Electrical Workers
ULP	Unfair Labor Practice
UMW	United Mine Workers
UNITE	Union of Needletrades, Industrial and Textile Employees
UPW	United Packinghouse Workers
URW	United Rubber Workers
USW	United Steel Workers
UTW	United Textile Workers
WEB	Women's Emergency Brigade
WTUL	Women's Trade Union League

SERIES EDITOR'S FOREWORD

The rise of organized labor in the United States in the twentieth century, with the formation of the Congress of Industrial Organization (CIO) in the 1930s and its later reunification with the American Federation of Labor (AFL) in the aftermath of the Second World War, presents one of the most dramatic episodes in modern American history. The emergence of a powerful labor movement changed industrial relations, reconfigured political alignments, and contributed to higher wages and better working conditions for American workers. Moreover, organized labor contributed to the integration of women and African-Americans into the workplace. At the same time, organized labor played an important role in progressive social movements, including the struggle for civil rights in the 1960s.

Organized labor formed through the struggles of common men and women who, in seeking their rights for collective bargaining and a place on the shop floor, often confronted hostile management and state authorities. At the same time, however, unusual social and political conditions created by war and depression accelerated the growth of unions and encouraged public authorities to pursue policies favoring unionization. Thus, the American Federation of Labor grew dramatically during World War I when the Wilson administration implemented pro-union policies to facilitate wartime production. Similarly, the Roosevelt administration in the depression decade of the 1930s supported legislation favorable to union organization. And during World War II union membership experienced rapid expansion.

Yet these advances came with setbacks. Following World War I, organized labor experienced a decline in membership during the 1920s, a decade in which unions faced the challenge of the Red Scare, management's anti-union call for an American Plan, and violent labor strikes in steel, coal, waterfront, and other industries. In the 1930s, the struggle to organize the CIO led to long and violent strikes in most of the nation's major industries, as well as in agriculture. The immediate aftermath of World War II brought renewed conflict as labor sought to reassert its power on the shop floor and in strategic management of industry. In these same years, organized labor experienced bitter ideological divisions between communists and noncommunists, as well as a divided movement created by the earlier split between the AFL and the CIO. The later reunification of these two organizations into the AFL-CIO did little to temper the gradual erosion of union membership in subsequent decades.

Steve Babson provides a vivid account of the ebb and flow of organized labor in the twentieth century. Although judicious in his approach, he remains sensitive to the position of labor and its struggle to gain recognition from management and the state. His account places the labor movement within a larger political and social context, but in doing so he emphasizes the importance of race, ethnicity, and gender in understanding the history of modern labor. As a result, this short history offers to its readers a richly textured narrative that integrates the latest scholarship in labor and social history.

Donald Critchlow
Series Editor

ACKNOWLEDGMENTS

A mong the individuals who supported my work on this book, I owe special thanks to Robert Zieger, whose recommendation brought the project my way, and to the people who read all or parts of the manuscript: Nancy Brigham, Robert Hullot-Kentor, Nelson Lichtenstein, and especially David Riddle, whose careful reading and critical comments were much appreciated. The staff at the Labor Studies Center at Wayne State University—Hal Stack, Geri Hill, Michelle Fecteau, Dave Reynolds, Loraine Alexander, and Onzell Patty—were equal parts forgiving and supportive of my endless fiddling with the manuscript. Their support has made this a better book, but in no way makes them liable for its flaws.

INTRODUCTION

The modern history of the labor movement holds many attractions for contemporary readers. At its best, it is the story of how steelworkers, garment makers, air traffic controllers, and janitors have collectively made history by putting people before profits. It is the story of how union wages and benefits dramatically widened access to the middle class and helped establish the basis for the broader prosperity that followed the Great Depression. It is also the story of how organizing for "worker solidarity" has often put unions at the forefront in opposing racial, ethnic, and gender discrimination. Even when the labor movement has failed this high calling, the history of that failing shines a unique light on the fault lines that divide our society. It is a dramatic story peopled by the everyday actors who join and lead unions.

A brief history of this movement may nevertheless provoke two dissenting responses. For those with little previous knowledge of organized labor, the history of this now declining movement may seem irrelevant. For those, on the other hand, who know that history in any detail, a "brief" recapitulation may seem impossible.

For readers who hold that unions are obsolete and destined for irrelevance, it is worth recalling a similar prophesy by George Barnett, past president of the American Economics Association. In an especially pessimistic speech, Barnett once described the many reasons for predicting the imminent demise of organized labor, citing unfavorable laws, the rising power of large corporations, and technological and occupational changes that undermined union organization. "It is hazardous to prophesy," Barnett concluded regretfully, since he counted himself a friend of labor, "but I see no reason to believe that American trade unionism will so revolutionize itself within a short period of time as to become in the next decade a more potent social influence than it has been in the past decade."[1] When students in my classes at Wayne State University's Labor Studies Center are shown these words out of context, they assume Barnett is speaking of today, and many find themselves agreeing (also regretfully) with his sober assessment. They are therefore startled to learn that Barnett was speaking in 1932—on the eve of the labor movement's dramatic recovery from near extinction. In the decade that followed, the labor movement did, indeed, "revolutionize itself," adopting new strategies and organizational forms as it grew exponentially.

It may be, as at least one student has speculated, that Barnett was simply ahead of his time, that the litany he cited in 1932—large corporations, hostile laws, technological and occupational change—will now finally overwhelm the labor movement. Perhaps so, but it is no less "hazardous to prophesy" this outcome today than it was in Barnett's time. Conversely, it is just as hazardous to predict a repeat of the stunning turnaround in labor's fortunes that occurred in the 1930s.

What can be said is that there is ample reason to pause before reading last rites over a movement that is still rather young by historical standards. After all, the modern labor movement took form in reaction to the unwanted state of dependency that industrial capitalism forced upon workers, and that state of dependency remains with us. The vast majority of people are still compelled by their relative lack of wealth to work for a wage or salary, and usually not under terms of their choosing. When this fundamental dependency compels them to work for corporate and government bureaucracies that dwarf the individual, then collective action—in some form—suggests itself as the means for securing individual prosperity on a socially equitable basis. Union activists have raised this call for workplace justice in many voices throughout the twentieth century, some by urging workmates to defend craft norms or adopt socialist politics, others (and over time the larger number) by their advocacy of collective bargaining and a reformed "moral capitalism." Their success in winning a wider following has ebbed and flowed, but even when the relative number of union members is small, they speak to issues that loom large.

One such issue, of special urgency at the start of the new millennium, concerns the global economy and the accelerating mobility of capital. Multinational corporations can now roam the world, abandoning old production centers and tapping new labor markets where desperate job-seekers are compelled to work for poverty wages. From a historical perspective, even this is not a disjuncture with our past, but another turning point on a familiar road. The constant theme in our nation's history has been the widening reach of market-driven capitalism, growing from subsistence farming and petty trading, to a national market linked by railroads and telegraph, to a world market linked by jumbo jets and satellites. With each outward jump in the size of the market, the conditions of work have been transformed. These workplace transformations—the rise of heavy industry in the late nineteenth century, the adoption of management-centered control in the early twentieth, the internationalization of production in our day—are turning points on an epochal scale. The turning points for labor that are the focus of this book occur against the backdrop of these momentous changes in the organization of work.

Workers have often benefited by the relentless widening of the market, but not without contesting the conditions of their labor and the distribution of its fruits. As the scale and scope of capitalist enterprise has grown, drawing in ever more varied people and regions, so has the labor movement been compelled to find more inclusive forms of organization, widening its mandate to include black and white, women and men, foreign- and native-born, skilled and less skilled. The current challenge is perhaps the most daunting—to find the basis for an international and multicultural unionism that can match the global stride of transnational corporations.

For those already persuaded that this story is important, the question isn't whether it is worth telling, but whether it can be told in so few pages. It is a pertinent question, for the necessity to compress and simplify does, in fact, threaten to reduce the story to a bland distillate of generalizations, drained of the ambiguity and contested evidence that make up the historical record. "It seemed a little too pat," as Raymond Chandler's fictional detective, Philip Marlowe, says of the evidence in *The Big Sleep.* "It had the austere simplicity of fiction rather than the tangled woof of fact." The danger is that Marlowe's words could apply to this slender book.

I have tried to retain something of the "tangled woof of fact" by focusing on turning points in labor's history. Some of the choices are obvious: the Great Strike of 1877 as the starting point of the modern labor movement; the Flint sit-down of 1937 as the seminal victory of a rising social movement; the defeat of PATCO in 1981 as that same movement's symbolic downfall. Each of these cases caused or marked an identifiable quickening in the pace of change, and contemporaries recognized them as obvious "turning points" in their day. Other, equally obvious turning points were external to the labor relations system—the 1929 market crash, or Pearl Harbor—but immediately changed the workplace terrain in which owners and workers defined themselves.

Focusing on "turning points" is a common enough device, each event providing an opportunity for closer examination of cause and consequence, while each in succession drives the narrative forward. When so much ground is to be covered in so few pages, two problems become especially acute: how to decide which "turning points" (beyond the obvious ones) deserve attention, and how to link them in a narrative that isn't simply a list of disconnected events. The choice of turning points is especially vexing. Readers familiar with the historiography of labor will recognize the many occasions where I have relied on the work of others to guide my choice and provide the evidence, and these debts are acknowledged in this book's notes and list of suggested readings. Most of these historians would agree, for example, that among the key turning points that defined the "New Unionism" of 1910–1922, the Lawrence Textile strike of 1912 and the steel strike of 1919 were seminal—the first demonstrating the potential of a broad-based multiethnic movement of industrial workers in the years before World War I, the second demonstrating the limits of that potential in the post-war era. In some cases, however, I have made choices where narrative continuity, rather than historical consensus, was my guide. In 1910, following mass strikes in New York City and Chicago, garment unions and employers agreed to a new system of grievance arbitration for the settlement of disputes, making both strikes a turning point for the "New Unionism" in the needle trades. I chose to focus on Chicago rather than New York because the former marked the arrival of Sidney Hillman and the Amalgamated Clothing Workers on the historical stage, and because Hillman and the ACW were later so prominent in the history of the 1930s and 1940s.

The narrative that links these turning points is asymmetrical in its organization, with the entire middle chapter devoted to the 1930s and the remaining four chapters covering all else between 1877 and 2000. In a book devoted to the modern history of organized labor, the focus on the 1930s is justified in part by the simple fact that the modern labor movement came into its own during that tumultuous decade. It could even be argued that the history of these years is sufficiently compelling that a book of this length should focus solely on the depression-era origins of the labor movement. Even if that prescription were followed, however, such a history would have to specify the "before" and "after" of this formative decade, since both the New Deal state and the Congress of Industrial Organizations had antecedents in the years preceding and antagonists in the years that followed. The present volume traces these on a telescopic scale.

Although it is never easy capturing this complex story in a few pages, it becomes especially difficult the closer the narrative comes to the present, and for the simplest of reasons. The present, after all, is unfinished business, its turning points incomplete or unconfirmed. It will be left to readers in the twenty-first century to determine which of these herald labor's demise or resurgence.

1

THE GREAT UPRISING, 1877–1910

Shortly after five o'clock in the afternoon of July 21, 1877, the First Division of Pennsylvania's National Guard opened fire on a crowd of strike supporters in Pittsburgh. Five minutes later, with the order to cease fire, the soldiers could see the ground before them littered with casualties, including three children among the twenty or so killed outright and the thirty or more wounded in the deadly fusillade.

In these few minutes of fatal violence the United States was crossing a threshold from one historical era to another. The headlines in the *Pittsburgh Sunday Globe* expressed the judgment of many that with this "Slaughter of the Innocents," the "Lexington of the Labor Conflict [is] at Hand."[1] The heated words did not exaggerate by much: the death toll in July 1877 would be higher than the original battle of Lexington, and the issues at stake would be contested for the next century and more.

In preceding decades, the nation had debated the issues of slavery and state's rights and then fought a bloody civil war to settle the matter. Half the men in Pennsylvania's First Division were veterans of that war, as were many in the crowd. Some had probably later served in the occupying army that protected the newly freed slaves in the South during the federal government's "Reconstruction" of the former rebel states. But the federal government had withdrawn its troops from the South and abandoned the

Freemen to the Ku Klux Klan just the year before the events in Pittsburgh. Now a new enemy haunted the imagination of editorial writers and elite opinion. In the fifth year of an economic depression that had driven millions of people to the edge of starvation, prompting bitter protests and violent countermeasures, it was the growing prominence and aggressive demeanor of "the laboring classes" that demanded attention. Their numbers had grown so dramatically and so recently with the expansion of American industry, and their poverty now so mocked the claims of America the bountiful, that workers—particularly the unemployed, "tramps," and strikers among them—had lately become the topic of worried speculation in board rooms and legislative chambers. A huge population of wage earners who owned no significant property and were dependent for their livelihood on capital—and worse still, were embittered by their dependence—did not fit the comforting agrarian vision of the independent yeoman farmer, long honored as the foundation of the young republic.

The Pittsburgh shootings and the events that followed made the specter of this nonconformist working class the new focal point of national concern. At the White Sulphur Springs resort in nearby West Virginia where Pittsburgh's elite summered, "congressmen, judges, merchants, farmers and all classes representing wealth and intelligence" discussed, according to the *Wheeling Intelligencer,* "the frightful condition of affairs" heralded by Pittsburgh, their concerns spoken "in bated breath and with serious aspect."[2] *The Nation,* a leading pro-business magazine, warned that "the time has never been more propitious for a rising of the worst elements."[3]

And rise they did, on a scale that would mark 1877 as the headwaters of the modern American labor movement. In Pittsburgh, crowds enraged by the shootings of July 21 fought the First Division's troops in a twenty-four-hour battle that killed twenty more townsmen and five soldiers before the guardsmen were driven from the city. Massive crowds then looted the freight yard and burned more than a thousand rail cars. In the next week, this "general insurrection," as Pennsylvania's governor described it in his plea for federal troops, rippled across the United States, overwhelming state militias and local police as it grew to a general strike of all industries in cities like Scranton, Pennsylvania; Toledo, Ohio; and St. Louis, Missouri. In Chicago, crowds of workers marched through industrial neighborhoods, shutting down factories and calling for an end to low wages and harsh conditions. When Chicago's mayor ordered his police to fire into these crowds, fighting erupted across the city, leaving more than thirty dead. Eleven states called out the militia to suppress the movement, mustering an estimated forty-five thousand soldiers. Many of these local troops proved to be unreliable, with soldiers deserting, stacking their rifles, or joining the crowds. Pittsburgh was "retaken" on July 29 by a federal force of three thousand soldiers, who met no armed resistance. Federal troops, some of them recalled from the Indian wars on the Great Plains, occupied Chicago, St. Louis, Baltimore, and other cities, ending the strikes and, with them, what contemporaries called the "Great Uprising." The final death toll exceeded one hundred, with many more injured.

"Capitalists may stuff cotton in their ears," the *Washington Capital* editorialized at the end of the uprising, "the subsidized press may write with apparent indifference, as boys whistle when passing a graveyard, but those who understand the forces at work in society know already that America will never be the same again."[4]

In the wake of the Great Uprising, the modern American labor movement took first form. Within ten years, workers had initiated the first Labor Day marches (begun in the 1880s and made a federal holiday in 1894), and the first May Day strikes (begun in 1886 to demand the eight-hour day, and subsequently marked as an international holiday to honor that strike's executed leaders in Chicago). The first truly national labor organization, the Knights of Labor, announced its presence the year following the 1877 strikes and grew to seven hundred thousand members by 1886, dwarfing the previous stillborn efforts to build a national movement. When the Knights began to falter, many union activists switched to the American Federation of Labor, founded in 1886. Fifty years later when the AFL faltered, it was the United Mine Workers—a union that traced its origins to the Knights of Labor and the years immediately following the 1877 rising—that formed the nucleus of the Congress of Industrial Organizations, founded in 1935.

The year 1877 marked the emphatic start of another, parallel trend that continued well into the twentieth century: the use of deadly force to suppress strikes and defeat union organization. Over the next sixty years, an estimated six hundred people would die in strike-related violence, roughly 550 of them killed by the police, National Guard, U.S. Army, or private guards. The death toll would become more lopsided decade by decade:

- In 1886, Chicago police fired on crowds supporting the eight-hour strike movement, killing two and wounding many more on May 3. The following evening, when police attempted to break up a protest rally at the city's Haymarket, a bomb thrown in vengeance (or by a rogue police agent, as many strikers argued) killed police and demonstrators and led to the hanging of four labor leaders. Among them was the printer and 1877 strike leader Albert Parsons—absent at the Haymarket, as the prosecution acknowledged in his case and others, but executed nonetheless for making "inflammatory" speeches.

- In 1892, the National Guard returned to Pittsburgh, this time to assist in breaking the strike at the Carnegie Steel works in Homestead, where strikers had previously repelled an assault by three hundred armed Pinkerton agents. At least nine people had died in that daylong battle, three of them Pinkertons. The strikers surrendered to the eight thousand troops who occupied the town.
- In 1914, striking coal miners and their families, having been evicted from the company housing owned by John D. Rockefeller's Colorado Coal and Iron Company, were attacked in their tent colony in Ludlow, Colorado, by the National Guard. Gunfire killed three workers, and eleven children and two women burned to death after guardsmen torched their tents.
- In 1937, Chicago's police returned to the headlines when they fired point-blank on striking steelworkers and their families during a peaceful Memorial Day picnic and rally, killing ten.

These and other episodes of fatal violence were the foreground events on a historical stage dominated by industrial revolution, boom and bust growth, world war, and fitful efforts at social and workplace reform. Over time, living standards would improve and the labor movement would grow, but not in evolutionary progression so much as spasmodic rounds of growth, decline, and renewed growth—with each ebb and flow marked by distinct turning points.

CAPITAL

The steelworkers of south Chicago faced the same adversary in 1937 as the strikers of 1877: the extraordinary and growing power of corporate capital. Nothing symbolized the arrival of this catalyzing force more powerfully than the sudden rise of the railroad corporation.

Corporations first grew to power in railroading for reasons well suited to their unique structure. Starting a railroad demanded more capital than a single proprietor could muster or borrow, and the corporation's "limited liability" spread the risk among hundreds or thousands of investors. Even so, railroad construction was so expensive and their operation so vulnerable (to accidents, cutthroat competition, and stock swindles) that it took massive public subsidies—land grants, loans, and tax breaks—to launch the railroad boom. In 1847, the national rail system had totaled less than six thousand miles, most of it concentrated near the Atlantic seaboard; thirty years later when the Great Uprising spread throughout the national rail system, mileage totaled nearly eighty thousand and stretched from New York to San Francisco. By 1907, railroad mileage topped 230 thousand.

This transcontinental network created a truly national market for the first time in American history, stretching from the Atlantic Ocean to the Pacific. The "Industrial Revolution" accelerated accordingly, spurred by the railroad industry's voracious appetite for steel, iron, coal, and lumber, and by the economies of scale that followed a widening market. Previously, large-scale manufacturers—meaning in 1850 rarely more than three hundred workers in the largest enterprises—were limited to a few eastern towns and the textile mills of New England; most artisans and small workshops served local markets within horse-and-wagon range. With the coming of the railroad, companies could now sell their products in distant markets and build ever-larger factories to supply this augmented demand. By 1900, America's largest factories each employed many thousands of workers, and their expanding productive power made the United States the world's leading industrial economy.

On this enlarged stage appeared the new leading actors of the industrial revolution: corporate capital, in varied costume as Robber Baron, philanthropist, and modernizing reformer; and labor, costumed in even greater variety according to skill, gender, race, ethnicity, and political ideology. The conflicts as well as the alliances between these diverse protagonists would define the modern labor movement.

At issue were sharply contrasting claims about who reaped the benefits of America's rapid industrialization, and who paid the costs. "*We* have made the country rich, *we* have developed the country,"[5] boasted railroad speculator Jay Gould during congressional hearings into business practices that brought him profits of $10 million in 1890. At a time when railroad workers averaged $560 a year and the average annual wage in manufacturing was only $439, the huge fortunes accumulated by Gould and others provoked bitter debate. "The officials can build palaces, the laborer can rent a hovel," observed *The Pittsburgh Critic* in 1877. "These railroad authorities can afford salaries that will secure the costliest luxuries but cannot grant enough to the beggared, starving, crushed laborer and his family to meet the commonest necessities of life."[6]

By the turn of the nineteenth century, even Gould's lavish income looked paltry compared with the fortunes amassed by John D. Rockefeller in oil, Andrew Carnegie in steel, and J. P. Morgan in finance. In 1899, Rockefeller's Standard Oil Company topped $45 million in profits; two years later, when Carnegie sold his industrial empire to Morgan's United States Steel, the sale netted him the unheard of sum of $300 million—the equivalent of $5 billion measured in the value of the dollar a hundred years later. The organization that emerged from this merger was equally unprecedented: capitalized at $1.3 billion, U.S. Steel controlled nearly two-thirds of the nation's steel industry and employed 168,000 workers. By 1904, as similar mergers consolidated corporate empires in other industries, the top 4 percent of American companies produced 57 percent of total industrial output.

Business leaders had little trouble justifying this enormous concentration of wealth and power. For those who had fought their way to the top from humble backgrounds, success marked a kind of rough justice, "the survival of the fittest." Academic theorists reinforced these self-congratulatory claims by drawing on Charles Darwin, whose book *Origin of Species* theorized that natural selection favored the evolution of those individual organisms most suited to survival in a harsh and unforgiving nature. "Social Darwinists" like Yale professor William Graham Sumner simply transposed this idea to economic life and broadcast it as scientific fact. "Millionaires are the product of natural selection," Sumner argued. "They may fairly be regarded as the naturally selected agents of society for certain work."[7] It mattered little to many of these millionaires that they owed at least a portion of their wealth to "selection" by their government allies—for protective tariffs, contracts, loans, land grants, and the frequent use of the National Guard (twenty-three times in 1892 alone) to break strikes and uphold the law. The "scientific" dazzle of Social Darwinism appeared plausible to many, particularly in the early decades of industrialization when technological change and rapid growth opened opportunities for men like Jay Gould (born to a farm family) or Andrew Carnegie (son of Scottish weavers) who were reared in poverty to acquire property and launch new companies. But these avenues of upward mobility narrowed over time as trusts and large corporations seized the economic heights, and by 1900 the ruling elite drew most of its members from the same narrow stratum. A study of two hundred leaders of the largest corporations in the early twentieth century found that 95 percent came from families of upper- or middle-class status, whereas no more than 3 percent came from immigrant or farm backgrounds. Even in a fast-growing city like Detroit, fewer than 20 percent of the city's top 115 industrialists at the turn of the century came from poor families, and fewer than 4 percent rose through the ranks. All 115 were white men, 85 percent of them sharing the same Anglo-Saxon heritage and Protestant religion (primarily Episcopalians, Presbyterians, and Congregationalists). Only 11 percent were Catholic, and 3 percent were Jewish.

Inherited or otherwise, the rich man's wealth manifested neither luck nor greed, but divine selection according to men like Rockefeller. "The power to make money is a gift of God," he once sermonized. "Having been endowed with the gift I possess, I believe it is my duty to make money and still more money."[8] George Baer, president of the Philadelphia and Reading Coal and Iron Company, elevated this claim to an assertion of "divine right" previously reserved for kings. "The rights and interests of the laboring man," Baer wrote in 1902, "will be protected and cared for by the Christian men to whom God has given control of the property rights of the country."[9] This patronizing claim justified two alternative responses to the widening gap between rich and poor. On the one hand, men like Andrew Carnegie spent considerable sums building libraries and sponsoring other acts of public charity to demonstrate that the rich philanthropist was the trustee of his "poorer brethren," as Carnegie put it, "bringing to their service his superior wisdom, experience, and ability to administer."[10] So long as the poor devoted themselves to individual self-improvement, they were deemed worthy charges by their wealthy "trustees." But for those who questioned "the laws of nature" and divine right, the judgment was harsh and the penalties severe. "No man in this land suffers from poverty," preached Henry Ward Beecher, pastor of Brooklyn's fashionable Plymouth Congregational Church, "unless it be more than his fault—unless it be his *sin*."[11] And sinners invited the wrath of God, no less, when they combined together in unholy protest. "Laborers' unions," Beecher sermonized in 1877, "are the worst form of despotism and tyranny in the history of Christendom!"[12]

Men who could so readily divide the world into extremes of "good" and "evil," placing themselves at the head of "Christendom" and dismissing their opponents as "sinners," were men who could readily justify the violence so frequently visited on workers. More so than their counterparts in Europe, America's business class possessed this unique certainty of mission, born in part of religious conviction, and in part of the open terrain in which they worked, relatively unimpeded by such "European" restraints as a landed aristocracy or a state-supported religion. America's business leaders had no need to compromise their acquisitive agenda or share power with titled nobles and mitered churchmen. Inspired, in some cases, to acts of Christian charity on behalf of their employees, they could also turn on the rebellious worker and invoke God's will in suppressing their unions. Particularly when the "lower orders" were doubly stigmatized for their immigrant status, their foreign speech, or their nonwhite skin, as they more often were in the United States, it became all the easier for the likes of New York socialite Edith Abbott to stereotype such "aliens" in 1905 as "a dangerous class: inadequately fed, clothed, and housed, they threaten the health of the community, and, like all the weak and the ignorant, they often become the misguided followers of unscrupulous men."[13]

Ever vigilant against the "unscrupulous men" who urged workers to collective action, America's corporate leaders waged a multifaceted campaign against union organization, either with ameliorative measures designed to pacify the discontented, or with violent suppression when all else failed. In this the United States differed by degree from Europe. There, class conflict was more politicized and the related violence more compressed into peaks of revolutionary (or counterrevolutionary) conflict. In the United States, "class war" centered less often on struggles for political power, and more often on workplace confrontations over something most of Europe's industrial societies would eventually take for granted—the very right of the union to exist.

LABOR

Workers could borrow from the same religious idiom as their employers to describe their place in the new industrial order, but many drew very different conclusions from their reading of scripture. "Every blow organized labor strikes for the emancipation of labor has the endorsement of Christ," declared Eugene Debs in 1893, the year he helped found the American Railway Union (ARU). "It is, reverently speaking, an alliance with Christ to oppose pomp and splendor."[14]

A year later, Debs was under arrest and the ARU destroyed after federal troops broke yet another national railroad strike. Once again, strikebreaking was backed by public authority, this time with the direct intervention of the U.S. attorney general—himself a corporate attorney and a director of several railroads. At the conflict's focal point in Chicago, a total of fourteen thousand U.S. soldiers and Illinois National Guardsmen forcibly reopened the lines, killing more than thirty Chicagoans in strike-related confrontations. The union's offices were ransacked by federal marshals and more than seven hundred union leaders placed under arrest. The American Railway Union never recovered.

Nevertheless, in this sharp encounter with the combined power of railroad capital and the state, the union had articulated something unique in the emerging culture of the labor movement: an all-encompassing concept of "solidarity" that defined an injury to any one worker as an injury to all workers. In fact, the 1894 strike was not called to protest the condition of railroad workers in that depression year, bad as these were. Instead, the ARU struck in support of workers in the model town that George Pullman had built around his factories in south suburban Chicago. The fleet of railroad sleeping cars manufactured by his company operated on virtually every rail line in the country, and with this growing business, Pullman had expanded his factory village to include employee housing, a library, churches, and utilities, all built at the company's initiative. This paternalistic arrangement had turned sour in the 1893 depression when Pullman began cutting wages by 30 percent and more, while still deducting from pay the same charges for rent and utilities. When Pullman summarily fired the three worker delegates sent to protest these conditions, the factory's five thousand workers went on strike and appealed to the ARU for a boycott of Pullman's owned-and-operated sleepers. Railroad workers responded in twenty-seven states, adding their own grievances to the widening dispute.

Debs called their solidarity the "Christ-like virtue of sympathy," a "fellow-feeling for the woes of others. . . [that] should be accepted as at once the hope of civilization."[15] Such "fellow feeling" grew out of the shared experiences of workers whose skills and physical force drove the industrial revolution forward, but whose hardest exertions still left them precariously perched between opportunity and disaster. Particularly in the recurrent depressions that plagued the economy in the 1870s and 1890s, when employers cut wages and unemployment soared to 20 percent or more, their common misery contrasted sharply with the extraordinary wealth of the new rich. In the recoveries that followed each down-turn, wages would creep back upward, but so too would mandatory work hours and injuries. Mechanization of production, rather than liberating labor from toil, had dramatically increased work hours as the economy shifted from agriculture to industry. Where the average farm laborer in medieval Europe had worked fewer than seventeen hundred hours a year, with hard labor frequently punctuated by festivals and sharply curtailed in winter, the average wage earner in American manufacturing worked more than twenty-eight hundred hours in 1901, when the ten-hour day and the six-day workweek were common. Workplace injuries and illnesses shadowed the life of every worker, particularly in mechanical industries where equipment was poorly guarded and safety procedures virtually nonexistent. In railroading alone, 2,451 workers died in collisions, derailments, falls, and shop accidents in the single year 1890; casualties mounted thereafter to a peak of 4,534 railroad workers killed in 1907, and averaged more than two hundred fatalities a month during these decades.

Life off the job could be nearly as dangerous. Industrial cities on the East Coast and throughout the Midwest saw urban growth race ahead of available housing, sewer capacity, and water supply, spawning some of the worst slums in the world. A report on New York tenement housing in 1903 described "foul cellars full of rubbish; . . . rooms so dark that one cannot see the people in them; cellars occupied as sleeping places; . . . pigs, goats, horses, and other animals kept in cellars; dangerous old fire-traps without fire escapes; . . . buildings without adequate water supply—the list might be added to almost indefinitely."[16] Outbreaks of diphtheria, scarlet fever, and other infectious diseases continued into the twentieth century, and although efforts to improve public health made headway, national life expectancy actually declined from fifty-two years in 1902 to fifty-one in 1917 as immigrant workers and internal migrants poured into city slums.

Individual striving was highly regarded by workers migrating to America's cities and mill towns, and opportunities to escape the long hours and uncertain rewards of wage work were eagerly seized. But "rags to riches" mobility was far less common than the geographic mobility that took "tramping" workers from one city to the next in search of work. The disabled railroader might be able to open a saloon next to the freight yards, the production worker might become a skilled tradesman in a metalworking shop, the skilled tailor might become a small contractor making clothing for wholesalers or department stores. Yet even these occupational advances left small proprietors and tradesmen within a working-class universe still dominated by insecurity and inequality. In this context, as employers organized themselves into ever-larger combinations of capital, and as many workers lost hope that their individual bargaining could improve their wages or job security, the appeal of collective action gained wider currency. "Each for himself is the bosses plea," as a parade banner of the barrel makers' union expressed it in 1880. "Union for all will make you free."

In America's cities and towns, in mining communities and lumber camps, a subculture of working class opposition was emerging in the closing decades of the nineteenth century and the opening of the twentieth. While Social Darwinists claimed scientific justification for inequality as part of "natural selection," this subculture proclaimed the transforming virtues of solidarity—captured in an 1886 Labor Day banner "Divided we can beg, united we can demand." While employers claimed the divine sanction of God almighty, some workers claimed the spirit of Jesus Christ—"a carpenter and a man of poverty." While employers invoked property rights, workers invoked the Bill of Rights, or more daring still, proclaimed the right of workers to collectively own the full fruit of their labor.

This oppositional subculture gave many worker protests an evangelical spirit, characterized by the emotional fusing of workplace and community solidarities against the prevailing culture of acquisitive individualism. The augmented solidarity and fellow feeling that flowed from these emotional bonds stimulated collective action at least as powerfully as the more rational calculation of low wages and long hours. In an industry like garment making, where immigrant workers sewed apparel in their own crowded apartments, or in nearby tenement sweatshops, or in factories never far removed from the immigrant ghetto, this merging of worker protest with ethnic and religious solidarities was especially evident. Beset by low wages, overwork, fourteen-hour days, and foremen who extracted fines and submission from their predominantly Russian-Jewish workforce, garment makers erupted in annual protests that galvanized the entire community. Lacking formal union organization, workers relied on the resources of the surrounding ghetto, with small synagogues serving as union halls and neighborhood parades serving as picket lines. Such protests were "organized with the fervor of religious fanaticism," as one participant recalled of the 1890 cloak makers' strike in New York

City. "We were sure the millennium was at hand."[17] Typically, the millennial fervor that carried these garment workers into the streets encompassed the entire occupational spectrum of the industry, from skilled cutters, finishers, and pressers, to basters and sewing machine operators—the latter overwhelmingly women, many of them prominent leaders in these community-based struggles.

It was the Knights of Labor who first harnessed this kind of cross-craft solidarity in the 1880s and gave it organizational form. In cases like coal mining and railroading, the Knights championed "industrial" organization that combined every trade in a particular company, industry, or town into a single body. In other industries, most workers were still organized into separate trade locals, but even here the Knights emphasized a new kind of solidarity by mobilizing citywide boycotts, mass picketing, and worker-owned cooperatives. These community-based mobilizations fueled the Knights' dramatic growth between 1880 and 1886, giving credence to the claim of Terence Powderly, the organization's national leader, that worker solidarity would "strike a powerful, telling blow at the base of the system which makes the laborer a slave of his master."[18] By Powderly's estimate, the combined growth of worker-owned factories, cooperative stores, and political reform would ultimately triumph over corporate power, but these grand expectations were almost immediately disappointed. On the heels of the 1886 strikes for the eight-hour day, employers launched a vigorous campaign to marginalize the Knights, and by the late 1880s a series of strike defeats and internal dissension had dramatically weakened the organization.

As the Knights declined, they were replaced by a rival coalition of unions, the American Federation of Labor (AFL). Formed in 1886, the AFL abandoned the reform-minded rhetoric and the all-encompassing organization of the Knights for more modest—but, its founders claimed, more winnable—improvements in the conditions of labor. Led by the Cigar Makers Union, whose leaders, Samuel Gompers and Adolf Strasser, helped found the AFL, craft unions established insurance benefits and strike funds to support their members in personal and collective emergencies; the centralized strike fund, in turn, gave the national union more control over local strike decisions, and by requiring higher dues, reinforced an organizational bias in favor of the skilled workers who could afford them. Rather than risk their organizations in industry-wide struggles that invited violent repression, many AFL unions retreated to the stronghold of craft, fortifying smaller but more strategic positions in the economy. Compared with Europe, skilled workers were in relatively short supply in the U.S. economy, making their craft knowledge all the more important in metalworking and construction, even as skilled labor declined in older industries like shoemaking or woodworking.

The industrial revolution had this paradoxical impact in many dimensions of economic and social life, creating both misery and opportunity, solidarity and fragmentation. Factories serving a national market could turn out cheap "ready-made" shoes, furniture, garments, simple tools, housewares, fabrics, food, and dry goods that undersold the customized hand-tool work of skilled artisans. Yet the very process of mechanization and specialization that marginalized the all-round craftsman in these industries also elevated new trades and new craft identities. Pattern makers, pipe fitters, boilermakers, machine builders, and toolmakers all gained ground installing and maintaining the new machines that powered factory production. The construction trades also grew as electrification and high-rise buildings created new skill categories and new craft unions—among them, the Electrical Workers, organized in 1891, and the Ironworkers, organized in 1896.

These AFL unions often sought alliances with allied crafts in the same workplace, and their frequent "sympathy strikes" in support of fellow craftsmen were a clear indicator of the wider solidarities that motivated many skilled workers. While generally rejecting anticapitalist ideologies or independent political action, the AFL's "House of Labor" still accommodated socialist and radical activists who led many of the affiliated unions and often mustered as much as a third of AFL convention votes. There was even room for "industrial" unions like the United Mine Workers and the Brewery Workers, both of whom transferred their allegiance from the declining Knights to the rising AFL. Still, there was no denying that the AFL's militancy was more narrowly focused on "pure and simple" trade issues, and its membership more narrowly focused on the skilled workers whose bargaining leverage could sustain unions through even the depression years of the 1890s.

For these skilled workers, the union was more than simply a vehicle for protecting wages. It was, in addition, a means for "legislating" the workplace and preserving the position of craftsmen who saw their skills as the driving force in the enterprise. Indeed, in the construction trades and many metalworking industries, skilled tradesmen supervised much of the work, provided their own tools, trained apprentices, and generally regulated the quality and quantity of production. Employers seeking to cut costs had to first contend with a shop culture that supported these craft regulations, even when there was no union. In a union workplace, the shop rules became all the more explicit; the Machinists Union, for example, prohibited helpers from performing journeymen's work, opposed piecework wages that tied earnings to output, and barred machinists from operating more than one machine at a time. Other union work rules were more detailed: the Amalgamated Iron and Steel Workers, for one, had fifty-eight pages of "footnotes" governing the Homestead Steel works of Andrew Carnegie in 1891.

Management could eliminate these rules by destroying the union, as Carnegie subsequently did at Homestead in 1892. In that pivotal struggle, the unskilled laborers in the plant sided with the Amalgamated's skilled workers, even though the union barred them from membership and left the largely Slavic laborers without representation. This exemplary display of solidarity was not easily reciprocated, however. Skilled tradesmen at the top of workplace hierarchies often regarded less-skilled factory "hands" with a mixture of sympathy, scorn, and distrust, the latter born of practical experience with employers who simplified operations and assigned the "greenhorn" laborer or "half-baked" mechanic to perform the low-end tasks of the craft. Technological change that threatened to blur distinctions between skilled and unskilled work further alarmed craft unionists who saw in these changes the employer's ultimate intention of destroying their craft.

The gap between skilled and unskilled workers widened all the more when reinforced by the ethnic, racial, and gender divisions that American workplaces exhibited in ever-wider profusion. In no other industrial economy in the world were ethnic cleavages, in particular, so pronounced and so often opposed to the promotion of workplace solidarity. As the immigrant stream widened after 1890, with 15 million people arriving in the next twenty-five years, its sources also shifted away from the North European nations of Britain, Ireland, Scandinavia, and Germany toward south and east European lands, especially Italy, Russia, and Austria-Hungary. Many new immigrants from the rural hinterlands of these regions were driven from their small-scale peasant holdings by population growth and the repeated subdivision of their tiny holdings. Whereas Russian Jews fleeing Czarist persecution and anti-Semitic violence usually arrived with every intention of staying, many immigrants from southern and eastern Europe planned only a brief sojourn in America's growing economy, intending to work a few years and return home with their savings to buy or protect the family farm.

In this sense, first-generation immigrants were ideal candidates for filling the worst industrial jobs: because many had no intention of staying, they viewed their condition as temporary and, therefore, bearable in the short term if they could save enough from their wages. This "instrumental" attitude contrasted sharply with the native-born and older immigrant groups who predominated in the craft unions of the AFL. To craftsmen, the immigrant laborer appeared as an unreliable opportunist, willing to accept harsh conditions that "spoiled the job." Bridging this cultural gap was all the more difficult when craftsmen and laborers spoke different languages, lived in separate ethnic neighborhoods, and belonged to different churches—the former often Methodist or Lutheran, the latter Roman Catholic or Greek Orthodox. Employers were well aware of the potential antagonism between such disparate groups and used immigrant workers as strikebreakers in coal mining, steel, and other industries. Though many immigrant workers refused this role (as at Homestead), others took the jobs and shunned the union. The union, particularly when it represented skilled workers, often refused to admit them in any case, either as a matter of trade policy (excluding the unskilled) or of prejudice (excluding, as one independent union of bricklayers put it, the "foreigners [who] take work away from us").[19]

Women found most craft unions even less accommodating. Reflecting the widely held opinion that women were suited only for domestic labor and motherhood, many AFL affiliates expressly forbade their membership in the trade and, in the case of the Iron Molders, even fined members who taught women the secrets of the craft. Women's participation in the wage economy was growing—from 15 percent of gainful workers in 1870 to 21 percent by 1910—but their role was often restricted to jobs deemed "feminine" by their approximation of household chores: sewing, caring for the sick, food service, or attending the needs of shoppers and office managers. When they ventured into the factory, it was expected to be a temporary sojourn before marriage or the next pregnancy; this expectation, in turn, was used to justify wages well below those paid men, even when jobs were closely comparable. In a social context where women had not yet won the right to vote, they were also disenfranchised in the wage economy and the labor movement. For many unions, a "living wage" meant a "family wage" paid to a man, the wage being sufficient to support "the wife at home." This ideal helped men justify their opposition to low wages and pay cutting, and it matched the aspirations of many women who saw in household work and child rearing a preferable destiny to the factory's low wages and dead-end jobs. Yet more women were taking such jobs, largely because household finances required it, and only a handful of unions welcomed them.

The chasm between white and black workers was all the wider and all the more difficult to bridge. Here, the labor movement reflected social trends that were moving rapidly toward racial segregation and "whites only" practices barring blacks from jobs, neighborhoods, schools, churches, theaters, and stores. In the 1880s, the Knights had struggled to overcome these barriers by opening their ranks to all workers regardless of race or gender. In the 1890s, however, as racial segregation intensified and lynchings took the lives of more than one hundred blacks each year, many unions retreated from this high ground and instituted constitutional provisions limiting membership to white males. Employers enforced the same segregation in their hiring practices and were no less discriminatory in the majority of workplaces that were nonunion. Most whites justified these policies by invoking the widely held belief that whites were the superior race, a claim some Americans of British and German heritage further elaborated by placing their Anglo-Saxon forebears a notch or two above the Slavic, Italian, and other so-called Mediterranean races. Relegated to the bottom rung of this racial hierarchy, African-Americans were deemed inherently incapable of skilled work—and were therefore denied training for it. Consequently, strikebreaking was often the only avenue for black workers seeking jobs in the citadels of whites-only employment, and here again employers were prepared to exploit the resulting antagonisms.

Despite these obstacles, some unions continued to agitate for the widest possible solidarity, none more so than the United Mine Workers (UMW). In mining as elsewhere, employers used black strikebreakers against white workers, but the UMW had learned an early lesson that applied equally to immigrant strikebreakers: rather than invite the antagonism and competition of other workers by excluding them from membership, white workers could counter the employer's divisive tactics by welcoming all workers into their ranks, regardless of race or ethnicity. The Knights of Labor, from which the UMW sprang, had not only recruited black coal miners into the union but had agitated for desegregating the mines and applying the same conditions to all workers. The UMW continued this campaign with such success that by 1900 over 20 percent of the union's ninety-one thousand members were black, with African-American miners holding office at all levels of the organization, including the union's National Executive Board. Richard Davis, a black miner from Ohio, was first in a field of fourteen running for national office at the union's 1896 convention, and he thereafter played a prominent role in advocating black-white unity. "It is high time for the color line to be dropped," Davis wrote in the union's national newspaper. "I think were we, as workingmen, to turn to fighting monopoly in land and money, we would accomplish a great deal more than we will by fighting among ourselves on account of race, creed, color, or nationality."[20]

In this he was as often opposed by conservative black leaders as by white bigots. Many prominent African-Americans, disheartened by the escalating violence and discrimination directed at blacks, advocated a strategic retreat and acceptance of segregation, preferring self-improvement within the ghetto or rural "black belt" of the South. "Agitation of the question of racial equality is the extremist folly,"[21] counseled Booker T. Washington, the former slave and founder of Tuskegee Institute, and many black church leaders followed his lead in seeking the protection and philanthropy of white industrialists. Their opposition to the UMW provoked bitter denunciations from Davis, who continually reminded nonunion black miners that "labor organizations have done more to eliminate the color line than all other organizations, the church not even excepted."[22]

Davis knew full well that the labor movement's record was mixed, that prominent AFL affiliates barred black workers altogether, and that even the AFL's national leader, Samuel Gompers, invoked the alleged superiority of "caucasian civilization" and its "uplifting" mission. But Davis also knew that unions were the only institutions in American life in which blacks and whites could meet as equals. Craft unions like the Machinists and the Electrical workers were "whites only," but a third of the members in the International Longshoremen's Union were African-Americans in 1902, some of them elected to office in locals with overwhelmingly white membership. Some unions that admitted black workers segregated them into separate locals, whereas others opposed all efforts to organize African-Americans. But when objections were raised in 1902 against the Carpenters Union for appointing a black organizer in the South, enough white carpenters supported the move to make it stick. "The mere fact that all of the boss builders in the South are advocating leaving the Negroes out of the unions is a good reason why we should organize them," as one Georgia union leader put it. "Let the good work go on, and let us hope for the day when there will be equal rights to all and special privileges to none."[23]

The solidarity this white carpenter invoked was not a "spontaneous" expression of workers' self interest. It was a deliberate project, a political ideal, and a social mission that required constant advocacy against the many forces fragmenting working-class communities. The "day when there will be equal rights to all" was still in the future, but as union membership underwent a revival in the opening years of the twentieth century, there was hope that such a day was not far off.

2

RISE AND FALL, 1910–1929

Union membership, after a short burst of growth in the first years of the new century, would rise dramatically in the second decade, more than doubling between 1910 and 1920. As it grew, the labor movement would take on new forms and confront new challenges as managers began to revolutionize the workplace, introducing "scientific management" and advanced mechanization to lay siege on the remaining realms of craft-based production. With the simultaneous rise of socialist politics, progressive reform, and broad-based unions, the stage was set for the labor movement's rapid growth during World War I, when the government intervened to regulate production and protect union organization. For a brief moment, the labor movement appeared to have won a secure place in the American polity.

But it was only a moment. In the war's immediate aftermath, in a context of economic recession, Red Scare, and official strikebreaking, the labor movement lost much of the ground it had gained in the previous decade. Thereafter, as the economy experienced unprecedented (if uneven) growth through the 1920s, and as courts and political conservatives backed a "business first" agenda, union membership fell and the labor movement grew more conservative.

Nevertheless, a tangible legacy survived from the years of growth between 1910 and 1920: a precedent for government regulation of the

19

economy and protection for workers; the first experiments with a system of collective bargaining centered on grievance arbitration; and broad-based industrial union organization, able to unify, if only briefly in many cases, diverse groups of workers previously divided by ethnicity, occupation, and gender. In all these regards, the stillborn initiatives of 1910–1920 awaited their fulfillment in the New Deal era of the 1930s and the wartime mobilization of the 1940s.

THE NEW UNIONISM

Hannah Shapiro did not appear to be one who could spark a citywide rebellion of garment workers. One of seven thousand employees at Hart, Schaffner & Marx, Chicago's largest garment maker, she toiled anonymously in shop no. 5 on South Halstead Street. In a workforce led by skilled cutters—the men who fashioned the cloth into patterns for sewing—Shapiro was a mere seamer, stitching pant legs in endless repetition for piecework wages. She was only eighteen years old in 1910, working "to better myself," as she later put it, and happy to have taken a job in a "modern" company like HSM, rather than the many sweatshops that crowded the industry.

Shapiro, however, was no greenhorn. Having started work at the age of thirteen, she was already schooled well beyond her years in the petty tyrannies of the garment trades: frequent wage cuts; arbitrary fines for lost or damaged garments; bottlenecks that interrupted work and reduced piecework earnings; foremen who ignored company rules, browbeat employees, and distributed jobs to family members and favored workers. On September 22, 1910, Shapiro had had enough. When her supervisor announced yet another cut in piecework rates, she stopped work and led sixteen other women out the door. "We all went out," Shapiro remembered. "We had to be recognized as people."[1]

At first, few recognized what these young women had done and fewer still took them seriously. "I remember we made fun of it, five girls working against HSM," recalled Sidney Hillman, a cutter who had been quietly organizing workers at the company. "But somehow the girls managed to take out the men after awhile."[2] Within four weeks the rebellion had spread beyond HSM and encompassed more than forty thousand strikers in a conflict that exemplified the continuities as well as the contrasts with previous struggles.

As in prior mass strikes, the 1910 walkout generated an intense bonding of separate occupations and ethnic groups. Strike meetings were conducted in a kaleidoscope of languages—English, Yiddish, Lithuanian, Polish, Italian, and Bohemian—punctuated by the enthusiastic reception of new strikers. "Hall doors opened, whistles sounded," the *Chicago Daily Socialist* reported of one mass meeting, "and in marched over 300 men carrying partly opened shears above the heads. The cutters had walked out. Deafening cheers."[3] Other strikers joined as neighborhood marches went from workshop to workshop. Marie Felski, a pocket maker at Kuppenhimer, recalled how her foremen restored pay cuts moments before such a march arrived at her shop. "We all rushed to the windows and there we could see the police beating the strikers—clubbing them on our account—and when we saw that we went out."[4] Police attacks were frequent and brutal, provoking a quickening cycle of revenge. Two strikers were shot and killed by police in separate incidents during early December; a week later, a strikebreaker was shot and killed in retaliation; days later, a union supporter was assassinated by private detectives; immediately following, there was a reprisal killing of a security guard at HSM.

Without formal union organization or leadership, the strike appeared to outside observers as a chaotic, spontaneous uprising, lacking even a list of grievances when the rebellion began. But as in previous upheavals, small groups of activists and organizers had prepared the ground. Most of these immigrant leaders were Russian Jews and Italians, many of them skilled cutters or pressers. Among them were socialists and veterans of the failed 1905 Russian revolution, like Hillman, who had suffered imprisonment in Czarist jails before fleeing to western Europe and the United States. Since the AFL's United Garment Workers largely ignored the foreign born and excluded all but the cutters from its tiny ranks, it was these ethnic radicals who took the lead in calling for a wider movement that included all workers and immigrant groups.

If their efforts had simply followed the pattern of previous garment strikes, the ending would have produced only a temporary restoration of wage cuts and the usual failure to win a "closed shop" (a settlement that would not only recognize the union but protect its base of support by obligating employers to hire exclusively from the union hall). In fact, the four-and-a-half-month walkout did end in defeat on both these scores for the majority of workers. But in several key respects, something different emerged from the strike: first, a settlement at Hart, Schaffner & Marx that salvaged a partial victory and established a new form of union representation; and second, an alliance with middle-class reformers and self-styled "Progressives" that helped sustain the strike and shape the settlement at HSM.

Instead of the "closed shop," the company agreed to implement a "preferential shop" in which union members would be given hiring preference over nonunion workers when they possessed comparable skills. More important, Hillman and other strike leaders persuaded their militant followers to accept a future ban on strikes or slowdowns in return for the company's promise to submit all unresolved disputes to a board of arbitration. The board, a tripartite body with representatives from the company, the union, and mutually acceptable public members, would issue decisions that were binding on all parties. Such a system of grievance arbitration was foreign to both management and workers in the garment trades, and every manufacturer but HSM rejected such power sharing. Many workers, in turn, believed that capitalist managers could not be trusted to abide by such a process. Critics within the Chicago union, like those who opposed a similar outcome in the 1910 garment strike in New York, advocated unyielding direct action in the workplace to force management compliance with workers' demands.

Hillman took the lead in advocating this new approach, but his efforts were strongly influenced by the middle-class allies who came to the workers' defense during the 1910 walkout. This too marked an important contrast with the more polarized conflicts of the late nineteenth century. Economic growth had generated not only extremes of wealth and poverty, owners and proletarians, as predicted by Marxist revolutionaries, but also a growing cadre of middle-level managers, lawyers, engineers, architects, economists, accountants, social workers, and others who managed increasingly complex corporate and public bureaucracies. Wedded to capitalist growth, many professionals and mass-market retailers were also critical of the inequities that restricted purchasing power and undermined popular support for the system. "Are those Bohemians, Poles, Italians, and Russian Jews to become loyal and law-abiding American citizens?" asked the Chicago branch of the Women's Trade Union League (WTUL) during the strike. The upper- and middle-class women of the WTUL worried, as they expressed it in one pamphlet, that "Despair is the surest road to Anarchy" and that "Indifference to this struggle on the part of the well-to-do is criminally selfish and short-sighted."[5] Many reform-minded women in the WTUL saw women's struggle to win the right to vote (finally achieved in 1920) as the primary battle, together with advocacy of protective legislation that would limit women's exposure to industrial work and protect their homebound role as wives and mothers. There were other WTUL activists, however, who also saw the need for union organization to improve conditions for women who had to work, and these WTUL women raised money for strike relief, marched in picket lines, and drew favorable media attention to the union's cause.

Hillman and other strike leaders were drawn into this circle and became frequent participants in forums and meetings sponsored by the WTUL and by Hull House, the center of Chicago's middle-class reform movement. There, Hillman met reform leaders like Jane Addams and Clarence Darrow, improved his broken English, and learned the language of liberal reform. From this alliance came a new union under Hillman's leadership, the Amalgamated Clothing Workers, which would later play a leading role in the many turning points of the New Deal era.

THE SPECTER OF SOCIALISM

Progressives saw something more tangible than mere "anarchy" threatening the future of American capitalism. "The growth of the Socialist Party in this country," as President and future Progressive Party leader Theodore Roosevelt warned in 1905, "is far more ominous than any populist movement in times past."[6]

Formed in 1901 from a merger of smaller left-wing parties, the Socialist Party (SP) initially posed no serious threat to status quo politics, boasting a membership of only ten thousand and a presidential ballot of just 129,000 votes in 1900. But four years later the vote for Eugene Debs, former ARU strike leader and SP presidential candidate, suddenly jumped to 402,000—prompting Roosevelt's warning—and thereafter doubled to 900,000 votes by 1912. In an election that saw a four-way race for president, Debs's 1912 tally made him an emerging contender, equaling 25 percent of the vote for incumbent President William Taft, 22 percent of the count for Roosevelt's Progressive Party, and 14 percent of the vote for winner Woodrow Wilson, the Progressive Democrat. That same year, the SP elected nearly twelve hundred local officials across the United States (including seventy-nine mayors), and its membership topped 118,000, a twelve-fold increase since 1901.

What alarmed Progressives and conservatives alike was not only the sudden rise of the SP but its wide and varied social base. Much of its support after 1912 was concentrated in large cities where immigrant workers joined the party's "language federations" for Russian, Polish, German, and other foreign-born workers. Yet the state with the largest percentage of votes going to the SP was rural Oklahoma, where farmers elected five SP candidates to the state legislature in 1914 and more than 130 Socialists to county and township offices. Although many SP candidates were avowed Marxists, many others were "soft" on doctrine and strong on a kind of moral suasion that combined populist sentiments opposing big business with a Christian faith in the moral bonds of solidarity. For members of the Christian Socialist Fellowship, this obligated the true believer to promote "the social message of Jesus, which in an age of machine production means Socialism, and nothing else."[7] Most Socialists believed in a nonviolent strategy of winning change through the ballot box, but a vocal minority argued that capitalists would never permit an elected Socialist government to take power and that workers should arm for self-defense or outright seizure of state power. Although a minority of bigots regarded socialism as the highest achievement of the "white race," the mainstream of the SP drew African-Americans A. Philip Randolph and Chandler Owen, editors of the socialist journal *The Messenger*, because the party "does not even hold race prejudice in the South."[8] The SP also recruited professionals like Margaret Sanger, the early advocate of birth control, who served as a leader of the Intercollegiate Socialist Society.

However prominent these intellectuals became in their appeals to middle-class voters, the Socialist Party's leadership and base was primarily working class: of the eighty-five Socialists elected to state legislatures between 1912 and 1920, more than 60 percent were workers (another 10 percent were farmers), and the vote for Eugene Debs spiked upward to four and five times the national average in mill towns and coal mining communities. Socialists called for democratic management of the economy, to be achieved by public ownership of railroads, banks, and mammoth corporations like U.S. Steel; in the meantime, Socialists advocated a mixture of municipal improvements and support for unions that appealed to many less ideologically committed voters. Socialist mayors who disarmed Pinkerton agents and ordered police not to protect strikebreakers won considerable support in working-class communities, and voters who supported programs to municipalize trolley service or lower utility rates elected Socialist mayors in Milwaukee, Minneapolis, Schenectady, and many smaller cities. A significant number of unions also elected Socialists to national leadership, including the Brewery workers,

Machinists, Western Federation of Miners, and (outside the AFL) the Amalgamated Clothing Workers. In 1912, the combined voting strength of left-wing delegates at the AFL national convention gave socialist printer Max Hayes nearly one-third of the vote in his challenge to Sam Gompers for the federation's presidency.

These gains were especially worrisome to Progressive leaders like Louis Brandeis, the prominent Boston lawyer and future Supreme Court justice who favored unions "as a strong bulwark against the great wave of socialism."[9] Brandeis and other progressives recognized that merely opposing socialists was not enough when underlying conditions of low pay and autocratic management drove many to embrace radical alternatives. "Every excess of capital must in time be repaid by the excessive demands of those who have not capital," Brandeis warned. "If the capitalists are wise, they will aid us in the effort to prevent injustice."[10] Brandeis found support among New York garment manufacturers in 1910, who accepted his proposal to establish the kind of grievance arbitration system implemented the same year at Hart, Schaffner & Marx in Chicago. Similar approaches found favor with the National Civic Federation, which brought corporate executives and AFL leaders together in 1900 to endorse trade agreements—treaties that replaced unilateral rules imposed by the company or the union with negotiation and neutral arbitration of disputes. "Our enemies," as NCF leader Ralph Easley put it, "are the Socialists among the labor people and the anarchists among the capitalists."[11] Rather than oppose all regulation, the NCF acted on the principle articulated by utility magnate Samuel Insull: if regulation in some form is likely, it is better to "help shape the right kind of regulation than have the wrong kind forced upon" you.[12] In this spirit, the NCF's corporate leaders lobbied for laws to regulate privately owned electric utilities (as an alternative to government ownership), to establish workmen's compensation for injured workers (to avoid more expensive liability in court suits), and to apply "reasonable" limits on corporate mergers (rather than prohibit them altogether). The NCF also added its voice to the growing support for Progressive legislation that set minimum wages and prohibited child labor.

Labor leaders like UMW president John Mitchell, who believed that relations between labor and capital had "become strained almost to the breaking point," hoped that the NCF could "bring into close and more harmonious relation these two apparently antagonistic forces."[13] It could not. The NCF's corporate leaders were only prepared to endorse unionism as an abstract principle, not as a living proposition in their own companies. Even as AFL unions grew at the turn of the twentieth century from a combined membership of five hundred thousand in 1898 to two million by 1903, most were still concentrated in competitive industries like garment making, coal mining, printing, and construction, where unions were more evenly matched against small-scale employers. The big corporations that supported the NCF's reform agenda—United States Steel, International Harvester, National Cash Register—remained adamantly nonunion, and most NCF-endorsed trade agreements eventually collapsed as workers conducted unauthorized strikes and employers reverted to unilateral rule making. By 1905, corporate leadership in labor relations was shifting away from the NCF to the National Association of Manufacturers and its open shop campaign of union breaking. In this context, as socialists gained support in many hard-pressed unions, AFL affiliates like the UMW, the Carpenters, and the Machinists voted to withdraw from the meaningless deliberations of the NCF.

"SCIENTIFIC MANAGEMENT"

With the NCF's failure to promote labor-management cooperation at the top of the industrial hierarchy, many Progressives turned their attention to the grass roots, endorsing a transformation of work relations that Louis Brandeis dubbed "scientific management" in 1911.

For several reasons, corporate managers were driven to continually reorganize their factories and workshops after 1890. First among these was the growing "mass" market created by the nation's expanding railroad system. Compared to Europe's smaller economies dominated by aristocratic tastes and custom-made goods, the United States was a huge "democratic" market growing by mass immigration and westward expansion, with a corresponding demand for cheaper and more standardized consumer goods. Second, the ever-growing scale and complexity of production produced stupendous logistical problems in the delivery of raw materials, the coordination of work flows, and the standardization of products. Third, the continuing shortage of skilled labor in the United States made it all the more expensive to expand output by hiring more craftsmen—a skilled metalworker in the United States averaged about $2.70 a day in 1910, compared to just $1.57 in Britain and only $1.30 in Germany.

For these reasons, employers increasingly saw skilled workers as a bottleneck that restricted access to the growing national market, particularly as these skilled workers tenaciously defended the craft norms that limited management's control of the workplace. In the minority of metalworking shops where craft unions had won recognition by the early 1900s, these norms were protected by work rules and the established "stint," or workload, that tradesmen deemed acceptable. Even in nonunion shops, managers had to defer to the expertise of skilled workers who cast, machined, and assembled complex metal machines. In some cases, companies had actually subcontracted the work of whole departments to craftsmen who hired their own workers and supervised production. Whatever the particular form of craft production, this routine authority wielded by foundry men, machinists, boilermakers, pipe fitters, and blacksmiths was galling to the emerging cadre of white-collar engineers who saw themselves, rather than skilled workers, as the bearers of economic rationality. Frederick Taylor, an engineer and a leading management consultant at the turn of the twentieth century, bemoaned the lack of control over costs and coordination that such craft methods implied. "The shop [is] really run by the workmen and not by the bosses," he complained. "The workmen together plan . . . just how fast each job should be done." Such "soldiering" by skilled workers was inevitable according to Taylor, who believed that most people strove to avoid work—and the more empowered the workers, the more diligently they avoided working. His solution to this lack of effort was to reformulate, in a more systematic way, the same approach that had already de-skilled production labor in older industries. "All possible brain work," as he put it in his 1903 book, *Shop Management,* "should be removed from the shop and centered in the planning or laying out department." Engineers, in short, would redesign every job and divide it into dozens of simple, repetitive tasks with detailed instructions for "not only what is to be done, but how it is to be done and the exact time for doing it." With this systematic de-skilling of the metal trades, most craftsmen could be replaced, in Taylor's words, by "men who are of smaller caliber and attainments, and who are therefore cheaper than those required under the old system."[14]

According to Taylor and a growing chorus of industrial engineers, management should do the planning and workers should simply follow orders. Most managers had little trouble accepting the elitist presumptions of this principle. "The average worker wants a job in which he doesn't have to think,"[15] claimed Henry Ford, who set about creating such "unthinking" jobs in the auto industry. Before 1910, groups of skilled metalworkers assembled chassis and engine components with hand tools and little mechanization, "fitting" the crude castings and machined parts together with hand files. Wooden coach and wagon bodies were also built by skilled craftsmen using hand tools. Ford's revolution began in parts making, where he introduced special machines, holding fixtures, and gauges that ensured more precise and consistent casting and machining. "The trend always was to cut down the number of operations to the smallest possible unit," as one stockholder report later observed of "Fordist" methods, "and then design a machine to do that operation with unskilled labor."[16] These specialized machines did require an expanding workforce of toolmakers and repairmen, but they could be operated by fewer and less-skilled workers to produce the standardized and "interchangeable" parts required by the moving assembly line. "In mass production," as Ford put it, "there can be no fitters."[17] Whereas before, a few skilled fitters assembled an entire engine with a toolbox of hand tools, by 1914 Model T engine blocks were being pulled past a line of more than one hundred assemblers, each performing a single repetitive task. The same minute division of labor and extensive mechanization was eventually installed in every department of the sprawling factory in Highland Park, Michigan, where Ford coordinated the labor of fourteen thousand workers in one continuous flow, from foundry to final assembly. Production time in the latter operation alone fell from 12.5 hours to ninety-three minutes when the moving assembly line replaced static assembly. Production costs fell and the price of the Ford Model T tumbled as well: from $780 in 1910 to $360 by 1916. Accordingly, sales skyrocketed from just twenty-one thousand Model Ts a year in 1910 to a stunning 585,000 in 1916.

Progressives like Louis Brandeis believed efficient work methods and lower prices would help rather than hurt workers. When he coined the term *scientific management* to popularize the work of Taylor and others, Brandeis welcomed "the perfect team play" that would occur once the employer "assumes the burdens of management and relieves labor of responsibilities not its own."[18] Managers trained in the "science" of job analysis and time-motion study could eliminate wasted motion and make work easier. Wages would rise with greater productivity—not from speedup, but from "removing the obstacles to production which annoy and exhaust the workman."[19]

Convinced that scientific "facts" could prevail over disorderly greed, Brandeis urged moderate union leaders to accept the new system as the basis for objective rule making. "Under scientific management men are led, not driven," he argued. "Instead of working unwillingly for their employer they work in cooperation,"[20] guided by scientific analysis. In effect, Brandeis was proposing to his AFL allies that unions adopt a kind of productivity bargaining, trading away their work rules in return for the incentive-pay bonuses that would reward higher output and create consumer purchasing power. Frederick Taylor, who opposed unions and collective bargaining (arguing in effect that "scientific facts cannot be negotiated"),[21] nevertheless claimed his methods would end labor-management conflict. "The great revolution that takes place in the mental attitude of the two parties under scientific management," he told congressional investigators in 1911, "is that both sides take their eyes off the division of the surplus as the all-important matter, and together turn their attention toward increasing the size of the surplus until . . . it is unnecessary to quarrel over how it shall be divided."[22]

Many workers found Taylor's claims of scientific impartiality hard to believe, all the more so when employers unilaterally imposed the new system with little of the "team play" Brandeis and other liberals hoped to see. "You can call it scientific management if you want to," one woman shouted at a 1911 meeting of the Boston Labor Council, where Brandeis addressed the issue, "but I call it scientific driving."[23] Her caustic remark expressed a widely held belief that the common goal of Taylor's scientific management and Ford's mechanization was not mere "efficiency," understood as more output from the *same* labor effort, but "speed up," meaning more output from *intensified* labor, forcibly driven by time study and the moving assembly line. Henry Ford admitted as much in later years, noting that with mechanization, "we regulated the speed of men by the speed of the conveyor."[24] Whether stopwatch or conveyor, such instruments of management control were not generally welcomed by workers. As early as 1904, the U.S. Commissioner of Labor reported widespread support among skilled workers, union *and* nonunion, for shop rules that protected "the workman in his legal and humanitarian right not to be considered as a mere automaton, used and driven incessantly, regardless of physical necessity."[25] Ten years later, N. P. Alifas, an AFL representative of federal workers, eloquently expressed his membership's distrust of the stopwatch and the time-study man. "If someone should discover they could run to work in one-third the time, they might have no objection to have that fact ascertained, but if the man who ascertained it had the power to make them run, they might object to having him find out.

"We haven't come into this existence for the purpose of seeing how great a task we can perform throughout a lifetime," Alifas added. "We are trying to regulate our work so as to make it an auxiliary to our lives and be benefited thereby."[26]

ONE BIG UNION

"There is at this time more restlessness, more aggression among the workmen . . . than there has been for several years past,"[27] warned J. J. Whirl, secretary of the Employers' Association of Detroit, in January 1912. Federal strike statistics were not compiled in that year, but there was ample evidence to support Whirl's claim. In April 1913, *Iron Age*, the industry newspaper for iron and steel, noted the same trend by reporting that the United States was experiencing "an epidemic of strikes."[28] In fact, the "contagion" would continue at unusually high levels for the next six years.

What made this strike wave noteworthy, besides the "aggression" reported by Whirl, was that it encompassed so wide a range of workers, and that they were so often willing to join their struggles with previously separate groups. The 1910 garment strikes in Chicago and New York had been early indicators of this turning point, and in both cases industrial unions emerged that united all the garment crafts in men's and women's clothing: respectively, the Amalgamated Clothing Workers (still an independent union outside the AFL) and the International Ladies Garment Workers (an industrial union within the craft-dominated AFL). Among metalworkers, the specter of "scientific management" provoked unified opposition even before its principles were widely adopted. When the Illinois Central Railroad introduced time cards and stopwatches to its repair shops in 1911, shop men from seven different craft unions immediately organized a joint federation to represent their combined opposition to time study and dilution of skills. This system federation of machinists, steamfitters, car men, sheet-metal workers, boilermakers, blacksmiths, painters, laborers, and even clerks eventually spread to other railroads and led to a prolonged strike of sixteen thousand workers. Though this strike ended in defeat, craft opposition to scientific management slowed its implementation in some metalworking shops and stopped it altogether in federal arsenals and shipyards after a series of strikes in 1911–1912.

At the same time, skilled toolmakers were joining with factory "hands" in the Pittsburgh area plants of Westinghouse to form the "American Industrial Union." Their 1914 strike over low wages and layoffs led to a fragile bargaining relationship with Westinghouse that lasted until 1916, when firings and a national strike of machinists for the eight-hour day produced a massive walkout of some fifty thousand workers in steel mills and metal working shops around Pittsburgh. Violent clashes at the gates of the Edgar Thompson steel works left three dead, followed by the arrival of the National Guard, the arrest of thirty strike leaders, and the collapse of the AIU.

To these struggles over scientific management and industrial organization, immigrant workers added an entirely new dimension. Although recent arrivals continued to swell their ranks, many immigrants were settling into permanent residence, establishing families and abandoning the prospect of returning to Europe. As temporary sojourners, they had endured the harsh conditions and the many indignities that characterized their work; now they were less inclined to do so, and the appalling conditions of immigrant life provoked repeated protests by Polish, Italian, Russian, and other workers from eastern and southern Europe.

Nowhere was this dynamic expressed more dramatically than in Lawrence, Massachusetts, the textile city thirty miles from Boston where some thirty thousand immigrants labored in the massive woolen and cotton mills along the Merrimack River. Ninety percent of the city's population were first- or second-generation immigrants, with fifty-one nationalities crowded within a mile of the mills. Many had been drawn from Europe by recruitment placards of the American Woolen Company depicting prosperous textile workers with bags of gold, standing in front of fine homes they supposedly owned. Instead, workers found the most crowded slums in North America, with rickety wooden tenements packed together along narrow alleys, untreated sewage dumped into the river, and four to five people crowded into most rooms. Rates of infant mortality and tuberculosis were among the highest in the country. Rent gouging and rising fuel prices forced families to take in boarders and send the children to work; as a result, one-half of all children between the ages of fourteen and eighteen labored in Lawrence's mills, earning little more than $5.00 a week. Their parents could count on little more: $8.75 a week, earned through fifty-six hours of hard labor in the heat, noise, and dust of the mills. "A considerable number of the boys and girls die within the first two years after beginning work," observed Dr. Elizabeth Shapleigh of Lawrence. By her estimate, "thirty-six out of every 100 of all men and women who work in the mill die before or by the time they are 25 years of age."[29]

Resentment over these conditions exploded in January 1912, when mill owners—forced by Progressive legislation to cut weekly hours from fifty-six to fifty-four—cut wages as well. With virtually no organization to direct their protest, strikers massed by the thousands in front of the plants, attacking strikebreakers and invading the mills to turn off the power and sabotage machines.

Their chaotic protest might have quickly dissipated if not for the arrival of organizers from the "Industrial Workers of the World." Formed in 1905, the IWW stood at the opposite pole from the AFL's espousal of craft organization and political moderation. "The *great facts* of present industry," the IWW had declared in its first convention call, "are the displacement of human skill by machines and the increase of capitalist power through concentration." To oppose these trends required "one great industrial union embracing all industries" and uniting workers of every craft, race, and nationality in revolutionary struggle. "This worn-out and corrupt system offers no promise of improvement and adaptation," the organization's founding manifesto brashly declared. Reform "offers only a perpetual struggle for slight relief within wage slavery."[30] Rejecting the reformist efforts of both the Socialist Party and the AFL, the IWW advocated a general strike of all workers as the only means for overthrowing capitalism and establishing workers' control of industry.

Although some Lawrence strikers were drawn by this apocalyptic rhetoric, others recognized that the IWW was their only option so long as the AFL's United Textile Workers union refused to expand beyond its tiny membership (208 in Lawrence) working in elite occupations like weaver or machine repairman. Only the IWW welcomed the "operatives," "hands," and machine tenders—half of them women—who dominated the production workforce in Lawrence and other mill towns. Led initially by IWW organizers Joe Ettor and Arturo Giovaniti and, after their arrest, by "Big" Bill Haywood and Elizabeth Gurley Flynn, the strikers' disordered ranks coalesced into a formidable organization. The 23,000 strikers divided into fourteen language groups (including Italians, French-Canadians, Poles, and Syrians), each of which elected four delegates to a general strike committee of fifty-six members, chaired by Ettor. Subcommittees for publicity, fund-raising, and relief were established on the same basis and set about organizing fourteen relief stations (by language group) to distribute groceries, medical services, and clothing. Five soup kitchens fed twenty-three hundred people daily in the winter months of the sixty-three-day strike, and daily meetings of the language groups and a massive Sunday meeting kept strikers informed.

Despite its fiery image, the IWW counseled peaceful mass picketing, even after Governor Eugene Foss (himself a mill owner) sent in more than two thousand National Guardsmen to keep strikers away from mill gates. "They cannot weave cloth with bayonets," Ettor cautioned. "By all means make this strike as peaceful as possible. In the last analysis, all the blood spilled will be your blood."[31] Two died in confrontations with police and Guardsmen—one of them an eighteen-year-old boy bayoneted in the back—but the strikers avoided additional clashes by adopting a new style of picketing. Because they were prohibited from "massing" at the mill gates, the picketers kept moving in long continuous lines that were not "massed" at any point, but still discouraged strikebreakers. With this "moving picket line," the strikers held out while public opinion slowly turned against the mill owners. In late January, a "bombing plot" initially linked to strike supporters turned out to be a clumsy framing by company agents. The following month, newspapers across the country reported on the exodus of hungry children sent by strikers to sympathetic homes in New York and Philadelphia; the subsequent police attack on mothers and strikers as they attempted to put more children on the outbound trains brought additional condemnations—and a congressional investigation—upon the mill owners.

When the companies finally conceded defeat and agreed to raise wages between 5 and 22 percent, Eugene Debs called the victory "one of the most decisive and far reaching ever won by organized workers."[32] This widely held view proved to be accurate, even though Local 20 of the IWW quickly lost its membership base in Lawrence. This decline, from sixteen thousand to seven hundred members by late 1913, was partly the result of retaliatory firings by the employers and partly the result of inflammatory rhetoric ("No God, No Master") paraded by some radicals—much to the distress of Local 20's many religionists. More fundamentally, the IWW placed so little store in permanently representing workers that it withdrew its organizers after the strike. Unlike the Amalgamated Clothing Workers or the AFL crafts that signed trade agreements, the IWW condemned any such contractual arrangement as a dishonorable "truce with the enemy." In its place, the IWW promised only continual agitation, and this crusading style characterized the mass strikes it led among steelworkers, farmhands, and lumberjacks. Though its strikes failed most everywhere but Lawrence and it rarely held a stable membership above one hundred thousand, it was the demonstrated militancy and "aggression" of these IWW supporters that so haunted J. J. Whirl and other management leaders.

The Lawrence strike also turned heads in the labor movement. Evidence that factory operatives and immigrant workers were not the unorganizable "mob" that some AFL craftsmen feared had been mounting over the years; Lawrence now proved the point beyond dispute, strengthening the hand of those within the AFL who supported industry-wide mobilization across craft and occupational lines. Lawrence was not only a turning point in this regard but also a storehouse of tactical inspiration, from the use of immigrant organizers like Ettor and Giovaniti, to the mobilization of public opinion, to the democratic conduct of strike deliberations. There was a sobering message for even the most narrowly self-interested craft unionist: "Either you must reach down and lift them up," said Ettor to craftsmen who would not support the unskilled, "or they will reach up and pull you down."[33]

Mary McDowell, an early Hull House reformer who later became a central figure in efforts to organize Chicago's meatpackers, saw what many others recognized in the Lawrence strike. Although she opposed the IWW's radical ideology, she pointed to the union's strike victory and warned that "it would be a great waste of time and energy if the A. F. of L. misses the point that has been so terribly emphasized at Lawrence. . . . In such industries as those of the steel, meat, textile & harvesters, etc., Industrial Unionism of a constructive type is surely the need of this moment. The A. F. of L. will lose out unless it wakes up and adds to the I.W.W.'s clever method, that of permanent and constructive organization."[34]

WORLD WAR AND CLASS WAR

AFL president Samuel Gompers also saw the need for a new labor strategy, but rather than look inward and adopt "Industrial Unionism of a constructive type," as McDowell and others advocated, he was more inclined to look outward, to a new alliance with progressive government regulators. The outbreak of World War I in 1914 reinforced Gompers's belief that such an alliance was not just possible, but necessary. "The present war has proved that one of the strongest emotions in men is patriotism," he wrote in 1915, two years before the United States entered the conflict. That even Europe's socialist parties would rally in support of national defense—despite their previous pledge to oppose military aggression with international solidarity—convinced Gompers that patriotism "was stronger than the fundamental tenet of socialism, stronger than the ideals of international peace, stronger than religion, stronger than love of life and family."[35] Therefore, Gompers concluded, to oppose military "preparedness" in the United States, as many in the labor movement did in 1915, would only invite a patriotic backlash. More important, it would miss an opportunity that Gompers and other AFL leaders had recently come to favor. Noting the failure of the NCF's voluntary approach to trade agreements and union recognition, many in the AFL now endorsed an alliance with Progressives in the Democratic Party that could make these goals a matter of public policy.

This, too, marked a turning point. For many years since its founding in 1886, the AFL had opposed public regulation of labor relations on the presumption, usually born out in practice, that the government would favor the employer—with bayonets if need be. AFL leaders had traditionally called for evenhanded laws that favored neither capital nor labor, leaving the actual content of labor-management relations to the *voluntary* initiative of unions and employers rather than government rule making. Until persuaded otherwise by business allies in the NCF, the AFL's "voluntarism" even opposed workmen's compensation laws that made the injured workman dependent on the government rather than the independent power of his union.

At the same time, the AFL had long held an officially nonpartisan stance of "rewarding friends and punishing enemies," rather than endorsing a particular party. Designed to minimize conflicts among the members, this policy had often been contradicted by the partisan efforts of local leaders, whose allegiance to Republicans or Democrats depended in part on the nature of their membership and in part on the narrow range of options in a two-party system. In Europe, workers had been denied the vote until very late in the industrial revolution and had therefore channeled more of their energies and self-awareness into independent forms of expression outside the status quo. Europe's Labor parties, Social Democratic parties, and revolutionary parties all built on this legacy of independence from political institutions that had until recently excluded them. In the United States, in contrast, voting rights were extended to white men far earlier than in Europe, and many workers were therefore integrated into a two-party system dominated in the nineteenth century by cultural rather than ideological conflicts. Republicans more often attracted Protestant and native-born workers who favored prohibition of alcohol and opposed parochial schools. Democrats more often attracted Irish Catholics and other immigrants who opposed the do-gooder meddling of evangelists and prohibitionists. Otherwise, both parties attracted voters with big-city machines that delivered jobs and other spoils to loyal followers; both parties were enthusiastically pro-capitalist; and both championed the virtues of small-scale enterprise long after the economy—and the leadership of both parties—had fallen under the predominant influence of corporate capital. Union activists who wanted to mobilize for political action found it difficult to break the well-established monopoly of the two-party system.

This barren terrain motivated the IWW to reject most electioneering as a waste of time, particularly when Democrats barred African-Americans and poor whites from voting in the South, and Republicans did the same to immigrant aliens in the North. In Colorado, for example, it was useless to urge coal miners savaged in the violent strikebreaking of 1914 to vote for pro-labor candidates—most of the miners were foreign-born aliens from the British Isles and eastern Europe and were therefore barred from voting. Armed self-defense made more sense to these UMW members, and they gave nearly as good as they got in the "Colorado coal wars" that preceded and followed the Ludlow massacre. In eight months of virtual civil war, ten guards, nineteen strikebreakers, and two militiamen were killed by armed strikers, nearly matching the thirty-three strikers and family members (including eleven children) killed by guards and soldiers.

When federal troops intervened to end this bloodshed, many anticipated a repeat of the 1894 Pullman strike, when the federal government openly sided with management. This time, however, was different. President Woodrow Wilson, a Progressive Democrat, pursued a more even-handed policy in the Colorado coal strike, in part to win labor and public support that would mute criticism of U.S. military preparations for the world war. In Colorado, federal troops prohibited picketing and permitted the mines to reopen, but they also disarmed company guards (as well as strikers) and prohibited management from importing strikebreakers across state lines. Federal mediators proposed a three-year truce, the rehiring of all strikers who had not violated the law, and elections for a grievance committee at each mine, with federally appointed commissioners to umpire unresolved disputes. This proposed solution, after winning approval from the union's district convention, was rejected by the company and was never implemented. But the federal government's constructive role was praised by many union supporters.

Gompers and others found additional reason to favor partisan support for Wilson's successful reelection in 1916. In its first term, the Wilson administration had established the Labor Department as a cabinet level position and appointed William Wilson, a former UMW leader, as the first secretary of Labor. Progressive Democrats had subsequently supported the Clayton Act of 1914, which declared that human labor "is not a commodity or article of commerce" and that unions were therefore exempt from prosecution under the Sherman Antitrust Act. Court injunctions to break strikes were also prohibited, "unless necessary to prevent irreparable injury to property." President Wilson's intervention to prevent a national rail strike in 1916 also led to passage of the Adamson Act establishing the eight-hour day on the railroads, at no loss in pay. The federal conciliation service established in 1913 was busy in many other disputes as well, mediating a total of 1,780 cases between 1915 and 1919, more than six times the 274 cases mediated by the NCF during the 1902–1905 peak of its private conciliation efforts.

Advocates for union endorsement of the Wilson administration pointed to these gains and compared them to the futility of supporting Socialist candidates. In the American context, they argued, a vote for the SP was wasted. Even after its stunning success in 1912, the Socialist Party had won only a single seat in Congress; in contrast, Britain's newly organized Labor Party, with virtually the same percentage of the national vote (6.4 percent), had elected forty-two members of Parliament in 1910. Among the reasons for these contrasting outcomes was the larger size of congressional districts, requiring more resources to run successful candidates, and the "winner-take-all" nature of presidential elections. Unlike a parliamentary system, with a prime minister selected by Parliament according to party coalitions, the direct election of the president meant small parties could not credibly elect their candidate and would therefore have no role in forming a government. The British Labor Party was further boosted by a secret agreement with the dominant Liberal Party, which backed Labor candidates in Scotland and other districts where they were more likely to defeat the Conservative opposition. No such friendly coalition awaited the SP in the United States, where Republicans and Democrats frequently united *against* the Socialists.

The AFL was all the more wedded to Wilson's Democratic administration after America entered the European war in 1917. Government intervention to manage the wartime economy was substantial, including temporary nationalization of railroads and telephone service and regulation of production, prices, and labor policies. In the latter case, the goal of federal labor policy was not so much support of either unions or the open shop, but the stabilization of labor-management relations to permit steady production of military hardware and essential goods and services. With four million men entering the armed forces, and with the wartime end of European immigration, an acute labor shortage would likely drive up wages and boost union organizing efforts. To prevent disruptive confrontations over the unions' right to exist, the Wilson administration established the National War Labor Board (NWLB) with representatives from labor, management, and the public (the latter represented by Frank Walsh, a pro-labor lawyer, and William Taft, the former Republican president). The NWLB, seeking a peaceful alternative to strikes or strikebreaking that would interrupt war production, promptly issued an unprecedented public endorsement of "the right of workers to organize in trade unions and to bargain collectively through chosen representatives." The NWLB further ruled that companies could not maintain blacklists, could not force individuals to sign the so-called yellow-dog employment contracts that barred them from joining unions, and could not use espionage and interrogation to oppose organization. Anticipating many of the New Deal's labor policies in the 1930s, the NWLB further provided that workers unfairly discharged for union activity could seek a federal hearing and, if their complaint was upheld, they would be reinstated with back pay.

By any measure, these regulations marked an unprecedented (if temporary) turning point: for the first time in the nation's history, the federal government was actively protecting union organization as a matter of policy. The NWLB would not force companies to recognize unions where there had been no previous collective bargaining, but the government's stated policy of protecting union rights dramatically boosted organizing efforts across the economy, doubling union membership between 1915 and 1920 from 2.6 to 5.0 million. In the latter year, unions represented an estimated 20 percent of the nonagricultural workforce—a higher proportion than eight decades later, at the close of the twentieth century. Contemplating these sudden gains, Gompers happily concluded that the war was the "most wonderful crusade ever entered upon in the whole history of the world."[36]

Left-wing activists in the labor movement drew very different conclusions about the war, and their contrary views gained considerable public support as the killing escalated to unprecedented levels. Some Americans strongly opposed U.S. entry into a European conflict over imperial boundaries and control of colonial possessions, and some ethnic groups specifically opposed U.S. support for the British and their allies—German-Americans because they favored their former homeland,

Irish-American nationalists because they opposed British occupation of Ireland. To these antiwar sentiments the Socialist Party and the IWW added the further objection that wartime mobilization would suppress dissent and force unions into collaboration with government policy; both the SP and the IWW therefore advocated draft resistance. Their antiwar stance provoked a withering repression by the Wilson administration and by vigilante groups that took their lead from government officials. Of five thousand Socialist Party locals across the country, at least fifteen hundred were destroyed by mass arrests, mob violence, burnings, and even lynchings. Left-wing union activists were branded as subversives under provisions of the Espionage and Sedition Acts of 1917–1918, which made it a crime to advocate draft resistance and opposition to the war; thousands were consequently arrested, fired, or assaulted during the wartime emergency. With one hundred of its national leaders imprisoned under the Espionage Act, the IWW closed most of its halls and went underground in 1918. The Socialist Party, in contrast, took its antiwar campaign into state and local elections and won dramatically higher votes: a fivefold increase to 22 percent in New York's 1917 mayoralty elections; a fourfold jump to 26 percent in Wisconsin's 1918 Senate race; and a tenfold jump to 34 percent in Chicago's aldermanic elections. Consistent turnouts of 20–35 percent for Socialist antiwar candidates were all the more significant given the fact that socialist publications were banned from the mails, public antiwar meetings were forbidden or physically attacked in many states, and some Socialists had to campaign while under federal indictment for their antiwar statements.

Although the AFL's wartime support of the Wilson administration won it an unprecedented measure of government backing, there was also mounting conflict over the kind of worker representation that the NWLB was imposing in war-related industries. The government favored elected shop committees in each enterprise, but there was little agreement among labor, management, and public representatives over the kind of "Industrial Democracy" these committees were supposed to establish. Followers of Frederick Taylor (who died in 1915) had moderated their previous emphasis on management control and saw elected shop committees as a mechanism for winning worker participation in a collaborative search for greater productivity. Yet, according to some Progressives and corporate leaders, worker participation did not always require a union; indeed, there were many managers who saw elected shop committees as a useful counter to union organization and were sponsoring employee representation plans (ERPs) in an effort to repel AFL or left-wing unions. Labor leaders naturally opposed these "company unions" as a form of sham democracy, lacking the power to pursue policies that management opposed ("We discuss matters but we never vote,"[37] as Charles Schwab later acknowledged of the nonunion committees he sponsored at Bethlehem Steel). Even so, the NWLB gave ERPs official standing in 1918, coequal with independent unions.

These disputes over what kind of worker representation the federal government should support were still unresolved when the war abruptly ended in November 1918. Within weeks of the guns falling silent, there followed the biggest strike wave to that date in American history. More than four million workers dropped their tools and went on strike in 1919, spurred in part by inflationary price increases that had doubled the cost of food and clothing since 1914, and in part by the widely held belief that workers' wartime exertions had not been recognized or compensated. Wage increases and collective bargaining were the immediate demands, but there was also a deeper spirit of rebellion that animated the mass strikes sweeping both Europe and North America. In Europe, general strikes and army mutinies overthrew the Russian Czar in 1917 and German monarchy in 1918, and thereafter flared during 1919 into revolutionary outbursts in central and eastern Europe. There was no such revolutionary potential in the United States, where war casualties were far smaller and war damage entirely absent, but many observers in 1919 detected the initial tremors of such an upheaval in the Seattle general strike, the Boston police strike, and the massive walkouts in steel, coal mining, textiles, telephones, construction, meatpacking, and metal fabricating.

The skilled metalworkers who led many of these movements were alarmed by scientific management and the wartime dilution of their skills, trends that had not *yet* gone so far as to eliminate their considerable power in toolrooms and many workshops, but had gone far enough to threaten *future* extinction. Their demand for "workers' control of industry" sometimes masked a narrow defense of craft privilege, but sometimes it merged with the organization of less-skilled operatives and laborers into powerful "all-grades" movements for industrial organization.

This rebellious spirit was especially evident in the nationwide strike by more than three hundred thousand steelworkers. Few imagined such a mammoth turnout was possible when union leaders—supported by strike ballots distributed in six languages—called for a walkout on September 22 to force an end to company unions, the twelve-hour workday, and the seven-day workweek. At the Colorado Fuel and Iron company's steel mill in Pueblo, Colorado, President J. F. Welborn had such confidence in his workers' loyalty to the Employee Representation Plan (formed after the 1914 Ludlow massacre to assuage public opinion) that he publicly conceded to the union any men who would picket outside come September 22—because "all those on the inside will be mine."[38] He later rued these words when only three hundred men crossed the picket lines, leaving six thousand union supporters outside the gates. Similar turnouts across the country swelled the strikers' exuberant ranks and partly compensated for the AFL's clumsy structure of union organization. Instead of a single industrial union for steel, the AFL had established a National Committee of twenty-four separate unions that claimed members (or hoped to) in the mills, mines, and related industries. Newly organized workers were distributed to their "appropriate" craft union or, lacking a craft, to the Amalgamated Association of Iron and Steel Workers. This unwieldy approach hobbled the National Committee from the start, since most constituent unions backed away from their initial pledges of money and organizers, leaving the committee without resources or staff. Some government officials supported the unions, including the mayor of Cleveland who banned strikebreakers from entering the city. In Pennsylvania's Allegheny County, on the other hand, local authorities deputized five thousand men who were armed and paid for by the companies; these irregulars subsequently unleashed a reign of terror in the Pittsburgh area, making it practically impossible to hold public meetings without inviting physical assaults and mass arrests.

Strikers pinned their hopes on the deliberations of President Wilson's National Industrial Conference, convened in the early weeks of the strike to find a compromise settlement for the general unrest sweeping American industry. Representatives from labor and the public favored extending the NWLB's wartime policies into the peacetime economy, with a declaration supporting "the right of wage earners to . . . be represented by representatives of their own choosing in negotiations and adjustments with employers."[39] However, even this compromise phrasing, which pointedly omitted reference to unions, was vetoed by management representatives who wanted an explicit disavowal of any obligation to negotiate with men "not of the number of their own employees,"[40] as corporate leader Frederick Fish described AFL leaders. The Industrial Conference ended in bitter disagreement, and with it ended any prospect for settling the steel strike on a compromise basis.

With employers refusing to bargain and with workers confronting hunger and cold, the strikers drifted back to work in growing numbers. The skilled men usually went back first, the less-skilled holding out even as the companies hired thirty thousand African-Americans as strikebreakers. For these newly hired men, AFL craft unions had no more appeal than the many other "whites-only" institutions that excluded them. The companies had little more credibility as "friends of the Negro," but at least mill owners were now—for whatever reason—offering jobs that few blacks could have entered before 1915. The wartime labor shortage had drawn them northward from southern agriculture, and many were now competing for jobs and housing in the industrial centers of the Northeast and Midwest. The same racial dynamic that rebounded against the AFL's steel unions appeared in other strikes during 1919, contributing to tensions that exploded in a series of deadly race riots across the country's urban landscape.

On January 8, 1920, with the strike already lost in the major mill towns, the steelworkers' National Committee sent a final telegram from union headquarters directing the remaining strikers to fold their tents. Even in defeat, the telegram sounded a hopeful note: "All steelworkers are now at liberty to return to work pending preparations for the next big organization movement."[41] There was no such movement that year, however, or in any other year of the decade that followed. Defeat in most of the 1919 strikes, particularly steel, marked a turning point, followed by a general retreat from the organizational heights of the war years. By 1923, union membership had fallen to 3.6 million, a 30 percent decline from the previous peak of 5.1 million.

THE AMERICAN PLAN

The labor movement that survived this postwar shakeout was still bigger than the one that had existed a decade before, but its internal composition was dramatically transformed. The UMW, the AFL's biggest and most militant industrial union, declined during the 1920s from five hundred thousand members to below one hundred thousand as the wartime protections of the federal government were annulled, the demand for coal slackened, and mine owners went on the offensive. As other industrial-union movements in meatpacking, steel, and metalworking were defeated or sharply contained between 1919 and 1922, the craft-oriented building trades emerged as the dominant affiliates within the AFL. The continuing high-rise construction boom in America's urban centers actually increased their membership during the 1920s, accentuating the AFL's bias toward craft organization. In an industry that built specialized structures with complex and unique installations of machinery, the construction trades were especially resistant to the standardized and de-skilled methods of scientific management. The ease with which small-scale contractors moved back and forth from journeyman status to small business-man also made tradesmen less receptive to radical visions of working-class solidarity, and their near total exclusion of minorities and women put them at odds with the growing numbers of both these groups in the wage-earning workforce.

For industrial workers, the postwar era was a time of especially dramatic transformations. This was partly the result of the ongoing industrial engineering that was replacing skilled work in many industries with semi-automatic machinery and simplified assembly processes. With the widening application of these mass production methods, many union leaders came to accept the kind of productivity bargaining endorsed by Louis Brandeis and other progressive proponents of scientific management, abandoning craft control of production for higher wages and purchasing power. Sidney Hillman's Amalgamated Clothing Workers led the way in the clothing industry, where grievance-arbitration procedures like those won at Hart, Schaffner, & Marx in 1910 found wider acceptance in the 1920s. But clothing was the exception, and AFL overtures to progressive business leaders for a détente based on the same approach largely fell on deaf ears. The transformation of work would be a top-down movement in the 1920s, imposed by management.

Accompanying this industrial engineering was a parallel social engineering that was just as relentlessly focused on remaking the working class. A primary target of these efforts was the immigrant worker. Even after defeating most of the 1919 strikes, industrial leaders viewed foreign-born factory operatives as an unpredictable genie, at once a highly profitable source of labor power, but also an increasingly volatile, alien force capable of collective resistance. Many government leaders concurred. "This is America," said Allegheny Sheriff William Haddock after suppressing the steel strike in the Pittsburgh area, and "my observation has been . . . that practically 90 percent of the offenders against the law are either aliens or naturalized citizens of foreign extraction, who are easily led into attacks on our government."[42] U.S. Attorney General A. Mitchell

Palmer further embellished this stereotype in his frequent attacks on foreign-born radicals. "Out of the sly and crafty eyes of many of them leap cupidity, cruelty, insanity, and crime; from their lopsided faces, sloping brows, and misshapen features may be recognized the unmistakable criminal type."[43]

Palmer's racist fulminations were no doubt inflamed by the dynamiting of his home in 1919, apparently the work of an Italian-born anarchist opposed to government attacks on antiwar radicals. Palmer and others also detected the work of foreign agents in the newly organized communist parties that sprang up during 1919. Modeling themselves on the Bolshevik revolutionaries who had seized power in Russia, foreign-born communists in the United States—especially those in the Russian language federation of the Socialist Party—denounced the reformist and nonviolent tactics of the SP and called on like-minded radicals to join a Communist International allied to Moscow. The Socialist Party split into warring factions over this call to immediate rebellion and finally expelled the communists in 1919.

Palmer, no less so than his revolutionary opponents in the communist underground, believed an armed uprising was possible, perhaps imminent, even though less-passionate observers saw little chance for such an occurrence. Palmer also believed that decisive action on his part could win him the presidential nomination of the Democratic Party. On January 2, 1920, he therefore launched a coordinated assault on left-wing organizations across the country, arresting more than four thousand people in thirty-three cities and twenty-three states. Only a handful of those taken into custody were charged with crimes or brought to trial; the overwhelming majority were held incommunicado for days in makeshift prisons, interrogated without counsel, and then either released or marched through the streets—wearing chains in some cases—to long-term detention and deportation. Thousands more were swept up in state-sponsored dragnets as part of a nationwide Red scare that grew out of the wartime suppression of the SP and IWW. By 1921, thirty-five states had passed criminal syndicalist or sedition laws that not only made illegal the mere advocacy of political violence, but in Ohio's case even made liable both the owner and the janitor of any hall where such views were expressed. Thirty-two states made it a crime to wave a red flag in public. New York state went so far as to declare the Socialist Party illegal in 1920 and refused to let five socialist legislators take their seats, even after all five were subsequently reelected.

The Communist Party underground, small to begin with in 1919, shrank to a tiny band of paranoiac and ineffective militants. The Socialist Party, although opposed to the Communists, was further weakened by the indiscriminate assault on the left. Eugene Debs again drew 920,000 votes in 1920 as the SP candidate for president, despite the fact he spent the entire campaign in the federal penitentiary, the result of his wartime advocacy of draft resistance. In 1921, the National Civic Federation found that socialist sentiment "has never been stronger," but the SP had "for the moment become a negligible force."[44] In the 1924 presidential elections, Senator Robert LaFollette of Wisconsin drew socialist and labor support in his run for president as an independent Progressive, winning 17 percent of the vote (36 percent in Pittsburgh and 44 percent in Cleveland). But progressive third-party efforts did not survive this single outing.

Cleansing the nation of foreign-born radicals and their native-born allies in the labor movement was only a first step in the eyes of many "Americanizers." The upheavals of 1919 and the lurid press accounts that accompanied them had so inflamed the popular imagination that many were now prepared to accept more thoroughgoing solutions. "We do not want to be a dumping ground for radicals, agitators, [and] Reds, who do not understand our ideals,"[45] said General Leonard Wood, commander of the federal troops that broke the 1919 steel strike in Gary, Indiana. The general added his voice to the many others calling for an end to unlimited immigration from Europe, and the Immigration Acts of 1921 and 1924 finally closed the door on federal policy that had encouraged immigration since the founding of the Republic.

Businessmen were now praised as the messiahs of a resurgent capitalism that would assimilate the working class and "Americanize" the foreign-born. "The man who builds a factory builds a temple,"[46] said Republican President Calvin Coolidge in one of his pro-business sermons of the mid-1920s, and both he and President Warren Harding before him placed the federal government at the service of this corporate "priesthood." During their administrations, the wartime excess profits tax was abolished and income taxes for the wealthy were cut dramatically. Treasury Secretary Andrew Mellon, founder of Gulf Oil and Alcoa, authorized billions in tax refunds and abatements for corporations during the decade. Harding, Coolidge, and (after 1928) President Herbert Hoover meanwhile vetoed numerous farm-relief and social service bills.

Administration of the law reverted to the prewar standards of "Business First." The Justice Department, far from opposing price-fixing conspiracies and other monopoly practices, openly encouraged corporate mergers and industry-wide associations to reduce competition and stabilize profits at high levels. The Supreme Court further buttressed business interests by voiding much of the Progressive legislation passed before 1920. The government, the court ruled, could not place restrictions on the hiring of child labor, could not set minimum wage standards, and could not otherwise "interfere" with business operations. In 1921, the Supreme Court all but declared peaceful picketing unlawful. The very word *picket,* according to the Court, suggested a "sinister" and "militant purpose" to deprive owners of their property rights. Thereafter, the court nullified the Clayton Act's prohibition of strike injunctions by declaring that, without judicial intervention, work stoppages might otherwise become an "irreparable injury to property." As a result, the number of antistrike injunctions soared to 921 during the 1920s, double the number in the previous decade.

Corporate leaders also offered a carrot as well as a stick in subduing the labor movement. "Take care of your men," Judge Elbert Gary, chairman of U.S. Steel, told his subsidiary managers in 1919. "Don't let the families go hungry or cold; give them playgrounds and parks and schools and churches."[47] It would cost money to provide these amenities, but it was well spent if it left "no just ground for criticism on the part of those who are connected with the movement of unrest."[48] Prodded by public criticism and the direct intervention of President Harding, the steel industry even abolished the twelve-hour day in 1923 and raised hourly wages 25 percent to compensate for the reduction to eight hours. The steel companies thereby granted what the strikers of 1919 had demanded, but as a gift rather than a right. Large corporations could afford this largess, paid for with the stunning productivity and profit increases of the decade, and some companies diverted a portion of these resources to corporate welfare programs like company housing, insurance benefits, company unions, and modest pensions. Few companies went so far as the Ford Motor Company, which had doubled wages to $5.00 a day in 1914 to counter the organizing efforts of the IWW and reduce labor turnover. Ford was also unique in compelling workers to open their homes to company inspectors, who searched for evidence that the $5.00 wage was spent on an appropriately "American" standard of living. In the 1920s, this style of coercive Americanization gave way to the positive inducements of corporate welfare, but even these were the exception rather than the rule. Fewer than 10 percent of all companies provided significant welfare benefits, and these were often restricted to skilled workers with high seniority. In 1930, just 2 percent of all retired workers received a pension from their employer.

Much more telling was the general atmosphere of growth, prosperity, and individual opportunity that characterized the 1920s. New industries and services grew as the automobile generated road building and urban sprawl, and new factories flooded the market with an ever-widening array of consumer goods. "Mass marketing" became a required component of "mass production" as corporations sought customers for their increasingly productive factories. The drumbeat of consumer advertising grew louder in the 1920s with the advent of radio broadcasting, which beamed the message of mass consumption directly into the home—along with *The General Motors Family Party and The Palmolive Hour.* Modern appliances were for sale, and with them an individualistic lifestyle that shunned the insular cohesion of immigrant cultures. "National advertising is the great Americanizer," declared Francis Alice Kellor, director of the American Association of Foreign Language Newspapers (AAFLN). "It is the answer to Bolshevism."[49] The AAFLN, founded by a consortium of corporations including Standard Oil and American Tobacco, was certainly no friend of immigrant culture. The ads it funneled to seven hundred foreign-language newspapers in the 1920s were designed to break down immigrant and rural values of thrift and home-based production of food and clothes. The diversity and self-sufficiency of these immigrant cultures contradicted the message of mass marketing, which stressed individual success, status anxiety, and conformity—whether you owned a *Leisure Hour* electric washer, or had the foresight to neutralize the "hidden wells of poison" in your mouth with Listerine. "The boss? . . . There with th' pipe," a worker says in a 1920 ad for Edgeworth Tobacco. "Men at the top are apt to be pipe smokers. Ever noticed?" Status was on sale at your local drugstore, and you had only yourself to blame if you didn't buy into it.

Although not immune to this relentless barrage of consumer propaganda, many workers also had reason to question it. The ad writers' surreal visions of consumer bliss contrasted sharply with the workplace reality of intensified labor in mechanized mass production. Coal miners and farmers, both mired in the decade-long depression of their respective industries, faced declining incomes and narrowing opportunities. African-Americans, on the other hand, had it both ways in the 1920s—for better and for worse. Fleeing the racism and rural poverty of the South, they found jobs and a vibrant urban culture in the North. But they also found segregated theaters, whites-only restaurants and housing, and discriminatory practices that denied them access to job training and skilled work. The revived Ku Klux Klan found its newest recruits in the North and grew to a national membership of more than four million in the early 1920s. Immigrants also found themselves targeted by the KKK's hate propaganda, but rather than identify with the principal victims of racist intolerance, many white ethnics assimilated the prevailing American ethos of white supremacy.

The ambiguous status of the Pullman porter personified the mixed blessings of black life in the 1920s. In that decade, the Pullman Company was the country's largest single employer of African-Americans, all of them as porters servicing the company's railroad sleeping cars. For many blacks, the job was a coveted opportunity to earn money while traveling the country, and the Pullman porter's starched white uniform became a badge of pride in a community only one step removed from the field hand's sweated work clothes. "Neckties were mandatory," remembered Ernest Ford, "and you have to understand, blacks were *elated* to get out of denims." But Ford also recalled the numerous indignities that shadowed his work. "The conductor was like a gestapo over the porter,"[50] he later recalled of his immediate supervisor, a whites-only position that paid twice as much. Earning a minimum of $60.00 a month in 1920 compared with the conductor's $120.00, the porter received only an additional $12.00 for the frequent occasions he was assigned the conductor's duties as well as his own. Tipping was supposed to supplement his income, but also obligated the porter to adopt a servile manner that whites found comforting. The constant travel that made him the envy of many African-Americans was also the porter's curse, exposing him to long stretches away from his family, frequent denials of service in restaurants and hotels, and night service on trains where the porter was prohibited from sleeping.

In 1925, a group approached A. Philip Randolph, the prominent socialist and editor of *The Messenger*, and asked him to assume the leadership of a nationwide organizing effort. The Brotherhood of Sleeping Car Porters (BSCP), organized in Harlem and spreading across the country to Chicago and Oakland, California, thereafter emerged as the largest black union in America. The Pullman Company responded with firings, beatings, and spies, but the BSCP continued recruiting under the motto "Fight or Be Slaves." "We were a handful of Negroes," recalled C. L. Dellums, an early organizer in Oakland who estimated that between five hundred and one thousand porters were fired for union activity. "[We] had nothing: no money, no experience in this."[51] Porters who feared for their jobs shied away from the Brotherhood and joined Pullman's company union, but in many cases the wives of pro-union porters would secretly carry on the organizational work while their husbands were on the road. "That's why I say that the women were the ones who were the backbone," recalled Rosina Tucker, who collected dues and organized teas and dances to raise money. "Of course, it was dangerous because it was possible that my husband would lose his job, if the people—we call them stool pigeons—if they knew. So that's why we had to be very, very careful about our meetings."[52]

In 1928, still organizing but unable to win recognition from the Pullman company, Randolph took his fledgling union into the AFL. Some porters criticized this move, noting that many AFL unions barred black workers. Randolph, however, took the longer view that social change—within the AFL and without—required black-white unity. "My philosophy was the result of our concept of effective liberation of working people," he would later say. "We never separated the liberation of the white working man from the liberation of the black working man. . . . The unity of these forces would bring about the power to achieve basic social change."[53]

That unity seemed a distant prospect in 1928. Unions were in decline, corporations were ascendant, and the commercial media welcomed both trends as harbingers of a new era. Charles Schwab of Bethlehem Steel proclaimed in *Nation's Business* that "it is a great joy to me to realize that humanity rules American industrial life today."[54] This optimistic assessment was widely shared by corporate leaders. "The end of the strike era is in sight," as one business spokesman predicted in 1929. Indeed, "the next five years will see an unparalleled gain in relationships of mutual understanding and good will between employee and employer."[55]

3

TRIUMPH AND CONTAINMENT, 1929–1941

The self-congratulatory optimism of Charles Schwab and other business leaders in 1929 was undeserved and certainly ill timed. Within a few short months, the economy was sliding into the abyss of the Great Depression, triggering an explosive social confrontation that would dramatically reshape American society and labor relations. Far from ending, the "strike era" was about to begin.

American workers entered this depression decade in the worst shape imaginable, victims of mass unemployment, near starvation, and, when they protested, violent suppression. They would end the decade with a new labor movement, far larger and more inclusive, and with supportive government policies establishing fair labor standards and a social safety net for the poor and unemployed. Sixty years after the "Great Uprising" of 1877, American workers would finally win recognition and legitimacy for their common interests, safeguarded by law and collective bargaining.

It would be, however, an uneven victory, and it would come at a price. Union organization was deep and wide in many manufacturing industries, especially in the North, but it was thin and precarious in most services, and especially weak in the South. Legislation protecting collective action would help subdue the fatal violence of police and antiunion employers, ending six decades of bloodshed, but these same laws would encourage a growing dependence on government protection as public support for unions waned in the last years of the decade.

THE GREAT DEPRESSION

In a decade of "turning points" for labor, the first and most fundamental transformations of the Depression era were psychological.

The initial reaction to the stock market crash in October 1929 and the mass unemployment that followed was not always rebellious. As layoffs swelled the ranks of the unemployed from just five hundred thousand in the fall of 1929 to an estimated eight million by 1931, the first response was often stunned disbelief, followed by deepening melancholia. "I have a definite feeling," said writer Louis Adamic of American workers in that second full year of the depression, "that millions of them, now that they are unemployed, are licked."[1]

That many saw their unemployment as a personal defeat, an individual rather than a social failing, was due in no small part to the repeated denials by "expert opinion" that anything was seriously wrong with the economy. Almost immediately, business and government leaders claimed that this "temporary downturn" would soon give way to renewed prosperity. "Manufacturing activity is now . . . definitely on the road to recovery,"[2] the esteemed Harvard Economic Society declared in March 1930, even as the economy careened downward. "Just grin, keep on working, [and] stop worrying about the future," advised Charles Schwab of Bethlehem Steel. "We always have a way of living through the hard times."[3] Thousands of unemployed tried to do so by selling apples in the streets, a polite form of begging that President Herbert Hoover welcomed with the nonsensical claim that "many persons [have] left their jobs for the more profitable one of selling apples."[4] Henry Ford had more blame than praise for the victims of unemployment, scolding "the average man" who "won't really do a day's work unless he is caught and cannot get out of it." By his estimate, there was no depression. "There is plenty of work to do, if people would do it."[5]

Against this backdrop of official denial, individual workers "experienced a private kind of shame when the pink slip came," as writer Studs Terkel described it. "No matter that others suffered the same fate, the inner voice whispered, 'I'm a failure.'"[6] Few could initially grasp the enormity of the crisis, particularly when the government did not publish unemployment figures. "One doesn't improve the condition of a sick man," Hoover's Secretary of Labor remarked in 1930, "by constantly telling him how sick he is."[7] According to the economic orthodoxy of the day, government intervention in the economy—even publishing unemployment statistics—would only discourage the natural recuperative powers of the free market. Instead of hard facts, President Hoover prescribed a steady diet of wishful thinking, repeatedly claiming that "recovery was just around the corner." In the meantime, Harvey Campbell, executive vice president of the Detroit Chamber of Commerce, expressed the opinion (and probably the hope) that "50 percent of the people in the United States don't know enough to know there is a depression."[8]

Henry Ford certainly knew, despite his public denials. By 1931 he had slashed his company's payroll from 129,000 workers to 37,000, and by the winter of 1932–1933 the auto industry was operating at just 25 percent of capacity. Annual production had fallen from 4.5 million cars in 1929 to barely one million, and estimated unemployment in the auto centers of Michigan and Ohio ranged between 40 and 55 percent of the workforce. The steel industry was worse still: in 1932, U.S. Steel was operating at just 17 percent of capacity with combined loses of $71 million, the first red ink in the firm's history. The company's full-time workforce simply disappeared, falling from 225,000 in 1929 to zero in April 1933, when all remaining workers (half the 1929 level) were working part time. Unemployment in steel towns from South Chicago eastward through Pennsylvania hovered close to 50 percent. Nationwide unemployment among construction workers rose toward 80 percent in the same year. Among textile workers, employment fell 26 percent between 1929 and 1933, much of it concentrated in one-industry mill towns in the South and especially New England, where unemployment in Lowell, Lawrence, and elsewhere soared beyond 60 percent. Layoffs here and elsewhere pushed the number of unemployed nationwide to an estimated 15 million in March 1933, representing 30 percent of the civilian labor force and 44 percent of all non-farm workers.

Fearing a complete collapse in consumer demand and a downward spiral that would lead to still more layoffs, President Hoover at first persuaded many large employers to hold wages at their 1929 levels. As sales and profits nose-dived, however, economic realities overwhelmed these voluntary measures. "None of us can escape the inexorable law of the balance sheet,"[9] said Schwab of Bethlehem Steel as his company cut wages 10 percent in 1931. By 1933, average wages in manufacturing had fallen to 44 cents an hour, 21 percent lower than 1929. Because most employed workers were on short-shift schedules, some working just five or ten hours a week to spread the available work, factory earnings fell even faster than wages, from a weekly average of $24.76 in 1929 to $16.65 in 1933—a 33 percent fall in just four years. Companies also cut prices in a mad scramble for sales, but the fall in the cost of living (24 percent) did not match the fall in weekly earnings.

Lower prices were small consolation to the unemployed, who had *zero* income and could not afford food or clothing at any price; only with their meager savings could they fend off starvation and eviction, and these reserves were soon exhausted. For most, the future was narrowing to a precarious, uncertain passage through the daily struggle to survive. Because the prevailing wisdom of the 1920s held that private enterprise rather than government would always provide for the future, there were no federally funded programs to cushion the blow of mass layoffs—no unemployment insurance, no emergency aid for food or mortgage, and no social security income for the elderly and disabled. Private charities and city welfare departments struggled to fill the gap, but the sheer scale of public need dwarfed their paltry means, forcing them into bankruptcy as well. It was the law of the jungle, harkening back to the "Social Darwinism" of the previous century. For a few who remained comfortable throughout, this brutish struggle had a positive side. "Some of the weaker, according to the law of nature, will naturally die under the stress of the times," observed Professor E. G. Conklin of Princeton University, but "the strong will survive and reproduce, and thus the human race will be strengthened."[10] Andrew Mellon, Hoover's treasury secretary and one of America's richest men, agreed that the crisis was "not altogether a bad thing" since "enterprising people will pick up the wrecks from less-competent people."[11]

This was cold comfort for those suffering the complete dissolution of their lives. The summary report of California's Unemployment Commission, issued in November 1932, captured the tenor of this nationwide catastrophe:

> Unemployment and loss of income have ravaged numerous homes. It has broken the spirits of their members, undermined their health, robbed them of self-respect, destroyed their efficiency and their employability. . . . Many households have been dissolved; little chil-

dren parceled out to friends, relatives, or charitable homes; husbands and wives, parents and children separated, temporarily or permanently. Homes in which life savings were invested and hopes bound up have been lost, never to be recovered. Men, young and old, have taken to the road. They sleep each night in a new flophouse. Day after day the country over, they stand in the breadlines for food which carries with it the suggestion, "move on," "We don't want you.". . . There is no security, no foothold, no future to sustain them.

Marriages and births declined. Malnutrition, typhoid, and tuberculosis all increased. Behind these statistics was the grinding, relentless degradation of poverty. "Literal starvation had been the lot of some," recalled Maurice Sugar, a union attorney in Detroit, "garbage cans and dumps the source of food for many. . . . Repossessions, evictions, bankruptcies, foreclosures had become the order of the day. Everywhere was suffering, misery, despair."[12]

COMMON GROUND

The insecurity and psychological trauma of the depression invaded every household in the country, scarring an entire generation of working Americans. The sea change in popular consciousness that flowed from this common experience would have profound implications for the future of the country. Above all, the seismic shock of mass unemployment would produce a noticeable "leveling" in gender, ethnic, racial, and occupational identities, preparing the ground for a more unified labor movement.

Underemployment was a near universal experience, but as its intensity and duration varied by degree for different groups of workers, their relative status and self-awareness changed accordingly. Men had predominated in jobs producing high-cost goods (houses, cars, and the capital equipment and materials to produce them), and because these were the first things hard-pressed families stopped buying, the unemployment rate among men was correspondingly higher than that among women, who were concentrated in service, clerical, and retail jobs where layoffs were less severe. As a result, the proportion of women in the wage-labor force grew during the 1930s from one-in-five workers to one-in-four, and in some cities to as much as a one-in-three.

For those who held to the traditional claim that men should remain the primary breadwinners, this was an unwelcome trend, and some companies and municipalities sought to reverse it by firing or refusing to hire married women. Their employment, it was argued, was "stealing" jobs from able-bodied men. In fact, many men were neither willing nor prepared to take "women's work" in clerical and service positions even if it were offered, and in many cases it was not—employers were generally happy to hire women at lower pay. Yet however low, women's wages became increasingly important in working-class households, and their status as wage earners grew as well. Many housewives likewise found themselves pushed into larger roles as their husband's workplace-world collapsed and the family's welfare depended on the household and neighborhood resources she could muster. For the labor movement, this augmenting of women's roles would lead to new possibilities in the nature and dynamics of union organization.

As gender roles partially overlapped, so did ethnic distinctions gradually fade. This had much to do with trends already evident in the 1920s, as legal restrictions on immigration curtailed the number of new arrivals, and as "Americanization" campaigns and corporate advertising projected a common, conformist culture of mass consumption. The depression dramatically accelerated both trends. With jobs no longer beckoning, the number of immigrants entering the United States in the winter of 1931 fell to its lowest level since 1820. At the same time, the depression overwhelmed many of the ethnic institutions that had preserved old-world cultures and identities. In Detroit by the winter of 1930, four of six Italian-owned banks were bankrupt, the Finnish Educational Association had lost control of its hall to creditors, and the Ukrainian Greek Church had closed both its parochial schools. As the depression deepened, ethnic groceries and mutual-aid societies also succumbed. Second-generation workers in these devastated communities still came from hyphenated cultures, but they now put increasing emphasis on the "American" half of their identity. If nothing else, labor's message did not always require translation into a half-dozen languages, as in past decades.

The depression also had a leveling effect on race relations as white workers found themselves victimized in ways previously reserved for America's nonwhite minorities. Here too, there was a backlash as the competition for jobs flared into racial antagonism whenever whites demanded the special considerations of white-skin privilege. In scores of low-wage jobs where African-Americans predominated, black workers were fired and replaced by whites, driving the unemployment rate among black workers to more than twice the level of whites—in some southern cities as high as 80 percent in the winter of 1932–1933. When the jobs at stake were relatively well paid, the struggle could become especially brutish; in Mississippi, whites terrorized black railroad workers in an attempt to drive them from their jobs as locomotive firemen, killing seven by mid-1933. Many Mexican-Americans were driven out of the country altogether, sometimes by forced deportations, more often by the blatantly discriminatory practices of municipalities and private charities that denied emergency aid to Latino families. By either means, five hundred thousand Mexican nationals and their U.S.-born children were returned to Mexico during the 1930s.

Yet the sheer enormity of the crisis also had a unifying effect. Although the suffering was indeed worse for America's minorities, it was nearly as bad for the whites who now joined them in the same breadlines, the same soup kitchens, the same "hobo jungles" on the outskirts of town. Misery was the common condition, and many blacks and whites found common cause in their shared predicament. The writer Meridel Le Sueur recalled one such occasion in Minneapolis, when a group of women broke the windows of an expensive grocery and began taking food; a black woman in the interracial group gathered as much bacon as she could carry, but rather than leave, called out, "Who has the most children here?"[13] The food went to families most in need.

The depression even humbled those whose previous prosperity had elevated them to "middle-class" standards of comfort and security. Tool and die makers, the skilled craftsmen who built the specialized machine tools that made mass production possible, fell the furthest as manufacturers postponed new models and canceled orders for new machinery. From an average annual income of $2,433 in 1929—50 percent higher than production workers in manufacturing—the toolmaker's income plummeted to an estimated $636 in 1933, actually below the earnings of many production workers. "They have lost their homes, they have had their automobiles repossessed, their furniture mortgaged," toolmaker Mat Smith testified in 1934 government hearings. "To eke out an existence, these men, the 'aristocrats of automobile labor,' arrange to go on welfare, try door-to-door selling, or plead for odd jobs."[14] Lawyers' income fell 30 percent in the same years, doctors', 43 percent, dentists', 48 percent, and every middle-class family suffered the depression's culminating blow in the winter of 1933, when the entire national banking system collapsed. Ted Hinckley, son of a California lawyer, remembered the day his father returned home with news their savings had been wiped out. "The back door opened and my father . . . slowly entered. His face was almost ashen. His eyes, usually filled with bonhomie, were filled with fear. My mother rose, but before she could say a word, he groaned, 'They have closed the banks.'"[15]

From this baseline misery emerged a widening resentment of the business leaders and government officials who counseled patience. Even the most liberal corporations, the few that had voluntarily implemented extensive benefit programs and company housing for their employees in the 1920s, now reneged on their promise of cradle-to-grave security. To protect its dwindling profits, General Motors abolished its employee savings plan and began to repossess company-built housing from unemployed autoworkers. General Electric initially increased funding for the unemployment benefits it paid to laid-off GE workers, but as the layoffs continued—eventually totaling more than half its workforce—GE canceled the program. "This was too ambitious a plan for any one company to undertake,"[16] admitted GE's president Gerard Swope. Further cuts followed in 1932 as the company abolished its attendance bonus, canceled paid vacations for blue-collar workers, and eliminated home-mortgage assistance. It was noted by many that although GE recalled these "gifts" from its hard-pressed workers, the company was dipping into reserves to continue paying stockholder dividends.

"The bankers and industrialists who have been running our country have proved their utter inability, or indifference, to put the country in a better condition,"[17] as V. C. French, an unemployed machinist about to lose his home, wrote AFL president William Green in 1933. French, like millions of others, had nowhere to turn. Corporations had canceled their benefit programs, municipal welfare departments were hopelessly underfunded, and private charities were bankrupt. The federal government made equivocal, half-hearted gestures to stem the crisis, boosting public works spending and providing emergency loans to businesses and states. But it was too little, too late, and popular resentment of the president's failure to take decisive action found expression in a lexicon of new phrases: a hobo camp was a "Hooverville," a meal of cheap horse meat was a "Hooverburger," and empty pockets turned inside out were "Hoover flags."

The labor movement was equally at a loss to provide direction or even a vehicle for protest. AFL membership, already diminished by the antiunion campaigns of the 1920s, fell further still after the crash, bottoming in 1933 at less than three million—a mere 6 percent of the workforce. The conservative, craft-oriented leaders of the federation bemoaned the deteriorating economic conditions, but as often as not blamed the victims, calling for deportation of illegal aliens and a ban on hiring women. In automaking, electrical appliances, meatpacking, steel, and rubber, where union membership hovered near zero, a handful of AFL craftsmen still regarded semiskilled workers "more as a threat to their security than as a field for missionary effort,"[18] as writer Paul Kellogg put it in the late 1920s. Surviving AFL affiliates in trucking and services were visited by even greater disaster as organized crime, having lost revenue from declining sales of bootleg liquor, seized control of local unions and began skimming dues, extorting employers, and distributing jobs to underemployed gunmen. In New York's clothing trades, Sidney Hillman and the Amalgamated Clothing Workers drove the mobsters out of cutter's Local 4 in 1931 with protest strikes, demonstrations, and physical confrontations. But the AFL mobilized no comparable countermeasures among its affiliates, as big-city gangs invaded local unions in New York City and Chicago.

Federation officials adopted the same do-nothing strategy in response to growing public demands for federal unemployment insurance. Government support for the unemployed, said the AFL Executive Council in 1931, was "a crutch that permanently weakens industry and keeps it from solving a problem whose solution is essential."[19] Only in 1932, when it was evident that voluntary efforts to stem unemployment had failed, did the AFL reverse itself and join—at the tail end—the movement for reform.

FIRST STEPS

There was no automatic turning point where resentment and anger "spontaneously" boiled into public protest. Some individuals and groups protested early and often, others only as protest movements gained momentum, and others not at all.

Indeed, many people endured their suffering in isolation, without protest, either because they believed that conditions should not be changed, could not be changed, or could only be changed at great risk. Rather than protest, they turned their anger inward and blamed themselves. Meridel Le Sueur recalled the unemployed women who suffered "without saying a word to anyone. A woman will shut herself up in a room until it is taken away from her, and eat a cracker a day and be as quiet as a mouse so there are no social statistics concerning her."[20] One statistic that did measure this kind of anguish was the steep climb in suicide rates after 1929, a telling indicator of the psychological depression that accompanied its economic twin.

For others, anger turned outward. "I myself would like nothing better than in broad daylight to heave bricks of patent dynamite into the windows of bureaus and agencies that are supposed to be established for the benefit of unemployed girls," fumed one Minneapolis writer, "Leah," in the pages of a pro-union newspaper, *United Action*.[21] Welfare supervisors in Detroit who had described the unemployed in 1930 as "orderly and . . . brooding," were by 1931 describing a "quickened irritability" among the city's 230,000 relief recipients.[22] Looting of grocery stores became more common in cities across the country, sometimes escalating into food riots as hungry crowds fought with police. "Nearly all my jobless acquaintances applauded the looting of stores,"[23] recalled Clayton Fountain, an unemployed autoworker who used to forage outside the city at night, stealing corn for resale at 15 cents a dozen.

Violence and lawlessness foretold a rising anger, but not the target of its fury. Although resentment of corporations and the rich was commonplace, it required organization and political mobilization to make it articulate, and no establishment party or group would provide leadership for such a movement. Individual politicians, liberals in both the Republican and Democratic Parties, sympathized with the plight of the unemployed and sponsored ameliorative legislation, but their piecemeal efforts did not stem the avalanche of layoffs, foreclosures, and evictions. Government failure to take effective action created a leadership vacuum in the political landscape, which the AFL's timorous officers neither wanted nor knew how to fill. It was into this void, therefore, that radicals stepped forward from all points on the political compass, setting in motion events that would shape much of the decade's labor and social history.

First in the field was the Communist Party (CP). Still closely identified with the Soviet Union, which it followed as model and guide, the party was self-consciously aligned with the policies and fate of a foreign dictatorship. Yet however closely it hued to Moscow's official line, the CP's mobilization of discontent in the depression years also attracted genuine homegrown radicals and a growing following among angry workers. Within six months of the stock market crash, the CP was calling for nationwide demonstrations of the unemployed to coincide with similar protests around the world, scheduled for March 6, 1930. Few imagined the call would generate much response, since the party retained only a minuscule membership (barely seven thousand) and the depression was not yet acknowledged for the disaster it would soon become. Authorities were therefore stunned by the turnout: thirty-five thousand in New York City, fifty thousand in Chicago, forty thousand in Milwaukee, fifty thousand in Detroit, and tens of thousands more in cities across the country. In Detroit, the demonstrators were met by three thousand police—"horsemen, machine gunners, and plain clothesmen" as reported by the *Detroit Times*—with the mounted police riding into the crowd, their clubs swinging and their horses stepping gingerly on their cork shoes."[24] Demonstrators in Washington, D.C., were teargassed near the White House, and in New York City the police attacked the protesters as they attempted to march on city hall. The *New York Times* conveyed the ferocity of the assault, as "hundreds of policemen and detectives, swinging nightsticks, blackjacks, and bare fists, rushed into the crowd, hitting out at all with whom they came in contact."[25]

The CP reported six thousand new members in the immediate aftermath of these demonstrations, and sixty thousand applicants altogether between the years 1930 and 1934. Most soon drifted out of the party (its total membership increased only sixteen thousand in the same period), but a far larger number of people followed CP leadership in militant protest of their work and living conditions. In the coalfields of Ohio, western Pennsylvania, and eastern Kentucky, the CP's National Miners Union (NMU) conducted major strikes in 1931 for the eight-hour day and better wages, temporarily winning the support of miners fed up with the factional infighting and inaction of the United Mine Workers. Over one hundred thousand miners joined these and other walkouts, representing one-third of all strikers in that depression year. The NMU's near-suicidal struggles against wage cutting ended in defeat as the National Guard (in Ohio and Kentucky) and local police (in Pennsylvania) counterattacked with fatal violence; in Pennsylvania alone, an incomplete list of casualties counted three miners dead, fifty-five hospitalized, and more than two thousand gassed or injured. Even so, in these and other CP-led strikes, the party gained a reputation for fearless (sometimes reckless) leadership of workers who felt they had little to lose. In Kentucky's Harlan County, miners' families in 1931 subsisted on beans and bread, supplemented by wild onions and grass. "We starve while we work," as one Harlan miner put it, so "we might as well strike while we starve."[26]

Organizing among the unemployed would produce more tangible results and a more lasting social impact. Here, the CP was an especially vigorous—but not the only—organization mobilizing the unemployed. Networks of self-help and mutual aid began forming among jobless workers in every major city and many rural townships in the early depression years, centered in churches, fraternal groups, and those ethnic halls that could still pay the light bill. A barter economy was often the initial basis for these grassroots efforts, with unemployed workers and family members exchanging services—carpentry, sewing, repair work—for food and fuel. As the depression deepened and resources dwindled, the focus shifted to protest and collective resistance, and radical activists gave these efforts an increasingly political hue. The Socialist Party, the ideological rival of the CP, mobilized Unemployed Leagues and Workers' Committees in Chicago, Baltimore, Oregon, and elsewhere against "capitalism, the outlaw system, which [has] brought havoc upon our beloved country."[27] The CP's Unemployed Councils mixed equally scathing denunciations of capitalism with the simple motto, "Fight or Starve."

True to their slogan, the Unemployed Councils were full of fight, mounting spirited direct action campaigns against landlords who gouged rents, sheriffs who evicted families, and city relief officials who denied or cut aid. "We would take members of the council and instead of a person going to the relief station alone, we went with them," recalled Fannie Goldberg, a Council leader in St. Louis. "And on evictions, if we heard someone was being evicted, we would gather a group and get there and put the furniture back in."[28] In Detroit, where evictions rose to 150 a day in the summer of 1932, the Unemployed Council had to back off when the police sent reinforcements—"but they couldn't stay forever," recalled Dave Moore, "and when they would leave, we'd put them back in again."[29] In Cleveland, Wyndham Mortimer recalled how similar wars of attrition finally dissuaded the local bank from further attempts to evict his neighbor, because "even if they did evict him, they knew the people would come back and put him in again."[30] But in Chicago, when five hundred Council members in a south side African-American neighborhood returned an evicted widow to her home, police fired into the crowd, killing three. The subsequent funeral procession reportedly drew sixty thousand marchers and, within days, twenty-five hundred new members to the Unemployed Council. The mayor thereafter ordered a halt to further evictions.

These episodes of community-based direct action did not herald a massive shift toward socialist or communist politics. Both parties experienced modest growth, but nothing to match their success in mobilizing the unemployed; as many as two million people participated in the Unemployed Councils and Leagues, yet membership in the Communist Party rose to just twenty-four thousand by 1934, while the Socialist Party grew to twenty thousand. Most people joined the unemployed movement because the radicals promised action and resistance. For the majority, "politics" was still a patchwork of ideas favoring government intervention "to do something" for the common people, mixed with anticorporate sentiments and resentment of the rich. Socialists and Communists were respected by many workers for their personal courage and their "large"—though sometimes esoteric—ideas (the latter including the CP's cryptic call for "Defense of the Chinese Soviets"). In most cases, however, respect did not inspire emulation among rank-and-file members whose principal aspirations were survival and employment.

Even so, the widespread mobilization of the unemployed marked a significant turning point for the country as a whole, and especially for workers. It marked, first of all, the reemergence in many working-class communities of a culture of solidarity, an organized expression of resistance and common purpose that would soon serve a revitalized labor movement. Networks of mutual aid, food banks, rent strikes, eviction blockings, sit-downs in city welfare offices, and demonstrations at city hall, together with the social gatherings and educational meetings that bonded the movement, were a continual schooling in the lessons of collective action. "I stood in the rain for three days and the Home Relief Bureau paid no attention to me," as one woman testified in a neighborhood meeting of Harlem's Unemployed Council. "Then I found out about the Council. . . . We went in there as a body and then they came across right quick."[31] Thousands of Council activists subsequently carried these lessons with them into a wide range of workplaces and political campaigns. The movement's community-based solidarities would also prove to be a crucial asset in mobilizing the unemployed to support—rather than replace—striking workers.

Second, this oppositional culture was established on a far more inclusive basis than most previous working-class movements. The active role of women in the Unemployed Councils, combined with their augmented role as wage earners, did not automatically inspire gender equality, but it did redefine "politics" and "solidarity" as household concerns rather than exclusively male prerogatives. The prominent role of African-Americans in this interracial movement was also unprecedented. Two decades of migration to cities in the North and South had created significant urban concentrations of African-Americans for the first time in American history, and this demographic change was now percolating into the social and political life of the nation. Even with the prevailing racial segregation that relegated blacks to separate and unequal realms, urban proximity allowed for increased, though still limited commingling. It took conscious political effort to widen interracial contacts still further, and the unemployed movement was the vehicle for this extended solidarity.

The Communist Party was the most aggressive advocate of racial unity, pledging to "organize Negro workers side by side with white workers,"[32] as leader William Z. Foster promised in 1930. Communist initiatives were often clumsy and self-serving, particularly as they castigated political opponents with scalding and dismissive rhetoric: black businessmen as "lap dogs at the table of the imperialists"; black ministers as "sky pilots"; and black socialists like A. Philip Randolph as "traitors."[33] Nevertheless, the CP won a begrudging respect as it elevated black communists to the party's central committee and expelled white members who refused to socialize with blacks—gestures no other white organization was willing to match. Eviction blockings and rent strikes won many black recruits to the Unemployed Councils, and the party's prestige soared in African-American communities for its national campaign to save the Scotsboro Boys. These youths, condemned to death in Alabama for rape on spurious evidence and dubious testimony (later recanted), were initially abandoned to their fate by an overly cautious NAACP, leaving the CP as the first national organization to champion their cause. African-Americans who were inspired by these actions and joined the CP thereby assumed a double jeopardy, particularly in the South, for being "Red" as well as black. Even a frequent critic like the *Amsterdam News* could understand the CP's appeal. "Denied an equal opportunity in his struggle for existence," Harlem's leading newspaper editorialized in 1931, "the Negro . . . is turning to Communism, even if it means death, which is not so much worse than the burden he carries."[34]

This emergent and precarious racial unity had implications far beyond the relatively small number of African-Americans who joined the CP. Discrimination and ghettoization were still the dominant norms in the depression era, but it was working-class organizations among the unemployed that first breached these segregated realms, integrating their membership and electing black leaders even when whites were the majority. "The history of this group of white and colored workers in a southern city is unique,"[35] the local leader of Baltimore's Urban League observed of the

Socialist-led unemployed movement in his city—and the same could have been said of councils and leagues in many other places. One concrete result for the labor movement was the sharp decline of strikebreaking by unemployed blacks. White members of the unemployed movement could return the favor as well: in 1933, when five hundred black women struck the Funsten Nut Company for better wages, white women from the St. Louis Unemployed Council walked the picket line and helped persuade hesitant white workers to join them.

Finally, the mobilization of the unemployed set the stage for much of the New Deal legislation that followed President Franklin Delano Roosevelt's election in 1932. This was not simply because the Unemployed Councils were among the first to raise—in 1930—the demand for federally funded unemployment insurance. Although important, this early endorsement was less significant three years later, when a lengthening list of liberals and reformers, including Gerard Swope of General Electric, had affirmed the concept. What gave the reform agenda a special urgency after 1932 was that there were thousands of protesters in the streets, their mood noticeably more militant as the crisis deepened. Demonstrations and hunger marches continually drew attention to the system's imminent collapse and repeatedly provoked violent countermeasures. A hunger march of three thousand members of Detroit's Unemployed Councils on Ford's main factory in Dearborn, Michigan, produced especially alarming results in March 1932 when police and company guards fired into the unarmed crowd on Miller Road, killing five and wounding fifty. Weeks later, thousands of unemployed Army veterans began a nationwide trek toward Washington, D.C., to lobby for early payment of their veteran's bonus; that August, police and U.S. troops using tanks and bayonets drove the twenty thousand "bonus marchers" from the capital, killing two and burning their encampment to the ground. At the same time, Midwest farmers—many of them armed—were invading courtrooms to forcibly prevent foreclosures, then barricading highways to block shipment of grain and enforce their "strike" against low prices. Unemployed miners in northeastern Pennsylvania were meanwhile occupying unused coal lands and digging hundreds of shafts to mine "bootleg" coal; eventually numbering upwards of twenty thousand, they were organizing a "bootleggers union" to physically defend their expropriated mines from police attack.

"Vast numbers of the unemployed are 'right on the edge'," observed Lorena Hickock, a Pennsylvania reporter hired by the federal government to report on social conditions. "It wouldn't take much to make Communists out of them."[36] Some professed to be there already. "I used to be a hundred-percenter," gasped one bonus marcher to a reporter, shortly after being teargassed in the nation's capitol. "But now I'm a Red radical. I had an American flag but the dammed tin soldiers burned it."[37] His words, undoubtedly inflamed by the adrenaline of the moment, were echoed in the many such moments of 1932. For Dave Moore, the Ford hunger march massacre marked "the turning point in my life," as he later recalled. "When I saw the blood flowing there on Miller Road, that was the point I became a radical. From that day on."[38]

Moore and his fellow radicals were still a minority, but a growing one. Their numbers, their organization, and their militant protests were the focal point of public attention. AFL president William Green, himself no radical, could sense the mood. If the country did not soon "get at the fundamentals in an orderly, constructive way," he observed in August 1932, three months before Roosevelt's election, "we shall be swept aside by the tide of revolt."[39]

THE FIRST NEW DEAL

"This nation asks for action, and action now," the new president proclaimed at his inauguration on March 4, 1933. "We must act, and act quickly."

Franklin Delano Roosevelt had won a landslide victory over Herbert Hoover the previous November by projecting this certainty of purpose. Yet even as he promised action, FDR remained vague and contradictory about the "New Deal" he pledged to implement. There was little evidence that he would soon preside over the most dramatic transformation of labor-management relations in American history—on the contrary, the evidence indicated he had every intention of avoiding such a radical outcome. Although he promised to repeal prohibition and make wine and beer legal again, his campaign platform had nothing to say about labor rights and collective bargaining.

Roosevelt was, in fact, a political conservative in many respects, only "a little left of center," as he put it. Even this seemed an exaggeration to some. Writing a year after FDR's inauguration, Senator Bronson Cutting of New Mexico recalled the president's first actions "with a sick heart. For then . . . the nationalization of banks by President Roosevelt could have been accomplished without a word of protest."[40] Every bank in the country had closed its doors that March, and many business leaders—bankers included—expected FDR to pursue at least partial nationalization. Instead, he pumped Federal Reserve notes into the bankrupt system and authorized the Treasury Department to reopen privately owned banks under federal licensing.

As governor of New York, FDR had favored unemployment insurance and emergency funding for public welfare, but during the presidential campaign he abruptly reversed field, promising to cut federal spending by 25 percent and balance the budget. He apparently meant it: in the first week following his inauguration, he sent an economy bill to Congress that reduced pensions for veterans and cut salaries for federal employees.

Neither FDR nor the Democratic Party were pledged to support the labor movement in its hour of crisis. Southern Democrats were often hostile to unions, and labor-liberals like New York senator Robert Wagner were the exception rather than the rule. Wagner was the immigrant son of a janitor, raised in the slums of East Harlem and educated at City University. "I lived among the people of the tenements," he later observed, and "unless you have lived among these people, you cannot know the haunting sense of insecurity which hangs over the home of the worker."[41] His remarks could have been directed at Roosevelt. Born to wealth and raised by a small corps of servants on the family's Hudson Valley estate, FDR was groomed for leadership at elite private schools—Groton followed by Harvard. In contrast to Wagner's partisan alliance with the labor movement, FDR held himself aloof as a patrician benefactor, sympathetic in tone during the campaign, but noncommittal in policy.

Nevertheless, the majority of labor partisans favored FDR, with only a few giving serious thought to the Socialist and Communist alternatives. Socialist votes totaled 882,000, and the CP tally only 103,000, compared with twenty-three million votes for FDR and sixteen million for Hoover. Roosevelt's candidacy generated little enthusiasm, however. The AFL made no official endorsement and actually denounced the campaign platforms of both major parties, whereas some prominent union leaders openly endorsed the Republican slate: notably, John L. Lewis, president of the United Mine Workers, and William Hutchinson, Carpenters Union president and national chairman of the GOP's labor committee. Lewis, who had supported Democrat Woodrow Wilson in 1916, was a calculating opportunist who would soon return (temporarily) to the Democratic fold, while Hutchinson's motives were undoubtedly conservative. Other labor leaders split their endorsements between the two major parties, usually by supporting congressional Republicans. Senator Robert La Follette Jr. of Wisconsin (son of the 1924 presidential candidate), Senator George Norris of Nebraska, and Representative (soon to be Mayor) Fiorello La Guardia of New York were members of a Progressive minority in the Republican Party that actually outnumbered their Democratic counterparts in the late 1920s and early 1930s. It was these Progressive Republicans who sponsored the AFL's singular legislative achievement of 1932, the Norris-La Guardia Act prohibiting federal court injunctions to break strikes.

In the context of this partisan confusion, with neither party committed to a coherent program for addressing the crisis, the actual content of the "New Deal" remained an open question in March 1933. In fact, FDR's advisors were still debating the alternatives as the new president took office. Any remedy for the deepening economic crisis would have to address its causes, and there were two contending diagnoses that shaped this debate, one focused on "underconsumption," the other on "overproduction." In effect, they were two sides of the same coin, and advocates on both sides shared a common commitment to saving capitalism. Each position entailed different policies for addressing the crisis, and each implied different consequences for labor.

Most agreed that the depression was caused by an imbalance between the system's accelerating capacity to produce goods and the faltering capacity of consumers to buy them. Manufacturing output had soared by more than 50 percent from 1920 to 1929, but as corporations used automation and "scientific management" to boost productivity, they could produce this expanding output of consumer goods with the same number of factory workers. Profits and dividends for large manufacturing firms had grown accordingly, tripling between 1920 and 1929; in contrast, annual earnings of full-time factory workers fell between 1920 and 1922 and only rose slowly thereafter, barely recovering the earnings lost at the start of the decade. By 1929, the richest 5 percent of the population was feasting on an estimated 33 percent of total personal income. When the corporations they owned could no longer find customers for their expanding output in the late 1920s, they had cut back on new investment and new hiring, further weakening consumer demand and contributing to the downward spiral.

"Underconsumptionists" focused on the lack of consumer purchasing power as the culprit. "Wages to labor have been so poorly coordinated with returns to capital," as Senator Wagner put it, "that recurrent failures of consumer demand have led to cyclical depressions and widespread unemployment."[42] Government spending would pump money into the economy and boost consumer demand according to a vocal lobby of liberal labor leaders, businessmen from mass retailing, and their allies in legal and academic circles. This spending approach was widely supported when it took the form of the Federal Emergency Relief Act, passed within months of FDR's inauguration to provide welfare assistance (usually food) to the unemployed. Some reformers wanted even more far-reaching policies, combining government spending on public works and unemployment insurance with government protection of union organizing to promote higher wages and purchasing power. A handful of liberals were already citing the theories of English economist John Maynard Keynes to support their contention that without such government intervention to support consumer demand, capitalist economies would tend toward permanent depression. These few "Keynesians" offered a theoretical justification for emergency measures like Senator Hugo Black's proposed legislation, passed by the Senate in April 1933, requiring larger corporations to limit the workweek to thirty hours; the curtailment in hours, it was hoped, would force companies to hire more workers. Sidney Hillman of the Amalgamated Clothing Workers criticized the Black bill for its lack of a minimum wage, but cited "Professor Keynes" in supporting the general principle of shorter hours. "Every two people re-employed at a decent wage," as he argued the case in 1933, will "make employment for another person"[43] simply by spending their earnings.

FDR was no Keynesian, and he moved quickly to block the thirty-hours bill as both impractical and extreme. He shared with most corporate executives a reluctance for government regulation of incomes and a preference, in his words, for "the regulation of production or, to put it better, the prevention of foolish over-production."[44] From this standpoint, the problem was the "cutthroat competition" that drove employers to seek market share for their expanding output by predatory price cutting, inevitably followed by lower wages and longer hours to compensate for the reduced revenue. To promote industrial recovery, it was argued, the government should allow employers to self-regulate their competition through private trade associations. Overproduction could then be prohibited, competitive price cutting would no longer be necessary, and the pressure on employers to cut wages would abate accordingly. The federal government had implemented a similar approach during World War I, when the War Industries Board coordinated military production through trade associations representing the major companies in each industry. Moreover, there were prominent labor leaders who favored self-regulation of production. John L. Lewis in particular wanted government backing for the creation of a trade association in the coal mining industry, where overproduction and predatory price cutting were chronic aspects of unregulated competition during the 1920s. Northern coal companies joined Lewis in lobbying for such an approach, and even agreed to recognition of the UMW as the price for Lewis's support.

The "National Industrial Recovery Act" that FDR finally proposed to Congress in May 1933 had something for all these contending interests. For those favoring government spending to stimulate the economy, the bill established a "Public Works Administration" with a $3.3 billion budget for construction of roads, schools, airports, and other public projects. The core of the bill, however, was Title 1 mandating "the organization of industry for the purpose of cooperative action among trade groups." Modeled after the War Industries Board, Title 1 suspended antitrust laws and called for industry trade associations to establish "codes of fair competition" permitting price fixing and restriction of production. Because Senator Wagner and other congressional liberals refused to support the bill unless these powers granted to business were balanced by protections for workers, Title 1 also included a last-minute compromise, Section 7a. Barely surviving business efforts to delete it, Section 7a required every code of fair competition to comply with minimum wage and maximum hour regulations prescribed by the president. More important, 7a specified that "employees shall have the right to organize and bargain collectively through representatives of their own choosing, and shall be free from the interference, restraint or coercion of employers."

Passage of the National Recovery Act and Section 7a marked a historic turning point. For the first time in American history, legal protection of "concerted activities for the purpose of collective bargaining or other mutual aid" was the law of the land, not a temporary expediency of wartime production, as during World War I, and not a right limited to a single group of workers, as with the Railway Labor Act of 1926. The law did not require companies to agree to union terms, but it did require them to tolerate and even talk with union negotiators chosen by their employees. Many labor leaders and workers, recognizing the momentous change that this heralded, agreed with John L. Lewis that Section 7a was, indeed, labor's "Emancipation Proclamation."

The hastily drawn statute, however, was full of vague, contradictory language, the fruit of hurried compromises. Business leaders, in particular, were mixed in their assessment, welcoming most of Title 1, but deploring the late arrival of 7a. The National Association of Manufacturers, for one, vowed to "fight energetically against any encroachments by Closed Shop labor unions."[45]

FALSE START

"The President wants you to join the union." Organizers proclaimed this message across the country, even when they knew better. Noting the corporate opposition to 7a and the lack of any mechanism to enforce the law, Sidney Hillman privately acknowledged to fellow officers of the clothing workers union that "you don't transfer power by statute. Section 7a can be enforced through strikes. You don't expect the Government to send the American working class to labor unions. That is the union's job."[46]

The United Mine Workers union was first to take up the task, and the most successful. There was much lost ground for the union to recover. UMW membership had declined from nearly five hundred thousand bituminous miners in 1921 to eighty thousand by 1928, and the depression had reduced the remaining membership by more than half. Before 1933, this rearguard was subordinated to the dictatorial rule of UMW President John L. Lewis, who expelled dissident leaders and took direct control of rebellious districts. With the passage of 7a, however, Lewis suddenly reversed field, reinstating left-wing opponents like John Brophy and sending more than one hundred organizers into the coal districts. "I suppose," as he later justified it to Brophy, "our differences in the past were largely ones of timing."[47] The timing now was certainly right in the coalfields, where "the people have been so starved out," in the words of organizer Garfield Lewis, "that they are flocking into the Union by the thousands. . . . I organized 9 locals Tuesday."[48] Membership spiraled upward, rising by more than three hundred thousand over the year.

True to Hillman's words, coal miners had to strike antiunion mine companies to win their rights under Section 7a, and Lewis skillfully used the threat of this widening militancy to negotiate for strong labor language in the soft-coal industry's "Code of Fair Competition." When finally approved by FDR and the National Recovery Administration (NRA) in September 1933, the code's provisions marked a stunning turnaround. The union won wage increases, the eight-hour day, the five-day week, the right for miners to chose their checkweighman (whose job determined a miner's "tonnage" pay), abolition of payment in company scrip, freedom from the obligation to shop at the company store, prohibition of child labor, and a grievance procedure culminating in neutral arbitration. In 1934, the UMW negotiated further code improvements, including elimination of substandard wages and conditions for black miners in the South. As Howard Brubaker of the *New Yorker* observed, "the defeated mine-owners agreed to all things that deputy sheriffs usually shoot people for demanding."[49]

Similar results followed the aggressive organizing efforts of the Amalgamated Clothing Workers (ACW) and the International Ladies Garment Workers Union (ILGWU). Like the UMW, both unions had declined in the late 1920s as employers shifted to nonunion operations, often moving the sewing work to sweatshops in Connecticut, New Jersey, and Pennsylvania, leaving only the skilled cutting of cloth in New York City. The ACW attacked these "runaway" employers from both ends, with a cutters' strike to starve the out-of-town shops of garments, and with community-wide mobilizations against the sweatshops. In Pennsylvania, where wives and daughters of coal miners worked eleven-hour days as shirtmakers, earning weekly wages of only $2.00 to $10.00, the miners union played a key role in boosting picket lines and pressuring town governments to support the clothing workers. In Connecticut, students from Yale University joined the picket lines. New Deal Democrats elected to state and local office also played a role in buttressing support, and Hillman's appointment to the NRA's Labor Advisory Committee gave the union sufficient stature to finally win admission to the AFL. More than two hundred thousand workers signed membership cards and the ACW and ILGWU parlayed this mushrooming support into strong protections for labor in the industry's codes of fair competition.

In other industries, workers were joining the first available union that might duplicate this success. "The entire valley is alive with unionism,"[50] reported a newly chartered local of the paperworkers union from the Ohio Valley. "I have so many calls for organizers," reported the national president of the same union, "that I have neither the men nor the money to take care of them all."[51] Two weeks after passage of the NRA, five thousand people attended the first public meeting of rubber workers in Akron, Ohio, and the weeks that followed were "something like a cross between a big picnic and a religious revival,"[52] reported Ruth McKenney. Upwards of forty thousand joined the union—roughly 85 percent of Akron area rubber workers. Similar growth in auto, steel, longshoring, textiles, chemicals, and dozens of other industries added as many as 750,000 new members to union rolls in 1933.

Many, however, were gone by the end of 1934. The success of the UMW and the needle-trades unions proved to be durable, but rather than heralding the revival of organized labor, it underlined the unique circumstances that had favored union growth in these exceptional cases. Both coal mining and clothing were older industries with long histories of union organizing; the unions in both cases were broad-based industrial organizations that unified diverse occupational groups; and in both industries, many of the small-scale producers still crowding the market were too weak to resist and too numerous too unify against the union. The very "anarchism" of competitive price cutting in both industries motivated some of the larger, more modern firms to favor union organization as the only industry-wide mechanism for disciplining the market. Hart, Schaffner & Marx had been under ACW contract since 1910, and could now—with its top executive chairing the code authority for men's clothing—impose on nonunion competitors the obligation to raise their pay and shorten their hours.

"The NRA protects your right to have a union and will punish the boss if he tries to stop you," proclaimed one ACW leaflet in 1933. In fact, because there was no government enforcement mechanism to uphold Section 7a, only the union could effectively punish the boss, and outside of coal and clothing, most AFL unions lacked the strength or will to make employers comply with the law. In steel, auto, rubber, and other industries where a few large corporations dominated the market, employers were quick to unify around a campaign to nullify Section 7a. "We don't intend to let any outside union get strong enough to tell us how to run our labor affairs,"[53] vowed one steel corporation vice president.

Employers could ensure this outcome simply by dominating the very NRA code authorities that were supposed to implement 7a. Although some coal and clothing companies had accepted the union as a partner in restraining cutthroat competition, in most other industries there was no union counterweight to corporate control. In automaking, for example, GM, Ford, and Chrysler already dominated the market and could restrain competition without government or union assistance. The National Automobile Chamber of Commerce therefore wrote an abbreviated code of fair competition that allowed companies to ignore Section 7a and treat employees "on the basis of individual merit, without regard to their membership . . . in any organization." Because management alone would evaluate "merit," the NRA's Labor Advisory Board protested the widening use of these merit clauses, fearing this loophole would be used to justify retaliation against union supporters. Such complaints fell on deaf ears. Thomas Emerson, the NRA's general counsel, later acknowledged that "the whole thrust of the NRA was industry oriented, and the labor influence was very peripheral."[54]

To keep it that way, many corporations sponsored "company unions." Despite Section 7a's prohibition of employer "interference, restraint or coercion" in how workers chose their representatives, management wrote the bylaws and constitutions for these company-controlled bodies, generally granting them only a limited capacity to adjust grievances. "They would fix the floors, they would fix the lighting, they would give us a large milk bottle," one worker later testified during Senate hearings, "but that was practically the extent of the company union's effectiveness."[55] Some workers valued even this limited role, especially at companies like Goodyear Tire and General Electric where the company union dated back to World War I. With delegates elected from each department, Goodyear's "Industrial Assembly" and GE's "Workers' Council" represented their respective workforces on a plant-wide basis, winning some degree of genuine support for this alternative to craft separation. But among the more than six hundred company unions that existed by 1935, many had been hastily organized in reaction to Section 7a, and these transparent attempts to evade the law had less credibility. At Weirton Steel, owner Ernest Weir imposed a company union on his employees in Ohio and West Virginia in July 1933—within three months, Weirton's ten thousand steelworkers had rejected this impostor and gone on strike to demand recognition of the AFL's Amalgamated Iron and Steel Workers.

Their walkout joined a widening protest. Strike activity jumped dramatically in 1933, marking the start of a five-year cycle of rising militancy that would transform industrial relations. Beginning with a chaotic, sometimes violent strike of fifteen thousand Detroit autoworkers in January—five weeks before FDR's inauguration—the year-long tally of strikes doubled to nearly seventeen hundred, and the number of strikers nearly quadrupled, to 1.2 million. Some of these walkouts, as in Detroit, had the character of "collective bargaining by riot," as crowds of workers with no official union massed at company gates to protest the most recent pay cut. After passage of the National Recovery Act, many more strikes focused on demands for union recognition and company compliance with Section 7a.

To head off these strikes and provide an alternative enforcement mechanism, President Roosevelt established the National Labor Board (NLB) in August 1933, headed by Senator Wagner. With corporate and AFL leaders also represented, this tripartite board (public, management, union) was supposed to mediate disputes and restore industrial peace. It failed in both, largely because many employers refused to recognize the NLB's authority. Weirton Steel was an especially prominent example. To end the strike by his ten thousand employees, Ernest Weir initially accepted the NLB's intervention in October 1933 and agreed to a board-supervised election to determine whether the AFL or the company union had majority support. Once the men were back on the job, however, Weir repudiated the agreement and held an election solely for delegates to his company union. Despite court action and talk of denying Weirton use of the "Blue Eagle" symbol signifying compliance with the NRA, Weir prevailed, winning a series of court appeals stretching into 1935. In the meantime, Roosevelt undermined his own NLB in the spring of 1934, ruling in the case of the Auto Code that company unions did not violate 7a and employers could give them "proportional" recognition along with competing AFL unions. Congress subsequently gave the president the power to replace the NLB with a National Labor Relations Board (NLRB) made up solely of government appointees, but this new body also had no enforcement mechanism and little standing. Few paid attention, therefore, when the NLRB subsequently contradicted the president's settlement in auto, ruling that company-dominated unions violated 7a and that an independent union with majority support had to be the *exclusive* representative of the workers. By then Section 7a was widely regarded as a dead letter, and the NRA—or "national run around," as many unionists described it—was on the verge of being nullified by the courts.

The AFL had no effective strategy for mobilizing opposition to these trends, though it did make halfway gestures. Most craft unions in the metal trades had already widened their charters to include intermediate grades and "amalgamated" crafts, and in 1933 the AFL opened the door to production workers outside traditional craft jurisdictions. In basic industries like auto and rubber, the AFL kicked off organizing drives by chartering large catchall unions combining every skill grade and production worker in the factory. These "federal locals," affiliated directly to the AFL rather than a particular craft affiliate, were a concession to Hillman, Lewis, and others who called for industrial organization that would unify workers rather than divide them. In practice, however, the new approach was undercut by the same craft agenda and jurisdictional squabbling that undermined the 1919 steel strike. Almost immediately, craft unions demanded that federal locals surrender the skilled workers that had joined in the first flush of enthusiasm for 7a, leaving the new recruits confused and demoralized. "The machinists and the electricians kept coming to the Federal local meetings," reported Ruth McKenney from Akron, where the AFL "could never make them understand why they were supposed to stay away, supposed to belong to a separate union."[56] Dan Tobin of the AFL defended the federation's decision to separate skilled workers from federal unions in rubber and auto, since otherwise the "fundamental principles" of long-established craft unions would be sacrificed to the organization of mere production workers—"men who have never been organized,"[57] in Tobin's words, and therefore did not deserve special consideration. Yet many of these workers, both skilled and production, saw the dismantling of their organizations as a betrayal, undermining the united front necessary to battle antiunion corporations. Failure to effectively challenge the conservative drift of NRA policy further demoralized new members. When the AFL canceled its strike deadline in auto and accepted the president's 1934 decision permitting company unions, thousands of members abandoned the autoworkers' union. Organizer Leonard Woodcock recalled that with the announcement of the decision at the union hall, "men [were] simply tearing up their membership cards and throwing them on the floor. . . . There was a deep sense of betrayal which carried over in the adamancy against the AFL for years afterwards."[58]

RISING

The AFL's paralysis and failure to lead, as with its previous failure to mobilize the unemployed, invited radical alternatives. Workers turned to these in 1934 by the thousands, launching mass strikes under left-wing leadership that openly defied the AFL and the NRA.

The most dramatic of these confrontations paralyzed the entire West Coast shipping industry, from San Diego to Seattle, as workers repudiated their national leaders and refused federal intervention. The primary focus of their anger was "the shape up," the practice of waterfront hiring in which men waited at the docks each morning for the foremen to pick his work crew, usually those who had bribed him. "The boys called this system 'Hanging a ham on the door,'" recalled longshoreman Gerry Bulcke, "which meant bringing a present to the boss—money or something else, maybe like painting his house."[59] The dockers wanted a union hiring hall that would equalize earnings among registered workers. When the AFL's International Longshoreman's Association accepted government-mediated terms that permitted company-dominated unions, local leaders rejected the settlement and mobilized a massive dockworkers' strike in May 1934 that spread to all the allied maritime trades, including sailors and dockside truck drivers. When police and National Guardsmen forcibly reopened San Francisco's port, killing two strikers and hospitalizing 115, the citywide labor movement answered with a general strike of 130,000 workers, closing the city for three days. When conservative leaders called off the strike and forced the dockworkers to accept government arbitration and a vaguely worded compromise, the longshoremen returned to work with a militant and effective campaign of "quickie" strikes and slowdowns that finally forced employers to accept a union-run hiring hall.

This spirit of defiance and grassroots militancy characterized many of the confrontations that rocked American cities and towns in 1934. Equally characteristic, however, was the official violence that crushed many strikes, often with the use of military force. By year's end, National Guard troops had been called into strikebreaking service in California, Ohio, Minnesota, Alabama, North and South Carolina, Maine, Massachusetts, Rhode Island, Georgia, Mississippi, Connecticut, Wisconsin, and Oregon. The combined death toll from picket line clashes in these and other confrontations totaled, by varied accounts, between thirty and fifty. Despite the fury of this repressive campaign, workers in some cases still managed to win significant victories, demonstrating the potential power of the new alliances and new forms of organization that were emerging at the local level.

In Toledo, Ohio, when an AFL strike faltered at the Auto-Lite parts plant, the picket lines were suddenly bolstered by the arrival of the Lucas County Unemployed League, affiliated with socialist A. J. Muste's American Workers Party. "It is nothing new to see the organized unemployed appear in the streets," newspaperman Roy Howard reported, ". . . but usually they do this for their own ends. . . . At Toledo, they appeared on the picket lines to help striking employees win a strike, though you would expect their interest would lie the other way—that is, in going down and getting the jobs the other men had laid down."[60] League members not only joined the picket line, but also stood their ground when the Ohio National Guard fired point-blank into their ranks, killing two and wounding fifteen.

In Minneapolis, where Teamsters Local 574 likewise confronted police and National Guardsmen during a series of strikes for union recognition, the local labor movement demonstrated an extraordinary resourcefulness in countering repressive force. Local 574's leaders were well aware that gunfire and tear gas were not their only, or even their most formidable, enemies. "Most strikes are lost," as one local leader reflected, "because the strikers lose touch with the strike. They sit at home watching the food give out and reading the newspapers telling them the strike is over."[61] To counter the corrosive effects of doubt and hunger, Local 574 organized the widest possible mobilization of community resources. A "Women's Auxiliary" recruited wives and family into the movement, with 120 women working around the clock to feed five thousand to ten thousand people daily at the union's strike kitchen. Area farmers donated food, and the city's Unemployed Councils pledged picket-line support. Local 574, with no backing from the national Teamsters and against the wishes of federal mediators, refused to sign any agreement that didn't also cover the "inside men" working in the warehouses, and this same spirit of solidarity brought thousands of supporters to the union's picket lines. Twenty thousand massed in May to repel police and special deputies attempting to reopen the city's central market, and construction workers and taxi drivers also struck in sympathy. To communicate with this growing movement, the union published a daily newspaper, *The Organizer*, with a circulation that peaked at ten thousand. Strike headquarters was a converted garage that served as food commissary, hospital, and auditorium for nightly strike meetings, with crowds of two thousand packed inside and more milling in the streets. From here, union dispatchers coordinated "flying squadrons" of motorized pickets that patrolled the city for nonunion trucks. By August, the union's mobilization was so deep and wide that when the National Guard seized the garage and arrested the union's top leaders, thousands of pickets continued to operate. "We established 'curb headquarters' all over the city," one organizer recalled. "We had twenty of them."[62] Unable to crush this resistance and alarmed by violence that had already left three dead (two strikers and one special deputy), the governor released the union leadership from jail and employers soon after capitulated.

In the many lesser strikes and organizing campaigns of 1934, local leaders and community-wide mobilizations were transforming the shape of the labor movement. In some cases, militants simply stretched AFL policy to suit their purposes, as in Barberton, Ohio, an industrial suburb of Akron, where local organizers treated the AFL's federal locals not as temporary bodies but as permanent unions uniting production workers and craftsmen. In January 1934, they opened a "Labor Temple" to house their newly organized Central Labor Union, and it was the CLU, not the national AFL, that initiated organizing campaigns, mobilized strike support, sponsored dances, and housed a growing network of women's auxiliaries, buying clubs, and political organizations. In Austin, Minnesota, on the other hand, local activists dispensed with the AFL altogether and organized an Independent Union of All Workers (IUAW), its locals representing truckers and warehouse workers, packinghouse workers and butchers, waitresses and bartenders, construction tradesmen and laborers, barbers and beauticians, laundry workers, department store clerks, and city employees. With a weekly paper, *The Unionist*, distributed free to every household in Austin, the IUAW became a focal point in the community, sponsoring dances, lectures, and classes in everything from public speaking and labor history to music and drama. An active Women's Auxiliary meanwhile ran the strike kitchen, organized boycotts of antiunion companies, and led the "Drum and Bugle Corps" in parades and rallies. From its origins in Austin, the IUAW spread outward to seven other communities in Minnesota, as well as to neighboring towns in Wisconsin, the Dakotas, and Iowa.

The variety of organizational forms in 1933–1934 matched the diversity of the workers who joined them. In many cases, the AFL was entirely absent. In California's fruit and vegetable fields, the Confederación de Uniones de Compesinos y Obreros Mexicanos, an independent union with ties to Mexico, organized strikes of Mexican and Filipino farmworkers. In New York City, the Communist Party's Food Workers Industrial Union led a massive strike of thirty thousand workers from fifty hotels. In Detroit, skilled tool and die makers of the Mechanics Educational Society of America (MESA) organized a multi-craft union of exceptional militancy, eventually forcing automakers to bargain an industry-wide agreement for toolroom workers. "We don't meander with the NRA," declared MESA leader Mat Smith, "but fight any encroachment of the bosses by direct action in the plants concerned."[63]

The men and women who organized these early movements came from distinct, sometimes overlapping, backgrounds. In many cases, they had grown up in union households. "I literally sucked this in with my mother's milk," recalled the Scottish toolmaker Bill Stevenson, an early leader in MESA, "because my father before me was interested in the labor movement."[64] The United Mine Workers was an especially important incubator of future organizers, as the coal industry's long-term decline scattered UMW families across the country. Children raised in these households were the most likely to consider union organizing a "natural" response to hardship, and their values and experience with the day-to-day practice of collective action buoyed the confidence of their "greenhorn" workmates.

Many early leaders were also skilled workers who had rejected the AFL's craft exclusiveness and excessive caution. Even in mass-production industries like automaking and electrical appliances, the semiautomatic machines that replaced craft work in direct production still required the skills of the toolmaker, the electrician, and the machine repairman, and these experienced workers possessed habits of self-assertion and planning that served them well as union organizers. The relative shortage of skilled workers also gave them added bargaining leverage as the economy made a slow recovery, and the same dynamic emboldened the many semiskilled autoworkers who machined parts, finished metal, or installed interior trim and upholstery. MESA's toolroom workers organized their independent union outside the AFL, but their strikes were often carried out in collaboration with production workers in AFL federal locals. The skilled waiters in San Francisco's Local 30 of the Hotel and Restaurant Employees (HRE) likewise made common cause with their less-skilled brethren, organizing a new local for the growing number of dishwashers, busboys, waitresses, and housekeepers previously excluded by the HRE's narrow charter. The IUAW, in contrast, organized an all-grades industrial union of meatpackers at Hormel, with skilled and less-skilled represented in the same local—but it was a skilled butcher, Frank Ellis, who served as chief organizer and principal leader of the IUAW.

Ellis was also a lifelong socialist and a former member of the IWW. A disproportionate number of early organizers shared his radical politics, though organizational rivalries often put these left-wingers at odds with each other. Harry Bridges, the Australian-born merchant sailor and longshoreman whose leadership of the West Coast dockers' strike elevated him to national prominence, was closely allied with the Communist Party. He rarely had anything good to say, however, about Ray Dunne and Karl Skoglund, the left-wing leaders of the Minneapolis Teamsters strike, because they were both followers of Leon Trotsky, the Russian revolutionary who opposed Soviet leader Joseph Stalin. The Socialist Party was likewise at odds with the CP, reflecting historical animosities (the 1919 expulsion of Communists) that were revived in the early 1930s as each party accused the other of deserting socialism and "paving the way for Fascism." Underlying these factional disputes, however, was a common political culture, a secular and optimistic faith in the historical inevitability of socialism, and it was this faith that sustained left-wing "missionaries" and impelled them toward leadership. By the end of the 1930s many would abandon radical politics for the concrete, if modest, achievements of the New Deal, but at mid-decade perhaps a third or more of early union leaders and organizers were still self-described socialists of some stripe. Among them were well-known leaders like Sidney Hillman of the Clothing Workers, A. Philip Randolph of the Sleeping Car Porters, and John Brophy of the UMW, with many more future leaders still working in relative obscurity: Walter Reuther, Emil Mazey, Wyndham Mortimer, and Leonard Woodcock in the autoworkers union; Julius Emspak and James Matles in the electrical workers union; and among women activists, Myra Komaroff (hotel and restaurant workers), Rose Pesota (garment workers), and Genora Dollinger (autoworkers).

They were joined by newcomers from the downwardly mobile middle class, younger men and women whose aspirations for professional or business success had been dashed by the depression. Douglas MacMohn, son of a New York realtor, was embarked on a Wall Street career when the stock market crash forced him to take a job as an unskilled maintenance worker on the city's subways. "What drove him to the union," one of his allies recalled, "was his personal unhappiness that he, the great Douglas MacMohn, would have to go around in a rat-hole there ten hours a day screwing [light] bulbs."[65] After joining the Socialist Party and later switching to the Communists, MacMohn became an organizer of the Transit Workers Union, eventually rising to top leadership. His personal journey was paralleled by others who turned their skills and ambitions toward the labor movement. Homer Martin, college graduate and seminary student, was a Baptist minister in Missouri until 1931, when he found work at General Motors, rose to leadership of his plant's AFL federal local, and later (1936) became the United Auto Workers' first elected president. James Carey was an aspiring electrical engineer and night-school student, attending the Drexel Institute and Wharton School before working as an inspector at the Philco radio factory and leading a 1933 strike for union recognition. Soon after, he was president of the plant's federal local, and later (1936) first president of the United Electrical Workers.

New leadership also appeared at the grass roots as workers attacked the status quo with increasingly radical tactics and rhetoric. Pennsylvania's unemployed coal miners digging "bootleg" coal on company property may not have been ideological radicals, but their struggle to survive led many to question the fundamentals of private property. "They stole the land in the first place," as one bootlegger said of the mine owners; "We weren't criminals," said another, "the companies were the criminals."[66] Organizers of the Southern Tenant Farmers' Union (STFU) also discovered a latent radicalism among the sharecroppers and cotton pickers of eastern Arkansas. Although the STFU initially limited itself to lobbying against federal subsidies that encouraged plantation owners to restrict production by evicting tenant farmers, organizers soon found that many of their members were openly advocating seizure of the plantations. Their growing militancy led to a cotton pickers' strike in 1935, which failed to win union recognition but did force plantation owners to raise wages to 75 cents per hundred pounds picked, up from the previous 50 cents. Even more startling to southern opinion was the unity between black and white members as the STFU spread to the delta regions of Tennessee and Mississippi. "Of course, there was still a lot of prejudice among the white people in those days," STFU President J. R. Butler recalled, "but hard times makes peculiar bedfellows sometimes, and so many of them were beginning to get their eyes open and see that all of them were being used."[67]

For a brief moment, it appeared a new sensibility might sweep through the South on a wave of union organizing, led by the region's textile workers. Southern mill hands played an especially prominent role in an industry that had been shifting production from the higher-wage mill towns of New England to the nonunion hill country of the Carolinas, Georgia, and Alabama, where living and working conditions were especially strained. Before the NRA, the *minimum* workweek on the first shift was fifty-five hours, with wages of $5.00 to $6.00 *a week* commonplace. Most workers lived in company-owned villages with company-owned housing, much of it dilapidated and without sewerage. No other industry employed as much child labor.

On paper, the NRA's Cotton Code had promised much: a forty-hour week, a minimum weekly wage of $12.00 in the South and $13.00 in the North, prohibition of child labor, and Section 7a. In fact, these promises were nullified by the simple fact that implementation of the code was left to the Cotton Textile Board created by the NRA, and the board was little more than a front for the employers. Consequently, the NRA did nothing to prevent widespread "code chiseling" by mill owners, who fired union supporters, reclassified workers as learners (therefore exempt from minimum wage protections), and doubled work loads to compensate for shorter hours. This stretch-out in workloads was the most common grievance among mill hands, who reported working at a feverish clip, eating lunch at their machines, their bodies "wet with perspiration, every muscle taut, every pulse beating hard,"[68] in the words of one.

In July 1934, twenty thousand textile workers in northern Alabama went on strike to win a $12.00 minimum wage for a thirty-hour week and recognition of the AFL's United Textile Workers (UTW), an industrial union previously limited to a small membership in New England. They called for a national walkout in support of these demands, and the timing seemed ripe, especially in the South. "Southern middle class opinion about labor matters has been remarkably changed," historian George Mitchell had written in 1931, shortly after mill owners had violently suppressed an earlier round of strikes in North Carolina. "The harshness of the repression . . . angered many." "We are sick of the whole business," an Alabama store owner confessed to the union newspaper, referring to the industry's low wages. "The workers have no money to spend; therefore our goods lie on the shelves and bankruptcy stares us in the face."[69] Buoyed by this public support and heartened by the promise—if not the practice—of 7a, more than one hundred thousand southern mill hands joined the UTW and forced the union's northern leadership to call a national walkout.

The biggest single strike to that point in American history began, appropriately enough, on Labor Day weekend. Employers, who had confidently predicted a weak turnout, were initially unprepared for the upheaval that followed; within one week, 376,000 workers were on strike in nine states, from Maine to Georgia. Southern mill owners were especially vulnerable to the "flying squadrons" that local militants used to spread the strike. "Moving with the speed and force of a mechanized army," the *New York Times* reported, "thousands of pickets in trucks and automobiles scurried about the countryside in the Carolinas, visiting mill towns and villages and compelling the closing of plants."[70] As many as fifty of these squadrons, each composed of two hundred to one thousand workers, kept employers off guard in the Carolinas, suddenly appearing to picket a plant, or fight company guards, or occasionally invade a mill and shut down the machinery.

Their efforts marked the high tide of union mobilization in the South, then and for decades thereafter. However bold and courageous, mill hands in the South and the North could not overcome the violent opposition of sheriffs and soldiers, the empty posturing of New Deal liberals, and the weakness of their own union. By the second week of the strike, the governors of South Carolina and Rhode Island had declared a state of insurrection and called out the National Guard to impose martial law. Georgia's National Guard made mass arrests of flying squadron members and interned them in a makeshift prison camp; the union's thirty-four top leaders in the state were jailed and held incommunicado. Company guards evicted strikers from their homes and drove organizers out of town. Sheriff's deputies and guardsmen in the South and the North began firing on unarmed strikers, who fought back with stones and bricks in desperate battles that gradually shifted against them. By the third week of the strike, the National Guard had been called out in nine states and the death toll was thirteen in the South, two in New England, and hundreds more injured and wounded.

Stunned by the violent countermeasures of state and local governments, and fearful they could no longer control the vengeful fury of the remaining strikers, UTW leaders welcomed federal intervention and called off the strike on September 22. In return, the Roosevelt administration promised it would address the workers' grievances and employers would not discriminate against returning strikers. Neither promise was kept. After much study, the government recommended that wages be raised and workloads decreased, and employers simply ignored the advice. In the meantime, the triumphant mill owners had their way with union supporters, firing thousands and evicting them (if they had not yet been) from their company homes.

The union never recovered. The very magnitude of its struggle in 1934 broadcast the totality of its defeat across the South, leaving a bitter legacy that would weigh on union organizing efforts for generations to come. Employers and local governments ensured that the lessons of this turning point were not soon forgotten; between 1936 and 1939, the Textile Workers Organizing Committee counted nineteen southern organizers murdered by Klansmen and vigilantes allied with local police and employers.

"Many of us did not understand what we do now," observed Patrick Gorman, the UTW's strike leader, "that the Government protects the strong, not the weak, and that it operates under pressure and yields to that group which is strong enough to assert itself over the other. . . . We know now that we are naive to depend on the forces of government to protect us."[71]

TURNAROUND

Government protection of labor, already rendered meaningless by employer domination of the NRA, disappeared altogether on May 27, 1935, when the U.S. Supreme Court declared the National Industrial Recovery Act unconstitutional. In their unanimous decision, the justices condemned the NRA for delegating legislative power to private code-making authorities, and for interfering in local commerce. Section 7a did not figure in the Court's ruling, but its provisions were nullified with the rest of the NRA.

Three days before the Court's decision, with the centerpiece of his New Deal recovery program on the verge of destruction, President Roosevelt belatedly endorsed Senator Robert Wagner's new legislation protecting Section 7a. First introduced in 1934, the National Labor Relations Act (NLRA) promised, in the words of its original preamble, "to ensure a wise distribution of wealth between management and labor, to maintain a full flow of purchasing power, and to prevent recurrent depressions." Because these prescriptions for boosting consumer demand could not, in Wagner's estimate, be achieved by individual workers confronting ever-larger (and hostile) corporations, the government would have to protect, as Section 7 of the new bill stated, the "concerted activities" of workers "for the purpose of collective bargaining or other mutual aid or protection." Unlike the NRA, the "Wagner Act," as it came to be called, also gave a reconstituted National Labor Relations Board (NLRB) the power to hold elections, certify majority support for the union, and seek court orders against employers whose "unfair labor practices" denied workers their Section 7 rights. Sponsors of the bill appealed for support not only on the grounds of social justice and "the full flow of purchasing power" but also on the claim that without government intervention, there would be no end to the social upheaval and economic disruption so evident in the mass strikes of 1934.

"It was not the president's idea,"[72] recalled his secretary of labor, Francis Perkins, regarding the Wagner Act. Indeed, Roosevelt "never lifted a finger"[73] to support the bill until it had already passed the Senate and

awaited House approval. Neither Perkins nor Roosevelt welcomed a permanent body like the NLRB, and both assumed the Supreme Court would
probably nullify this law as well. Business leaders moved quickly to make
that so, filing suit in district courts across the country to enjoin the NLRB
and prevent implementation of the bill. Within less than a year, the courts
had issued nearly forty injunctions nullifying the board's powers and, in
some cases, even preventing it from holding hearings. Corporate lawyers
confidently predicted that the Supreme Court would overturn the Wagner
Act and advised their clients accordingly. "When a lawyer tells a client that
a law is unconstitutional," said Earl Reid, counsel to Weirton Steel, "it is
then a nullity and he need no longer obey that law."[74] Reid's advice had
no legal basis—only the Supreme Court, not private lawyers, could nullify
a law of Congress—but his advocacy of unlawful behavior was widely
endorsed by corporate attorneys. For the next two years, the Wagner Act,
in the words of NLRB general counsel Charles Fahy, existed "as little more
than a vehicle for protracted litigation."[75]

Yet it was in these very years, 1935–1937, that the labor movement
would achieve the most dramatic organizing victories in its history. This
unexpected turnaround gathered much of its momentum from four crucial events. First, despite the near-total paralysis of the NLRB's administrative machinery, the Wagner Act had nevertheless resurrected and validated Section 7 as a civil right, sanctioned by law even though not yet
enforced by the government. Second, in the absence of government
enforcement, an alternative means for defending workers' rights would
finally take form within the AFL: the Committee for Industrial Organization, with new strategies and new tactics that would suddenly (if only
temporarily) tip the balance of power in favor of workers. Third, the
economy was finally (if, again, only temporarily) on a genuine upswing.
And fourth, the 1936 elections would soon provide a stunning ratification
of the New Deal, capping a political trend that put business leaders and
their conservative allies on the defensive.

The second of these events followed within months of the first as
AFL delegates gathered in October 1935 for the federation's annual convention in Atlantic City, New Jersey. Recent passage of the Wagner Act
buoyed advocates of industrial unionism, who urged fellow delegates to
support all-inclusive organizational campaigns that would mobilize
unskilled as well as skilled workers, tapping into the enthusiasm and militancy evident in the big strikes of 1934. As in past conventions, these
proposals were politely turned aside, blunted by amendment, or openly

derided by craft unionists and conservative leaders. Outvoted by the AFL establishment, younger delegates from the surviving federal locals in steel, auto, and rubber turned to mineworker leader John L. Lewis as their last best hope. He did not disappoint them. On the convention's final day, when Carpenters union president William Hutchinson tried to suppress the dissenting remarks of a rubber worker delegate, Lewis challenged Hutchinson and—in a move calculated to dramatize his break with AFL orthodoxy—suddenly punched the oversized craft unionist and left him sprawling.

The next morning, Lewis convened a meeting of industrial union leaders that included Sidney Hillman of the Clothing Workers and David Dubinsky of the Garment Workers. The following month, the UMW, ACW, and ILGWU—the three principal industrial unions within the AFL and the only three to have successfully organized their industries in the previous three years—drew in additional supporters and founded the Committee for Industrial Organization, the CIO. Although still formally a part of the AFL, the new committee promised to directly contradict federation policy by supporting the organization of auto, rubber, and steel workers on an industrial basis. Crucial to this effort would be the financial support of the UMW and the charismatic leadership of its president. Lewis had been an industrial unionist all his life, and he now believed that failure to act would not only jeopardize the potential demonstrated by the events of 1934, but might also undermine his own union if the steel industry—with its "captive" coal mines—remained nonunion.

The industrial union movement had finally found its voice. "Let him who will, be he economic tyrant or sordid mercenary, pit his strength against this mighty upsurge of human sentiment now being crystallized in the hearts of 30 million workers," Lewis intoned over NBC radio in 1936. "He is a madman or a fool who believes that this river of human sentiment can be damned by the erection of arbitrary barriers of restraint."[76] Lewis, in fact, knew better than most that antiunion employers would not surrender to mere "human sentiment." The CIO would need organizers—hundreds of organizers prepared to take on the world's biggest corporations in a no-holds-barred campaign. To bring these grassroots leaders to the CIO's banner, Lewis was prepared to adopt the wide range of locally based organizing efforts that had sprung into being after 1933, and with them, the many Socialists, Communists, and independent radicals who had helped initiate these efforts. Demonstrating a remarkable flexibility—and opportunism—Lewis, a one-time Republican and a recent supporter of Herbert Hoover, was prepared to work with the kinds of radicals he barred from his own union. "In a battle, I make arrows from any wood," Lewis responded when asked about his collaboration with Communists. "Who gets the bird?" he later added, "the hunter or the dog?"[77] There was little doubt which role Lewis saw himself in.

The Communists, for their part, had stopped attacking their socialist and liberal rivals as "Social Fascists," and resolved instead to join a Popular Front with their former labor adversaries. CP leader Earl Browder acknowledged that the party's holier-than-thou posturing had isolated it from the mass strikes of 1934, and that, consequently, "Communists in the main were unable to exercise a decisive influence in the leadership of the workers."[78] Critics pointed out that the CP was also responding to a shift in policy by the Soviet Union, alarmed by the rise of Hitler, and seeking allies against a rearmed Germany. For whatever reasons, American communists dissolved their independent "Red" unions in 1934–1935, downplayed their revolutionary rhetoric, and joined the AFL unions they had previously condemned as sellouts to capitalism.

The new movement's organizers could not have picked a better time to launch their campaign, for the economy in 1936–1937 was finally recovering from the depths of the depression. In the latter year, the auto industry sold 3.9 million automobiles, its second-best year on record, topped only by 1929. The total number of nonfarm employees was at near record levels, a hair shy of the 1929 peak, and actually higher in manufacturing and whole-sale-retail trade. The recovery was by no means complete, however. Although employment had regained much of the ground lost by 1933, continued population growth meant unemployment still hovered at nearly eight million jobless workers, or 14 percent of the ever-growing labor force. Hourly wages had returned to 1929 levels in many industries, but weekly work hours still lagged, depressing overall income. Even so, the upward trend was undeniable, and for the first time in years many workers felt secure enough to demand better of their boss. Some even enjoyed a seller's market. "You know the employers are short of skilled men," as one organizing leaflet put it to Detroit's toolmakers in 1936. "This gives you the advantage right now to sell your skilled labor at a higher wage."[79]

The political climate also improved as congressional liberals, led by Senator Robert La Follette of Wisconsin, launched an unprecedented campaign to expose corporate resistance to the Wagner Act. Beginning in April 1936, a lengthening procession of witnesses testified before La Follette's Senate committee to the illegal use of industrial spies and coercive methods to suppress union organization. There were, according to Senate investigators, more than two hundred espionage and strikebreaking firms in business, offering corporations the services of as many as forty thousand undercover agents. General Motors alone employed the services of at least fourteen detective agencies, with upwards of two hundred spies posing as workers in its plants. Not only did they report the names of union sympathizers, but many were instructed to win the confidence of their workmates and seek election to union office. Senate findings indicated they were often successful; in GM's home base of Flint, Michigan, the thirteen-member executive board of the citywide autoworkers' union included five undercover agents from two well-known espionage firms, Pinkerton and Corporations Auxiliary. There was little doubt that the work of such spies was effective in creating a climate of fear. With an undercover Pinkerton agent serving as treasurer of the newly formed union at the Fruehauf Trailer plant in Detroit, the company—as management admitted under oath—was able to acquire membership lists and subsequently fire nine workers and threaten others if they didn't abandon the union. "The mystery and deadly certainty with which [espionage] operated," as NLRB Chairman J. Warren Madden testified in the Fruehauf case, "was so baffling to the men that they each suspected the others, were afraid to meet or talk, and the union was completely broken."[80] The La Follette Committee's dramatic revelation of these illegal methods—along with wiretapping, opening of personal mail, and surveillance of worker homes—created a public climate more sympathetic to labor organizing and less forgiving of company resistance.

Many corporations found their options narrowed still further after 1935 as they lost control of their company-union Employee Representation Plans (ERPs). The Wagner Act specifically declared that the kind of management-dominated ERPs formed at many companies in 1933 were a violation of workers' Section 7 rights to independent representation. As yet, the law had little practical impact, but elected worker delegates to the ERPs were by now emboldened to seek genuine improvements in wages and working conditions. At U.S. Steel, local ERPs were taking steps by late 1935 to form a company-wide ERP, despite management objections. In Chrysler's Detroit-area plants, employee delegates to the company-sponsored Works Council were also asserting their independence. "We bargained for clean windows and floors without grease," as one Works Council delegate complained, but "when it came to dollars and cents . . . we were powerless"[81]—blocked by the veto rights that council bylaws reserved for management. In 1935, worker delegates formed their own independent union, but they continued to attend council meetings for the next two years, "using it as a medium to win support." When they finally resigned as a group, the union took with it all but seventeen of the 120 elected delegates in Chrysler's main plants, destroying the council's legitimacy. In General Electric, where the company's Workers' Council was an older and more credible arena for airing worker grievances, union organizers concluded that their boycott of company-union elections had simply isolated them from the many high-seniority workers who still identified with GE's paternalistic managers. In 1935, therefore, union candidates began to run for seats on the Workers' Council, and the following year organizer Bill Turnbull, a turbine inspector at GE's Schenectady, New York, plant, could report that "inroads are being made in the company union," with "members, including the President of our local, elected to the Workers' Council."[82] From this vantage point, the union—still a minority among plant workers, but gaining ground rapidly—called for a 10 percent wage increase "on the company union floor in so sharp a manner," as Turnbull described it, "that plant executives themselves had to speak on the question, dropping their pose of impartiality in order to defeat it."[83]

ELECTION 1936

The rising confidence and independence of workers came to a crossroads in the 1936 elections. Widely regarded as a referendum on the New Deal and the Wagner Act, the November elections also marked a decisive turning point in the twentieth-century history of the labor movement, both in how political action was mobilized and how it set the stage for the union growth that immediately followed.

Unlike in 1932, when FDR campaigned on vague and contradictory promises, the New Deal was now concrete policy, highlighted by the emergence of a "Second New Deal" following the demise of the NRA. In short order during 1935, Congress passed and Roosevelt signed the Social Security Act, creating publicly funded pensions and federal unemployment insurance; the Banking Act, consolidating government control of the national money supply and reducing the power of private banks; the Works Projects Administration, employing millions of workers in their professions or in the construction and maintenance of schools, roads, bridges and other public structures; a revenue bill that paid for these measures by, among other things, raising taxes on corporations and wealthy estates; and finally, the National Labor Relations Act.

Conservative politicians and business leaders bitterly denounced all of these initiatives, assailing the New Deal in apocalyptic terms that demonized the president. William Randolph Hearst, owner of the nation's largest chain of daily newspapers, condemned the tax bill to his editors as "essentially communism," attributing the "bastard" proposal to "a composite personality which might be labeled Stalin Delano Roosevelt."[84] The American Liberty League, led by Alfred Sloan of General Motors and Pierre du Pont of the Delaware Chemical Company, called the Social Security Act "the end of democracy," predicting that if Roosevelt were reelected in 1936, Congress would soon be reduced to little more than a "Congress of the Soviets."[85] The Republican Party's candidate for president, Alf Landon, made equally dramatic claims as the 1936 campaign progressed, finally predicting that the expanded powers and spending of the federal government would soon compel Americans to wear identification tags around their necks, the better to administer Social Security. Most employers openly sided with the Republican opposition to the New Deal, hanging anti-Roosevelt placards in the workplace and stuffing pay envelopes with dire warnings of higher taxes if the president was reelected.

Republican rhetoric condemning the New Deal as "a socialistic state honeycombed with waste . . . and ruled by a dictatorship"[86] polarized the campaign in ways that destroyed the opposition's credibility, while also obscuring the real achievements—and limits—of FDR's reform agenda. The federal government had, in fact, grown dramatically in size and economic importance, nearly tripling its budget since 1929 and increasing its share of the Gross National Product from 3 to 10 percent. But these growing expenditures had been driven by political expediency as much as policy, with Roosevelt struggling to preempt more radical propositions. The president was harried on his left by two especially prominent rivals for public attention, Huey Long, the "soak-the-rich" Senator from Louisiana, and Upton Sinclair, the California socialist who captured the Democratic nomination for governor in 1934 and nearly won the state's general election. "I want to save our system, the capitalist system," Roosevelt said in defense of the New Deal, but "to save it is to give some heed to world thought of the day. I want to equalize the distribution of wealth." He did so, as he confided to his aides, by "stealing Long's thunder,"[87] signing a tax bill that originally proposed much steeper levies on accumulated wealth, but finally accepted relatively minor adjustments.

Rather than killing capitalism, the New Deal's reform measures helped save it. Indeed, as corporate revenues rose nearly 60 percent, corporate after-tax profits climbed from a *negative* $3.8 billion in 1932 to a healthy $6.5 billion in 1936. Given this turnaround, Roosevelt had little patience for the insulting invective hurled his way. "In the summer of 1933, a nice old gentleman wearing a silk hat fell off the end of a pier," as Roosevelt characterized his business opponents. "A friend"—Roosevelt—dove in the water and saved the man, but could not retrieve the hat. "Today, three years later, the old gentleman is berating his friend because the silk hat is lost."[88] Most Americans agreed with the import of this parable. "The bosses had to get used to the fact that they were no longer dictators," as one Ohio chemical worker recalled of employer opposition to the Wagner Act and collective bargaining. "They had to treat people like human beings and not like animals."[89] That Roosevelt was not the first or the most vigorous defender of the many New Deal initiatives for which he was blamed or blessed mattered little to those who saw him as a benevolent savior. "Every house I visited—mill worker or unemployed—had a picture of the President," reported Martha Gellhorn, a federal relief investigator, from the Carolinas. "The portrait holds the place of honor over the mantel; I can only compare this to the Italian peasant's Madonna."[90] In the 1936 campaign, the president skillfully reinforced this image of the people's savior, now embattled on all sides. "Economic royalists," as FDR called corporate conservatives, "are unanimous in their hate for me—and I welcome their hatred."[91]

Many union activists and leaders were well aware that FDR was an unpredictable ally with no clear commitment to independent union organization. They recalled the 1934 press conference in which he endorsed company unions and stated his belief that under Section 7a workers could choose to be represented by "the Ahkoond of Swat . . . , the Royal Geographical Society, . . . a corporation, a union, or the Crown Prince of Siam."[92] However much these remarks rankled union activists, in the polarized atmosphere of 1936, FDR now symbolized to many the hopes of a resurgent labor movement. AFL leaders, including most of the CIO rebels, approved of the New Deal's reformist agenda to save capitalism, because it matched their own aspirations for business-like collective bargaining, rather than root-and-branch social transformations. The socialist minority, in the meantime, splintered into at least three camps. Stalwarts like Norman Thomas, the Socialist Party's presidential candidate, ridiculed the claim that Roosevelt was a socialist—if FDR, said Thomas, had carried out the SP program, "he carried it out on a stretcher."[93] Communists, in contrast, abandoned their harsh criticism of Roosevelt and, for the time being, endorsed the president as "a bulwark against Fascism." Other radicals, however, abandoned their socialist faith altogether and joined the Democratic Party. "Labor could not afford to let FDR lose," recalled David Dubinsky, a long-time Socialist Party member and head of the ILGWU. "The venom with which reactionaries were ganging up against him made me decide I had to align myself openly with his reelection campaign."[94] Dubinsky resigned from the SP in 1936 and lobbied heavily for labor support of the Democratic ticket. He was joined by Sidney Hillman of the ACW, who warned that "defeat of the Roosevelt Administration means no labor legislation for decades to come."[95] For Dubinsky, Hillman, and many others, 1936 was a personal turning point in the long-term shift of labor allegiance from socialism to the Democratic Party (see Table 3-1).

With opinion polls in the spring and summer of 1936 predicting a close election and possible Republican victory, Hillman and John L. Lewis launched an unprecedented mobilization of labor support for the New Deal. Rather than subordinate their efforts to the official Democratic Party campaign, however, the CIO leadership established Labor's Non-Partisan League (LNPL) as an independent organization that could galvanize worker support for Roosevelt without abandoning the political autonomy that many union activists and socialists still valued. Some even viewed the LNPL as an embryonic third party, and in New York State this potential took form in 1936 when the local LNPL transformed itself into the American Labor Party.

Sentiment for a national labor party had grown dramatically among union activists during 1934 and 1935, particularly in communities and industries where strikers had been subjected to violent countermeasures by the police and National Guard. "The New Deal was supposed to give

Table 3-1 Political Preference of Labor Leaders

	1900	1925	1946
Democratic	21.3	13.7	69.4
Republican	21.3	11.2	13.4
Socialist	37.7	27.5	8.1
Progressive/Labor	11.5	25.0	0.5
Nonpartisan	8.2	21.0	8.6

Source: Gary Fink, *Biographical Dictionary of American Labor* (Westport: Greenwood Press, 1984), 21–23.

us the right to organize," as the Massachusetts Committee for a Labor Party declared in March 1936. "Yet when the textile workers went on strike in 1934 for recognition of their union and to stop the speed-up, Democratic governors in 12 states called out the militia to drive the workers back to work and break the strike."[96] Textile union leader Patrick Gorman carried this same message to the AFL's 1935 convention, calling for approval of a Labor Party resolution that would strengthen "people's resistance to tyranny, to the destructive efforts of the bosses, and their agents, the Democratic and Republican parties."[97] The Labor Party resolution narrowly lost by a delegate vote of 108–104, opposed by most of the national unions, but supported by a majority of citywide and state federations. Many of these local bodies attempted to field candidates in 1936, running Labor slates in those cities and states where they could gain ballot status. Typically, these efforts merged the same varied strands of community and workplace organizing that was evident in the 1934 strikes. In Hamtramck, Michigan, an industrial suburb of Detroit and home base for Chrysler's Dodge division, The Peoples' League ran community activist Mary Zuk for city council in April 1936 on a platform favoring the CIO and opposing police interference in strikes. Zuk, leader of the Housewife's Committee against the High Cost of Living, and organizer of a citywide boycott against meat prices, handily won election.

With the political issues in the November presidential ballot posed in the most class-oriented terms of any U.S. election in the twentieth century, the results proved to be a stunning endorsement of the New Deal. Roosevelt carried every state but Maine and Vermont with the largest margin of victory, to that time, in American history: twenty-eight million votes compared to Landon's seventeen million (Thomas, the Socialist, garnered only 190,000 votes, barely a fifth of his 1932 tally). From a party that had previously relied on big-city political machines in the North and one-party "whites only" dominance in the South, the Democrats emerged in 1936 with a new coalition of urban reformers, unions, ethnic workers, minorities, and women, grafted on top of the party's older, conservative foundations. The realignment of the black vote was especially notable. Historically aligned with the "Party of Lincoln," black voters in the urban North had been abandoning the GOP in growing numbers since 1932, when the New Deal began distributing services and jobs to African-Americans on something like an equal basis—with exceptions that widened as one moved South. ("My friends," as Robert Vann of the *Pittsburgh Courier* advised his African-American readers, "go home and turn Lincoln's picture to the wall."[98]) For labor, 1936 also marked an historic realignment, as both the Socialist Party and Progressive Republicanism lost adherents to the New Deal coalition.

Union supporters were exhilarated by the election results. There was no doubting that the vote represented a public mandate for the New Deal—including the Wagner Act—and a repudiation of the business practices that had obstructed reform. Although Roosevelt's overwhelming margin meant no single group could claim the decisive role in engineering his victory, few doubted the importance of the money, organizers, door-to-door canvassing, and radio appeals sponsored by Labor's Non-Partisan League. Some regarded labor's mobilization as the key to FDR's victories in Illinois, Indiana, Ohio, Pennsylvania, and New York, with the LNPL in the latter state drawing 275,000 votes for Roosevelt through the American Labor Party, and many more through support of the straight Democratic ticket. The New Deal's congressional majority had grown dramatically, and statewide offices had also shifted to the liberal column with the election of Governor George Earle in Pennsylvania and Governor Frank Murphy in Michigan. Murphy, the former mayor of Detroit, campaigned in the heartland of the Republican Party's traditional base on the pledge he would never call out the National Guard to break strikes. "If I worked for a wage," Murphy announced to union supporters celebrating his upset victory, "I'd join my union."[99]

Labor had arrived at a momentous turning point. "The first reelection campaign of Franklin D. Roosevelt in 1936," as David Dubinsky later observed, "was the start of the American labor movement's systematic, year-round involvement in politics."[100] It was also the spark for the most successful union organizing campaigns in U.S. history. "You voted New Deal at the polls and defeated the Auto Barons," as union organizers announced in Michigan after Murphy's November victory. "Now get a New Deal in the shop."[101]

THE SIT-DOWN ERA

Less than forty-eight hours before Frank Murphy's inauguration as governor of Michigan, fifteen hundred autoworkers barricaded themselves inside two GM factories in Flint, Michigan, vowing to continue their "sit-down" strike until the company recognized their union and began national negotiations over wages and working conditions. The shutdown of these crucial Fisher Body plants immediately disrupted GM's assembly operations, forcing a dramatic showdown between the world's largest manufacturing corporation and the fledgling union that represented only 10 percent of its workers.

The United Auto Workers (UAW), barely one year old when the Flint sit-down began, was one of several national organizations established by the AFL to consolidate the membership of its federal labor unions in mass production industries. The AFL's inept and cautious leadership had squandered the initial hopes of autoworkers, however, and membership had remained low until the UAW aligned itself with the CIO. Thereafter, the autoworkers were a focal point of CIO strategy, along with the United Rubber Workers, the Steel Workers Organizing Committee, and the United Electrical Workers.

The sit-down strike was the key innovation that gave these organizing efforts their extraordinary dynamism in 1936–1937. It was not an altogether new tactic—meatpackers in Austin, Minnesota, had used it in 1933 to win union recognition, and rubber workers in Akron, Ohio, briefly used it for the same purpose at Goodyear and Firestone Tire in the spring of 1936. But it was not until the immediate aftermath of the November elections that the tactic gained a sudden and widespread currency among labor activists. Brief sit-down strikes began to flare in GM factories and supplier plants for the next two months, culminating in the Flint occupations on December 30. More than a dozen other GM plants around the country would eventually join the strike, but it was here, in the company's home base, that the widening confrontation between GM and the UAW came to a head, drawing national attention to a struggle that was widely recognized as the CIO's most critical test.

For the sit-down strikers who were risking their jobs and possible arrest in this illegal seizure of company property, wages were not the primary motivating factor. "I ain't got no kick on wages," as "Red" Mundale, sit-down leader in the Fisher #2 plant, put it. "But I just don't like to be drove."[102] Speedup was their primary grievance, along with the tyranny of supervisors who were, in the estimate of one Chevrolet worker, "just people with a bullwhip. . . . They treated us like a bunch of coolies." In the frenzied, machine-driven pace of auto production, with GM cutting the workforce to the minimum, "we didn't even have time to go to the toilet," as one Buick worker complained. "You have to run to the toilet and run back." Frequent layoffs and recalls also rankled autoworkers, particularly if their foreman played favorites deciding who did or did not work.

"If he happened to like you, or if you sucked around him and did him favors," as one Chevrolet worker put it, "you might be picked to work a few weeks longer than the next guy." For many, it was a matter of dignity. "We were treated like a bunch of dogs," as one worker later recalled, "and we resented it so much that the people with principle . . . were grabbing for anything to try to establish themselves as men."[103]

They "grabbed" the sit-down tactic because it perfectly suited the strategic circumstances facing the union. From just 150 members in October 1936, UAW Local 156 had grown rapidly after the November elections, enrolling forty-five hundred by the end of December. Even with these gains, however, union members were still a small minority of Flint's forty-five thousand GM workers. An opposing minority remained loyal to the company, some of them because they saw sufficient benefit in GM policies that favored skilled and senior workers, others because of their hostility to an outside organization that included radicals. A larger number, perhaps the majority, favored the UAW but hesitated to join a union widely known to contain company spies. Fear of company espionage, which had contributed to the demise of the AFL's federal labor unions in Flint, and which had been dramatically confirmed by the La Follete Committee, meant the majority of workers held back. Company executives actively fanned these fears by announcing that Flint workers who wore UAW buttons would be fired—an action clearly illegal under the Wagner Act, but of little concern to GM, which had secured a court injunction against the NLRB.

The UAW could not win the majority's active support without first confronting GM's unlawful intimidation of union supporters, but the legal means for doing so were paralyzed by court proceedings. Strike action was the only alternative, but a conventional walkout would expose picketers to police counterattack, as demonstrated in a previous strike at Fisher Body, in 1930, when Flint's mounted policemen rode down picketers, dispersed their lines, and arrested union leaders. A sit-down, in contrast, would prevent the use of strikebreakers and give strikers more protection, since the company was less likely to attack its own property—particularly if sit-downers made clear their intention to resist. Barricaded inside the plant, the militant minority could, in effect, put the company's property under "house arrest" for management's failure to abide by the National Labor Relations Act.

"Well, it is illegal," President Roosevelt said when asked his opinion of the Flint sit-down. "But shooting it out and killing a lot of people because they have violated the law of trespass . . . [is not] the answer. . . . Why can't those fellows in General Motors meet with the Committee of workers?"[104] Governor Murphy also urged company and city officials to forgo violent countermeasures, and when city police nevertheless mounted a nighttime assault on Fisher #2 with gunfire and teargas (an attack the strikers repelled with fire hoses and repeated volleys of thrown auto parts) the governor sent in the National Guard to prevent further violence—but not, as the company demanded, to evict the sit-downers and break the strike.

The standoff lasted six weeks, with the company and the union continually maneuvering for public support and legal leverage. GM secured a court injunction ordering the plants to be evacuated, but had to abandon this option when union investigators revealed that the judge owned $220,000 worth of GM stock. The company also sponsored a "back-to-work" petition that supervisors circulated in Flint plants not yet impacted by the strike, securing (or coercing, as the UAW charged), thousands of signatures. The union countered by organizing the widest possible community mobilization, including a Women's Auxiliary to bring wives and women workers into active strike support. In addition to picketing, public speaking, and working in the strike kitchen, the most militant of these new activists formed a Women's Emergency Brigade (WEB) to join the men in the picket-line battles that flared around the occupied plants. Their role was especially prominent in the daring maneuver that won the union control of a third plant, Chevrolet Engine. By feeding the company false information through a suspected spy, the union lured company guards and police to a distant plant, allowing their activists to occupy Chevrolet Engine and, with the WEB, hold it against counterattack.

After forty-four days, GM finally surrendered. The company agreed to begin national negotiations with the UAW for a contract covering the seventeen plants where UAW strikers had stopped production (three in Flint and the rest scattered from Atlanta to Cleveland to Detroit) and to refrain in the meantime from recognizing any other bargaining representative, including its discredited company union. All strikers and union supporters would be rehired, and there would be, in the words of the settlement, no "discrimination, interference, restraint, or coercion" against union members, including those who wore union buttons. "Even if we got not one damn thing out of it other than that," said one Fisher Body worker of the nondiscrimination clause, "we at least had a right to open our mouths without fear."[105]

The UAW's victory had an electrifying effect on union supporters across the country, especially in nearby Detroit, where news of the Flint victory sparked excited debate among workers in a wide range of industries. "Little by little we were getting information," recalled Estelle Gornie Cassily, a machine operator in one of Detroit's largest cigar factories. "And we figured, if they can do it, we can also do it. . . . So we decided on a certain day, a certain hour. And we sat down. . . . We got rid of the manager and took the factory over."[106] Estelle and her militant coworkers at General Cigar were not alone as they fortified their plant against possible counterattack. By February 20, 1937, little more than a week after the end of the Flint GM sit-down, two thousand women cigar makers had occupied Detroit's five largest cigar plants. They were soon joined by thousands of others in every major Detroit industry as "sit-down fever" spread across the city. All nine of Chrysler's Detroit factories were simultaneously occupied in a carefully planned sit-down on March 8, with seventeen thousand sit-downers taking control of the factories within minutes of the 1:30 p.m. strike call. A week later, the waiters and waitresses union occupied two of the downtown's major hotels, emulating the 250 saleswomen who had already sat down inside Woolworth's department store. According to newspaper estimates (the *Detroit News* ran a daily box score in the month of March of "Plants Closed by Sit-downs") a total of thirty-five thousand workers joined sit-down strikes in the two months following Flint, closing fifteen major auto factories and twenty-five parts plants; a dozen industrial laundries; three department stores and over a dozen shoe and clothing stores; five cigar plants; five trucking and garage companies; ten meatpacking plants, bakeries and other food processors; warehouses, restaurants, coal yards, bottlers, and over a dozen miscellaneous manufacturers. In all, nearly 130 factories, offices, and stores were occupied and held for a few hours or up to six weeks, constituting a virtual "rolling" general strike.

Business leaders were naturally alarmed by this widespread disregard for property rights and called on Governor Murphy to forcibly suppress the movement. "If lawless men can seize an office, a factory, or a home and hold it unmolested for hours and days," as one business publication editorialized, "they can seize and hold it for months and years; and revolution is here."[107] Murphy, however, refused to invite the bloodbath that military intervention would have provoked and worked instead to mediate the larger disputes. Detroit's police did evict some of the cigar workers and meatpackers from their factories, but a massive rally of over one hundred thousand people discouraged further attempts. In Hamtramck, where six thousand autoworkers had barricaded themselves inside the Dodge plant on the first day of their sit-down, Councilwoman

Mary Zuk of the Peoples' League sponsored a motion that put the city—and its police—officially on the side of the sit-downers.

However revolutionary these events appeared to some business leaders, the actual sentiments of most sit-downers were neither anticapitalist nor seditious. The majority favored a more equitable "moral capitalism" and regarded corporate leaders as "lawless" for their refusal to comply with the Wagner Act. "Laboring people justify the sit-down on the grounds that it is effective," as Governor Murphy observed. "They contend it is moral."[108] Workers paraded in the streets with American flags, and Woolworth's strikers reportedly sang "America" when their boss refused to negotiate. Even so, these patriotic symbols held very different meanings for the sit-downers than they did for most employers. In practice, union militants acted on principles of solidarity and group commitment that stood in sharp contrast to the dominant ideology of individual upward mobility. Without rejecting individual striving, their goals were defined more often in terms of collective security and dignity. "We weren't for getting rich," recalled Bill Mileski, a sit-downer at Dodge Main, "because you never can get rich working. We wanted seniority, so the guy didn't have to be a kiss-ass to keep his job."[109]

Although it was certainly not revolutionary to demand a seniority system—one that regulated layoff and recall solely by the standard of how much time each worker had invested in the company—the winning of it seemed to require revolutionary means in the winter and spring of 1937. Across the country, workers emulated the sit-downers in Flint and Detroit with nearly five hundred stay-in strikes of one day's duration or longer, representing 10 percent of the record number 4,760 strikes in that year. In the majority of cases, whether sit-down or walkout, the goal of this unprecedented strike wave was union recognition, and with the movement's new tactics and political success, membership climbed dramatically. By April 1937, the UAW boasted 250,000 dues-paying members, a fivefold increase from the previous November. Few other unions could match this pace, but most experienced a hothouse growth unknown in previous years. By the end of 1937, union membership in the United States had grown from four to seven million workers, representing a climb from just 7 percent of the labor force to 13 percent.

Not all of this growth required strikes. In the steel industry, the CIO won a sudden, bloodless victory when Myron Taylor, head of U.S. Steel, agreed in early March to recognize the Steel Workers Organizing Committee (SWOC) and establish a formal grievance procedure to resolve workplace disputes. Taylor's decision, reversing decades of determined opposition to independent unions by the industry's leading company, followed his conviction that multiple trends were shifting the balance of power against the company. The management-dominated Employee Representation Plans, which had been established to repel independent unionization, had by now boomeranged against their creator; workers had grown accustomed to electing delegates to a plant-wide body that unified all steelworkers regardless of craft, and by the winter of 1936–1937, they were electing pro-SWOC candidates who were pushing for wage increases, adjustment of grievances, and negotiated work rules. FDR's reelection and the success of New Deal candidates in Pennsylvania and elsewhere had weakened the company's claim to government protection, and the UAW's Flint victory further emboldened steelworker activists. Within one week of GM's capitulation to the sit-downers, Taylor entered secret negotiations with CIO leader Lewis, hoping to avoid a similar confrontation in steel. Lewis, for his part, accepted terms that still permitted the company to simultaneously recognize its ERPs, and thereby potentially limit SWOC to a minority status. But Lewis was confident that SWOC was winning control of these bodies and that steelworkers, sensing the same trends as Taylor, would switch to the union banner. Events proved him correct at U.S. Steel and in many—but not all—companies in steel and allied metalworking industries. By the fall of 1937, SWOC had chartered one thousand local unions and signed collective bargaining agreements covering five hundred thousand workers.

The month following SWOC's surprising triumph at U.S. Steel, the Supreme Court capped the labor movement's phenomenal string of political and organizational victories by upholding the constitutionality of the National Labor Relations Act. No doubt aware that, in the absence of a legally prescribed system for regulating labor relations, a growing number of workers were turning to militant actions that threatened private property, the justices ruled in April that employees had as much right to chose their own representatives as business owners had to select their own managers. Since, in the court's words, a single employee was "helpless in dealing with an employer," only collective organization could give workers the opportunity "to deal on an equality" with management.

On the crest of this labor upsurge, A. Philip Randolph and the Brotherhood of Sleeping Car Porters (BSCP) finally overcame the opposition of the Pullman company and signed the first collective bargaining agreement negotiated by a black union. It had been a long journey from the

BSCP's founding in 1925, marked by the union's near collapse in 1933, when national membership totaled just 658, to the final confrontation with Pullman's company union in 1935, when the BSCP won a head-to-head election with 81 percent of the seventy-four hundred votes cast. It took two more years, however, for Pullman to agree to contract terms, and then only after the issuance of a strike threat and the intervention of federal mediators. The August 1937, agreement won higher wages, maximum hours, overtime pay, and seniority rights.

The BSCP's very survival, however, had already highlighted the whites-only foundations of the American Federation of Labor. Randolph and his BSCP colleagues had openly challenged the AFL at its 1934 convention, calling on the federation to expel any affiliated union that refused to eliminate the whites-only membership criteria still common in many craft unions. The motion failed, gaining only the support of Lewis's United Mine Workers and Dubinsky's Garment Workers. Thereafter, the federation added insult to injury by ordering the BSCP to dissolve and make way for the newly chartered Order of Sleeping Car Conductors—a whites-only union. Remarkably, AFL leader William Green told BSCP officers he had every confidence they would give the conductors' union "a full measure of cooperation and support."[110] Randolph simply ignored the order.

By 1937, the BSCP, although still formally affiliated with the AFL, was closely allied with the CIO and Lewis, who had been among the BSCP's lone supporters in 1934. The BSCP had ample reason to side with the rebel movement, since newly chartered CIO unions publicly declared themselves open to black as well as white members. Although some CIO unions were slow to make good on this promise, others were determined to demonstrate their racial egalitarianism in practice, and none more so than the Packinghouse Workers Organizing Committee (PWOC), formed in the fall of 1937. In an industry where 25 percent of the workforce was African-American, and where past failures to incorporate black workers in the World War I era had been repaid by black strikebreakers and union defeat, PWOC made every effort to bridge the racial divide. The union's chosen symbol in Chicago was telling: two hands clasped in a handshake, one black and one white. More than symbolic, racial unity "was an integral part of the union's thinking from the word go,"[111] recalled Herb March, PWOC's left-wing leader in Chicago. While signing up members on the job, PWOC sponsored integrated picnics, dances, and softball teams, and sent "flying squadrons" of black and white members to desegregate bars near the stockyards. At the Armour plant employing seven thousand workers, two thousand of them black, white workers who opposed an integrated union began to change their minds in June 1938 when black workers supported a threatened work stoppage protesting the firing of a white union supporter. In turn, blacks who well knew the whites-only history of AFL unions began to change their minds about PWOC when white workers joined a sit-down protesting the layoff of senior black workers. PWOC reaped the goodwill it sowed in both Chicago communities as young black preachers and young Catholic priests both endorsed the union.

Crucial to the success of PWOC was its practice of organizing a tight network of union "stewards" who worked on the killing floors and in the processing departments, each representing the twenty or thirty workers in their immediate area. These unpaid activists were the union's frontline leaders, and PWOC recommended the widest possible spread of the steward system so that "more men are given responsibility, and our organization becomes more powerful and more closely knit."[112] At Armour, stewards represented the union on the job long before Local 347 won formal recognition or a written collective bargaining agreement. Buoyed by the Supreme Court's validation of the Wagner Act, they were demanding to meet with supervisors on a wide range of grievances, often involving work pace or seniority preference in job assignments. If managers refused to meet, Herb March recalled, "when we got enough of the workers organized, we'd have work stoppages."[113] This immediate, direct-action approach was characteristic in many newly organized workplaces in 1936–1937, where the use of "quickie" sit-down strikes lasting a few minutes or hours was a popular tactic for "disciplining" antiunion foremen.

Where these tactics worked, union success motivated many skeptics to join. Alfred Lockhart, a GM worker who initially opposed the UAW, was one doubter who changed his mind after the sit-down. "The inhuman high speed," he wrote, "is no more. We now have a voice, and have slowed up the speed of the line. And [we] are now treated as human beings. . . . It proves clearly that united we stand, divided or alone we fall."[114]

CONTAINMENT

The surge of union growth and success that appeared so irresistible to Lockhart and others at the peak of the sit-down wave suddenly slowed after the spring of 1937, and then it stopped. Just as multiple factors had favored union supporters in the upswing, there were manifold reasons why the movement now faltered.

First and most dramatically, with the successful organization of industry leaders like GM and U.S. Steel, union organizers now confronted the violent resistance of companies like Ford, Republic Steel, and Youngstown Sheet and Tube—companies that were still huge in their own right, but less concerned with public image and less prepared to compromise their shop floor control. In the spring of 1937, these secondary companies vigorously counterattacked the union drives in auto and steel, blunting further gains in both cases. Their resistance was front-page news after May 26, when UAW organizers leafleting Ford workers in Dearborn, Michigan, were assaulted at the Gate 4 overpass by members of the "Ford Service Department," a private force of three thousand armed men led by the company's security chief, Harry Bennett. Over the protests of Edsel Ford, Henry's son and nominal president of the company, Bennett launched his campaign against the UAW with the backing of the elderly and psychologically unstable Henry, who vowed never to recognize the union. Ford's security chief had ample resources for sustaining the antiunion assault. As a member of Michigan's parole board until Governor Murphy removed him, Bennett had recruited gangsters from Michigan's prisons and put them on the Service Department parole. These men had already demonstrated their capacity for fatal violence in the 1932 Ford hunger march massacre, and they thereafter waged a campaign of espionage and intimidation that led not only to the firing of union sympathizers, as elsewhere, but often to their physical pummeling before they were thrown (literally in some cases) into the street. In the attack of May 26, Bennett's thugs severely beat Walter Reuther, a former Ford worker and future UAW president, along with dozens of men and women who were peacefully leafleting Ford workers. Stunned news photographers recorded the "Battle of the Overpass" in vivid detail, and the subsequent publicity tarnished Ford's civic reputation. Even so, Ford would not be organized in 1937.

Neither would Republic, Youngstown, Bethlehem Steel, Inland, and National Steel, the so-called Little Steel companies that refused to follow Myron Taylor's lead in recognizing SWOC. Their refusal led to a strike that began the same day as the events in Dearborn and ended six weeks later in defeat for the union. In what turned out to be the last major round of fatal violence in the twentieth-century history of the labor movement, police and company guards shot and killed eighteen strikers, effectively breaking the picket lines and defeating the union. Ten of these workers died in the single incident that came to be known as the Memorial Day massacre, when police opened fire on an unarmed crowd in front of Republic Steel's Chicago plant. Newspapers initially justified the killings, describing the demonstrators as "an armed mob" (the *New York Times*) and "a trained military unit of a revolutionary body" (the *Chicago Tribune*). But subsequent examination of newsreel footage showed, as the *St. Louis Post-Dispatch* reported, "uniformed policemen firing their revolvers pointblank into a dense crowd of men, women, and children, then pursuing and clubbing the survivors unmercifully as they made frantic efforts to escape."[115] Of the ten killed, seven had been shot in the back and three in the side.

A second factor that took the wind from labor's sails was the economic recession that deflated job prospects in late 1937 and revived fears of mass unemployment. Few agreed on the causes of the downturn. Many businessmen blamed the New Deal and argued that sit-down strikes and corporate taxes discouraged investment. Many New Dealers, in turn, blamed the near-monopoly control of investment wielded by large corporations and argued that, with the richest 1 percent of all Americans still taking a combined income greater than the bottom third of the population, consumer demand remained too weak. Some reasoned that President Roosevelt, in a mistaken effort to balance the budget when the unemployment rate was still over 10 percent, had erred in cutting public works and job programs when more spending, not less, was called for. Whatever the causes, the results were unmistakable by 1938, when national unemployment ballooned to over ten million people, representing 19 percent of the civilian labor force.

In these depressed conditions, workers grew more cautious and companies less accommodating. Unions that had barely won recognition the year before now struggled to survive as employers cut payroll and resisted strikes, or shuttered their plants altogether and locked out the union. In electrical manufacturing, where the United Electrical workers (UE) had won representation elections at GE and Westinghouse plants but had not yet signed national agreements, prospects dimmed as sales fell 30 percent in 1938 and companies laid off sixty thousand workers. There was little chance of a national contract at Westinghouse, but GE's more liberal management, led by Gerard Swope, was willing to stabilize labor relations by signing a unique agreement with UE. In the seven plants where UE had won majority support, the union said it was willing to accept the company's existing handbook of work rules and wage rates as the basis of a one-year national contract if, in turn, the company would recognize UE's steward system and add a grievance procedure. Swope agreed and UE members voted to accept these modest terms, which at least protected current wages and union representation.

A third dimension of labor's retreat was evident in the altered political climate that followed the sit-downs. Although the public generally supported the initial stay-in strikes and opposed the violent methods of Ford and Republic Steel, the continuing disruptions of the strike wave and the recession that arrived soon after finally produced a backlash. The only significant pro-labor legislation to follow in the late 1930s was the Fair Labor Standards Act of 1938, establishing the minimum wage, abolishing child labor, and requiring payment of overtime premiums for work beyond forty hours a week. Otherwise, public opinion was moving against unions and their New Deal allies.

The difficulties in winning majority support for pro-labor candidates and legislation were underlined in Michigan. In the 1937 primaries for Detroit's municipal elections, a Labor slate featuring UAW organizers finished strongly in the first round of voting for mayor and city council. However, the prospects of a CIO city government alarmed conservative workers, small-business interests, and salaried professionals, and the Labor slate's opponents won a decisive victory in the runoff by urging these voters to simultaneously "Defeat the CIO" and "Defeat Communism." It was cold comfort to CIO supporters that the new mayor and his superintendent of police both went to prison in 1940 for skimming money from illegal gambling operations. By then, the mounting crusade against the "state of anarchy", as congressional conservatives called Michigan, had turned against Governor Murphy and his pro-labor policies. In 1938, in the midst of his reelection campaign, the newly formed House Un-American Activities Committee (HUAC), chaired by Democrat Martin Dies of Texas, began hearings on the role of Communists in the Flint sit-downs and Murphy's failure to suppress them. Witnesses hostile to the governor dominated the headlines, charging Murphy with "treasonable action," as Flint's city manager termed the governor's decision not to attack the sit-downers. In the November election, Detroit still gave Murphy 59 percent of the vote, but statewide returns gave the Republicans a 53–47 percent victory and returned Frank Fitzgerald to office—the same man under whom Bennett had previously served on the state parole board. Murphy thereby became HUAC's first victim in a prolonged

"Red scare" that would later hound an entire generation of New Dealers and left-wing labor activists. Nationally, the Republicans also recorded their first gains since 1932, adding seventy-five House seats and seven senators to their congressional minority.

Yet another factor contributing to labor's faltering step was one that came from within the movement, as a bitter factionalism began to split workers into warring camps. Craft distinctions and organizational rivalries that had been temporarily submerged in the sit-down wave now bobbed back to the surface as union growth slowed, touching off fierce battles over "jurisdiction" in scores of industries. The rift between AFL leaders and the Committee for Industrial Organization had previously been an internal affair, even after William Green announced in August 1936, the suspension of ten unions affiliated with the rebel committee. During the sit-downs, the labor movement remained unified despite the suspensions as local activists regardless of affiliation cooperated in the political and workplace mobilizations that drew millions to labor's cause. By mid-1937, however, AFL directives to local bodies were forcing an open breach, and the rupture became complete the following year when the CIO officially reconstituted itself as the "Congress" of Industrial Organizations.

Galvanized by the CIO's stunning organizational success, the AFL had also grown during the heady months of late 1936 and early 1937. Retaining those craftsmen who still viewed themselves as a privileged elite and drawing in workers who viewed CIO radicals with alarm, many AFL unions had borrowed from the CIO's playbook, adopting more militant tactics (at least one hundred sit-downs in 1937 conducted by AFL workers) and widening their base to include production workers. Some AFL unions also advanced their organizational growth by striking an opportunistic bargain with management, offering themselves as a compliant alternative to the militant CIO and signing "sweetheart" deals that forestalled CIO intervention. In shipyards, sawmills, aircraft factories, meatpacking, electrical manufacturing, and elsewhere, competing AFL and CIO affiliates spent as much energy battling each other as they did contesting management. In meatpacking, the AFL's Amalgamated Meat Cutters simply replaced the Armour Company's management-dominated company union, absorbing the discredited "Employee Mutual Association" in 1938 and launching a wave of bombings, shootings, and beatings against the CIO's PWOC. That same year, AFL leaders made common cause with congressional conservatives, testifying before Martin Dies's HUAC investigation and delivering the names of more than fifty CIO officials alleged to be Communists. Labor unity in electoral politics was virtually impossible in these poisoned circumstances as the AFL opposed CIO-endorsed candidates in Democratic primaries and local elections, including Detroit's Labor slate.

In the auto industry, labor factionalism nearly destroyed the UAW as opposing camps within the union aligned themselves with the competing national federations. Internal splits were evident within months of the sitdown wave, as workers impatient for change ignored the negotiated grievance procedure and conducted unauthorized quickie strikes to win workplace improvements. Pressured by corporate management to subdue these militants, UAW president Homer Martin touched off a stormy battle within the union by branding all his opponents as Communists. With little support in the membership, Martin's efforts to silence the opposition grew increasingly clumsy as he first censored local union papers, then abolished them altogether, and finally removed rebellious local leaders from office. Widely perceived as an unstable and erratic personality, with little understanding of the industry he had only briefly worked in, Martin came to rely on two outsiders with even less experience in the auto union: former Communist leader Jay Lovestone, now a prominent anti-Communist advisor, and David Dubinsky, garment union leader and former Socialist, who was now taking the ILGWU out of the CIO. Isolated within the union, Martin finally overplayed his hand when he secretly began negotiations with company security chief Harry Bennett to establish a "sweetheart" union at Ford. Martin suspended the executive board members who discovered and denounced his unauthorized backroom deal making, and in 1939 announced he was taking the UAW out of the CIO and back into the AFL. When the suspended officers countered by forming a "UAW-CIO" to oppose Martin's far smaller "UAW-AFL," companies like GM and Chrysler withdrew recognition from both the rival claimants. The union's demoralized members, already battered by layoffs that emptied two hundred thousand of them from Detroit's plants by January 1938, appeared on the verge of losing all the gains of 1937.

In a telling measure of what the CIO gained by uniting production and skilled workers in the same union, the UAW-CIO was able to recover the initiative by relying again on the militancy of a strategic minority. In 1937, it had been the production workers who took the lead by sitting down inside GM's Flint body plants; in 1939, it was the turn of the skilled tool and die makers to fill that role by preventing the preparation of new machinery and tooling for GM's anticipated 1940 models. Representing

only six thousand of GM's two hundred thousand workers, these craftsmen were in short supply when they struck in July, halting preparations
for the new model just as the economy was recovering. Unlike many AFL
craftsmen, these former member's of Detroit's MESA were predominantly
left-wingers who identified more strongly with working-class unity than
with craft exclusiveness, and their strike demands reflected this larger
agenda by calling on GM to recognize the UAW-CIO in all of its plants, not
just the tool and die shops. Only these skilled workers, as a UAW-CIO
leaflet put it, could "make GM talk turkey with production workers."[116]
After a month, GM agreed to a face-saving compromise, agreeing to negotiate exclusively with the UAW-CIO in the forty-one plants (out of fifty-
nine total) where the union was unopposed by the UAW-AFL. In April of
the following year, the matter was definitively settled when NLRB elections gave GM workers a choice between three alternatives: the UAW-CIO,
the UAW-AFL, or no union. Heavy majorities favored the CIO affiliate in
forty-eight plants, whereas just five voted AFL and only one no-union.

The NLRB's role in certifying this victory reflected the augmented
power of the federal government to regulate labor relations. Backed by
Supreme Court decisions that finally freed it from the paralyzing clutch of
lower-court challenges, the NLRB now gave the labor movement, particularly the CIO, critical support that partially countered the adverse circumstances of 1938–1939. NLRB rulings favored industrial organization at
the expense of AFL crafts and even overturned some of the "sweetheart"
contracts that employers had hurriedly rigged with AFL unions. By the
end of 1941, workers and unions had filed nearly twenty-four thousand
charges of unfair labor practices (ULPs) against employers, many of these
leading to NLRB orders—backed by the courts—to reinstate workers illegally fired for union activity. Republic Steel alone was forced to reinstate
seven thousand union supporters, and Ford was forced to take back four
thousand. The NLRB also conducted six thousand elections to determine
whether the union had majority support, with CIO unions winning 82
percent of all such contests where they were on the ballot and the AFL,
56 percent. In cases where unions from the two federations ran head-to-
head, as at GM, CIO affiliates won 75 percent of the contested ballots.
Sweeping victories in meatpacking, where PWOC's Local 347 defeated
the Amalgamated Meat Cutters 4–1 at Armour, and at Chrysler, where the
UAW-CIO defeated the UAW-AFL by a vote of thirty-seven thousand to
four thousand, ended the AFL challenge in both cases. For this reason, as
well as the many NLRB rulings favoring industrial organization over craft

separation, the AFL joined with southern Democrats and conservative Republicans who wanted to abolish or curtail the NLRB's powers. Their efforts were turned back by the Democratic majority, but to mollify his business critics, President Roosevelt appointed more conservative members to the board. By late 1940, *Business Week* was satisfied that "subtly, perhaps, but surely, the Board may be counted upon to change its line . . . [and] from now on business can expect to find the Board's agents more tolerant of its problems and points of view."[117]

Even so, the NLRB continued to backstop the labor movement in the critical period when economic recession and political reaction imperiled the fragile gains of 1937. To Philip Murray, the former UMW official who now headed SWOC, the fact that "unionism in the steel industry was able to survive the tribulations which beset it in 1937 and 1938 . . . is due in no small part to the existence of the National Labor Relations Act."[118] It was also due in no small part to the continuing direct action of workers who were willing to strike Ford (April 1941) and Bethlehem Steel (February and March of the same year) to force both to submit to NLRB elections. The landslide victories for the UAW and SWOC that soon followed marked the end of Ford and Little Steel's violent resistance to union organization.

It also marked the consolidation of a new and portentous relationship between the labor movement and the government. NLRB and court decisions helped protect the labor movement as it finally overcame employer resistance, but they also made unions increasingly dependent on such government intervention. For the time being, the outcome was positive insofar as it sustained a movement that might not otherwise have survived. In this respect, 1938–1941 stood in sharp contrast with 1917–1920, when wartime gains in the labor movement's power and membership had suddenly collapsed in the counterrevolution that followed. But government support that sustained unions as quasi-public institutions, certified and legitimated by NLRB elections, also entailed government regulation that potentially compromised the labor movement's autonomy. A reliance on the NLRB's legal procedures, combined with a simultaneous use of direct action and mass mobilization, was still a potent combination, and remained so as long as government policy supported union growth. Yet even in such favorable circumstances, there were a few who questioned the wisdom of relying on government intervention. "No federal agency intervening in the conflicts between employers and employees can be expected to fairly determine the issues of labor's rights," Roger Baldwin of the American Civil Liberties Union had written Senator Wagner in 1935, explaining his initial opposition to the NLRA. "We say this from a long experience with the various boards set up in Washington, all of which have tended to take from labor its basic right to strike by substituting mediation, conciliation, or in some cases, arbitration.

"The pressures on any governmental agency from employers," Baldwin continued, "are so constant and determined that it is far better to have no governmental intervention than to suffer the delusion that it will aid labor in its struggle for the rights to organize, bargain collectively, and strike."[119]

Wagner's response reflected the prevailing opinion of liberals and labor activists in the 1930s and helped persuade Baldwin to drop his opposition. "Government in every country is going to be forced to play a more important role in every phase of economic life," Wagner wrote, "and for that reason it seems to me more useful to attempt to direct the nature of that role rather than merely to state the truism that government is likely to be influenced by the forces in society that happen to be strongest. Certainly these forces cannot be checked by governmental self-limitation, nor do I believe that governmental action in such matters . . . serves to check the struggles that labor must carry on by extra-legal means."[120]

With the U.S. government mobilizing the nation for world war and global ascendancy, these opposing assessments would delimit labor's existence for years to come.

4

GROWTH AND
ACCOMMODATION, 1941–1965

The labor movement gained new ground in the years after 1940, establishing union representation in virtually all of heavy industry and transportation and winning important beachheads in retail and communications. But renewed growth after the economic recession and political reaction of 1937–1939 only settled the matter of labor's survival. Still to be determined was the nature of its relationship to government regulators and corporate adversaries.

Between 1941 and 1965, this emerging labor relations system was defined in a series of legal, workplace, and legislative confrontations that narrowed the labor movement's social and political agenda, even as unions negotiated for an ever-widening share of material prosperity. Increasingly, these turning points for labor were shaped not only by the contending aspirations of workers and managers but by the emphatic intrusion of world war, Cold War, and the struggle for black civil rights. In a context defined by the labor movement's increasing dependence on bureaucratic procedure and the political agenda of the Democratic Party, unions gained an apparent permanence as they were transformed into publicly regulated "partners in production." At the same time, with the institutionalization of their role, unions relinquished much of their capacity to mobilize for social change.

CONTENDING CLAIMS

Business leaders had to accept unions forced upon them by strike action and government decree, but most were unreconciled to this forced marriage in the early 1940s. Indeed, some expected the worst. John Scoville, staff economist for Chrysler Corporation, described collective bargaining to Detroit's Kiwanis as "an assault on liberty, as an evil thing which is against the public interest, as . . . one chick in the foul brood of vultures that seek to pick the meat from the bones of honest men."[1] Scoville, like most business spokesmen, was less concerned with wage demands than he was with the challenge unions posed to management control of the workplace. "You don't run your factory if it is unionized," complained James Lincoln of Lincoln Electric Company, "you merely cooperate with the union and try and get it to do the things you would like to have done."[2] For men accustomed to unilateral control of "their" workers, this was exasperating and unacceptable. "We do a better job alone than when you interfere with us," exclaimed one Allis Chalmers executive during labor board hearings. "You are trying to tie management up in knots."[3] Congressional conservatives sympathized. "Industry could not, any more than an army, take orders from every private in the rear ranks and operate successfully,"[4] declared one irate congressman.

Union supporters saw things differently. "It was like the South didn't want to give up the slaves," as rubber worker Dale Ray recalled of management hostility to the union at Seiberling Tire. "They hated to give up power to poor workers." And with a measure of power now in their hands, workers at Seiberling and elsewhere wanted to settle grievances on the spot: speedup, unsafe work, unilateral discipline, unequal pay, arbitrary job classifications, supervisory favoritism in everything from job assignments to promotions to layoff and recall—all demanded immediate attention, and all at once. It was this frontal assault on the "old way" of doing things that so alarmed corporate spokesmen like Scoville and Lincoln, particularly as union stewards challenged the authority of frontline management. "With the coming of the union," proclaimed the UAW's steward manual in 1940, "the foreman finds . . . his small-time dictatorship has been overthrown, and he must be adjusted to a democratic system of shop government."

There was, however, virtually no language in the sparsely worded collective bargaining agreements of the late 1930s that specified what this "democratic system of shop government" actually was. The grievance procedures outlined in most of these contracts had little agreed-upon structure, time limits, or appeal process and could not, therefore, accommodate the explosive conflicts that erupted in the wake of union organization. Workers who took their complaints through the multi-step procedure, first to the foreman and finally to top executives, usually found management ignoring, delaying, or, in the final step, denying both the grievance and the remedy, with no appeal. Because many workers were unwilling to accept these outcomes even when their grievances had no contractual standing, they resorted to direct action—to the "quickie" sit-downs, slowdowns, departmental walkouts, and plant-wide confrontations that had proved so effective before the 1938 recession.

This sporadic militancy presented union leaders with a difficult dilemma. On the one hand, immediate shop floor mobilization was the more reliable and timely means for countering management hostility to the newly arrived union. The alternatives were often unreliable (especially grievance procedures) and woefully slow (especially NLRB proceedings), and risked alienating member support for the union and its incumbent officers. On the other hand, unplanned eruptions of militancy, particularly departmental squabbles over the pace of work or job assignments, could shut down an entire plant, impacting the paychecks of workers far removed from the source of conflict. Continuous confrontation could create conflict within and among local unions, disrupt long-term strategy for national bargaining, and force officers to focus on saving (or abandoning) workers fired for unauthorized "wildcat" strikes. Of equal importance, perpetual disruption weakened the incentive for management to continue recognizing the union, and it also undermined public support.

In steel as elsewhere, union leaders began to address this situation by concentrating power at the national level and disciplining local wildcat leaders. This emerging emphasis on orderly procedure was typified in the case of Stanley Orlosky, a pipe fitter and steel mill worker expelled from the union and fired in 1941. "His idea of a grievance settlement was to get everything or strike," as SWOC officials described the matter. "Stanley's leadership was essential to the establishment of the union against bitter resistance, but after it had been fully accepted by management, such leadership was a handicap to the development of cooperative, union-management relations."[5] SWOC's top-down structure was especially suited to imposing this kind of discipline on Orlosky and others, and when SWOC was reorganized as the United Steel Workers (USW) in

1942, the same centralized control characterized the new organization. All of the USW's five hundred national staff were appointed by President Philip Murray (rather than elected by district, as some locals demanded); three-quarters of each dues dollar went to the national office; local strikes could only be authorized by national leaders; and USW conventions were tightly scripted to discourage resolutions or amendments from the floor.

USW leaders defended these measures as necessary to maximize the union's power and unity for national bargaining with corporations that were only recently—and still precariously—committed to collective bargaining. Similar arguments were mustered on behalf of centralized authority in other unions, with varying results. In meatpacking, local unions withheld their dues in 1941 to protest the CIO's imposition of SWOC-like controls, eventually winning (in 1943) a union charter that made the United Packinghouse Workers (UPW) more decentralized and democratic. In the UAW-CIO, opponents of Homer Martin had written a 1939 constitution that scaled back the power of the president, strengthened the rights of local unions, and established bargaining councils of worker delegates to guide negotiations. Democratic debate remained vigorous, even chaotic, at UAW conventions in the 1940s, but the establishment of orderly collective bargaining also changed the union. Many of the earliest UAW locals had organized on a come-one, come-all basis, with citywide bodies like Flint's Local 156 representing workers from five different GM plants, dozens of smaller factories, dime stores, hotels, restaurants, the city bus system—in all, forty thousand workers. This was bound to change over time as individual GM plants sought separate local charters and as non-autoworkers transferred to unions representing their trade or industry. What they thereby gained in specialized attention to their particular needs came, however, at the expense of a direct and wider class affiliation with "one big union." Citywide mobilizations were not precluded by this parceling of workers to separate locals and national unions, but the shift made it more likely that union members would focus their primary attention on bargaining issues unique to their industry and plant, while community-based concerns common to all workers became secondary.

While the union's external ties to the Flint community were fragmented by these structural changes, inside GM's plants bitter confrontations still boiled over work rules and discipline, prompting heated contract negotiations between the company and the union. In the company's view, there was little prospect for stabilizing labor relations so long as union stewards contested the authority of company supervisors. GM therefore took the lead in asserting "basic management prerogatives," as Chairman Alfred Sloan termed them, by refusing to acknowledge any role for union stewards (other than dues collection) in the 1940 contract it negotiated with the UAW. With the union's victories in the toolmakers' strike of the previous year and the NLRB vote of 1940, GM had reconciled itself to recognition of the UAW, but not on the terms conceded at Chrysler and elsewhere permitting line stewards to negotiate one-on-one with foremen. GM would only tolerate a "shop committee" representing workers in a ratio of one to 250, instead of the common steward ratio of one to twenty-five. Although these shop committee members were given some latitude in moving around the plant, in most cases they could only—given their small number—react to problems brought to them, rather than organize for the kind of day-to-day improvements a working steward could address. To further legitimate supervisory authority, GM also insisted that the contract include a "management rights" clause that officially acknowledged "the sole responsibility of the company . . . [to] hire; promote; discharge or discipline for cause; and to maintain discipline and efficiency of employees."

In return for these concessions to management control, the union negotiated a more detailed prescription for the kind of "democratic system of shop government" it hoped to establish in the workplace. Its model was the system of grievance arbitration first negotiated by the Amalgamated Clothing Workers in 1910. As at Hart, Schaffner & Marx, the Chicago clothing manufacturer where Sidney Hillman helped pioneer third-party arbitration, the UAW proposed that the grievance procedure, rather than ending in impasse when company and union could not agree, would end with binding arbitration by a mutually acceptable third party—a permanent "umpire" with the contractual power to impose decisions on the disputants. "The contract is your constitution," the UAW counseled its GM stewards, now relegated to unofficial status, "and the settlement of grievances under it are of an industrial supreme court. A complete record of such decisions is sometimes more important than the contract itself."[6] Against critics who favored direct action and opposed the umpire as a "dictatorship," UAW Vice President Walter Reuther argued that without such a system of workplace jurisprudence "instead of having democracy, you have 'mobocracy.'"[7] Drawing directly from the experience of the ACW, Reuther and others hoped to build a relationship that would duplicate the clothing industry's system of codetermination, where union representatives and management jointly determined production standards, piece rates, selection of foremen, and investment in new technology. The prospects for such an evolutionary development under the guidance of a neutral umpire seemed all the more realistic when management agreed to fill the role with Harry Millis, a former arbitrator in the clothing industry and a man well schooled in the principles of "industrial democracy."

The 1940 UAW-GM agreement would prove to be a model for a wide range of industries, but this did not lead in the hoped-for direction of codetermination or industrial democracy. Unlike clothing, where some employers valued the union's role as an industry-wide regulator of otherwise chaotic and cutthroat competition, the auto industry was dominated by just three modern corporations and led by just one: General Motors. GM executives, rather than pursue an ever-widening agenda of codetermination, were determined to limit the umpire's role to a narrow application of the contract. Nevertheless, GM's acceptance of a neutral umpire marked an important turning point. At a time when fewer than 10 percent of all collective bargaining agreements included third-party arbitration, even a partial surrender of unilateral action by the world's largest manufacturer was noteworthy.

Within less than five years, the system would become nearly universal in unionized industries—if not by negotiation, then by government order.

MIXED BLESSINGS: GOVERNMENT WARTIME REGULATION

With Japan's attack on Pearl Harbor in December 1941, the government's expanding regulatory role in labor-management relations became all the more predominant. Whatever the contending claims of labor and management, they were now subordinated to a single overriding imperative: stability. Above all else, national defense required the uninterrupted production of military hardware, and government regulators had little tolerance for any agenda that disrupted the flow of arms.

The labor movement immediately pledged its cooperation. Unlike in 1917, when the clash of pro- and antiwar sentiments divided the nation, in 1941 there was near unanimous support for a struggle that pitted the United States and its allies against the expansionist and genocidal aims of Nazi Germany and Imperial Japan. Even John L. Lewis, whose prewar opposition to military preparedness led him to oppose President Roosevelt's 1940 reelection, now publicly declared his support. Philip Murray, who became CIO president after FDR's reelection and Lewis's subsequent resignation, went further. "Labor," he announced in the days after Pearl Harbor, "is determined to place itself in the forefront in the battle of achieving maximum production."[8] Joined by the AFL, CIO unions pledged to forswear all strike action for the duration of the war.

With collective bargaining effectively suspended, labor and management agreed to submit unresolved disputes over contract language and grievances to the National War Labor Board (NWLB), the emergency body created by President Roosevelt within weeks of Pearl Harbor. For the next four years, the NWLB would take the lead in structuring labor relations in the United States, establishing precedents that would remain in place long after the war had ended. Modeled after the emergency board of World War I, the NWLB drew its twelve representatives in equal numbers from management, labor, and the public, the latter consisting of lawyers and academics who often cast the deciding votes when labor and management were deadlocked. Such impasse was not uncommon, and both sides therefore had much to oppose, and welcome, in the tie-breaking deliberations of the NWLB's public members.

Business leaders were especially incensed by NWLB measures that forced companies to accept union shop provisions in their collective bargaining agreements. Unlike a closed shop (which required companies to hire only union members) and the far more common open shop (which placed no restrictions on who the company employed), a union shop required workers (however they were hired) to join the union as a condition of continued employment. With the notable exception of Ford in 1941, no major corporation outside of coal mining and clothing had agreed to such a provision before the war, but the NWLB now imposed a variant of the union shop (called "maintenance of membership") on whole sectors of the economy. The logic was simple: if the union could not use the threat of strike action to improve the working conditions of its members, there would be less incentive for workers to join or continue paying dues, making the no-strike pledge suicidal for the union and its elected officers. "Too often members of unions do not maintain their membership because they resent the discipline of responsible leadership," as NWLB public member Frank Graham put it. "A rival but less responsible leadership feels the pull of temptation to obtain and maintain leadership by relaxing discipline, by refusing to cooperate with the company."[9] The

union shop would ensure stability and continued production by rewarding "responsible union leaders" for their commitment to the no-strike
pledge. For much the same reason, the NWLB also forced companies to
accept the kind of third-party arbitration established in the UAW-GM
agreement of 1940. Again, as an alternative to strikes, grievance-arbitration
would ensure uninterrupted production. "Collective bargaining is not con-
fined to the making of an agreement once a year," observed NWLB public member George Taylor, a former arbitrator in the clothing industry and
briefly a UAW-GM umpire. In the "day-to-day process" of interpreting the
contract, grievance-arbitration should "make unnecessary unresolved disputes over the application of the agreement."[10]

   With their membership base protected and their access to grievance-
arbitration enlarged by NWLB decree, unions grew in lockstep with the
rapidly expanding wartime economy. The UAW doubled in size between
1941 and 1944, topping one million members; the Steelworkers nearly
matched the UAW's pace and grew to seven hundred thousand; and the
United Electrical workers tripled their ranks, growing to 432,000 members. Overall, in the three short years from the beginning of 1942 through
the end of 1944, U.S. unions grew from ten to fourteen million members,
representing 21 percent of the labor force—more than triple the percentage of ten years before. Despite a strict ceiling on wage increases
imposed by the NWLB, earnings grew as well, with overtime and rising
piecework rates outpacing inflation. The NWLB also softened the impact
of its wage controls by supporting union demands that companies stan-
dardize their archaic classification and pay systems, closing the wide disparities in pay for workers doing the same jobs. By establishing a simplified ladder of pay progressions (thirty steps in the steel industry,
twenty-five in meatpacking) to replace thousands of old rates, union bargaining backed by the NWLB eliminated the previous inequities and
favoritism that animated so many grievances.

   Workers, of course, paid a price for these gains. More than two hundred thousand former members of the steelworkers union were serving in
the armed forces by 1944, but until the Normandy invasion of that year,
more steelworkers were killed inside the mills than in battle. Nationally,
53,000 workers died in workplace accidents in the first three years of the
war, three hundred thousand more were permanently disabled, and an
unknown number died from exposure to metal and coal dust, toxic chemicals, and fumes. The six- and seven-day workweek was commonplace,
inflation was especially high in mill towns and working-class communi-

ties, many necessities were rationed, and overcrowding was the common curse of neighborhoods bulging with war workers. Even so, for many people, especially women, African-Americans, and an entire generation of depression-era workers, the wartime boom was the first time in their lives when high-wage jobs were plentiful and prosperity beckoned. Kate Archibald would later recall that for most of her fellow shipyard workers, "the war was an experience of opportunity rather than limitations. Their wartime income was larger than ever before, and they ate more abundantly and lived more agreeably."[11]

Business leaders had even more reason to regard the war as a time of opportunity. Although they chafed at government-imposed mandates for union growth, they were otherwise happy to be restored to prominence in Washington, D.C., as captains of industry, serving on wartime production agencies that mobilized the nation's economy for war. The depression-era stigma attached to Big Business was a receding memory, and with cost-plus military contracts and government-imposed wage ceilings, corporate pretax profits were rebounding to record levels, tripling to $27 billion between 1940 and 1943—in the same years, the average annual earnings of all employees grew only half as fast. The NWLB's focus on stability could also work to the company's advantage, with the board taking steps to strengthen management control of the shop floor. NWLB policy recognized management's right to promulgate and change work rules governing transfers, production standards, work pace, schedules, and other matters without the union's prior consent and even exempted some of these job-control issues from arbitration. As stated in a 1944 ruling, the NWLB endorsed the general principle that "management retains the right to discipline employees for cause and as necessary for the efficient conduct of operations."[12] To ensure that unions held their members to these canons of management control, the NWLB further ruled that strike action and other disruptive tactics would mean the withdrawal of union shop provisions and possible suspension of union recognition.

For these reasons, many unions came to see the NWLB in particular, and government regulation in general, as a mixed blessing. Without the right to strike or, in some cases, even arbitrate issues, and with the NWLB unable to review in a timely way the ten to fifteen thousand disputes that came before it *each month,* unions were often left to deal with employers who claimed patriotic necessity for every unilateral action, justified or not. Worse, unions had to choose between acting as disciplinarians of their own members, at the risk of alienating their support, or acquiescing to (if not leading) unauthorized strikes, at the risk of losing the NWLB's union shop protections. Price controls on business were widely regarded as inadequate and poorly enforced, while wage ceilings were backed by the full force of the government. Efforts to lobby on behalf of more equitable wage and price controls failed, prompting a smoldering resentment among labor representatives who noted their second-class status as "advisors" to government bodies led by corporate executives.

"Why should the agencies of government in Washington today be virtually infested with wealthy men," CIO president Philip Murray complained to steelworker delegates in 1942. "What are we running? A war production organization to win the war, or a war production organization to destroy labor?"[13] Mineworker leader John L. Lewis likewise condemned the government's "paradoxical policy that runs to the premise of rewarding and fattening industry and starving labor."[14] However, unlike Murray and most other union leaders, who never wavered in supporting FDR's overall war aims and policies, Lewis had already broken with the president in the 1940 elections, supporting the Republican peace-first candidate, Wendell Wilkie. In 1943, Lewis repudiated his union's no-strike pledge, refused to appear before the NWLB and, when contract negotiations with the mine operators ended in impasse over wage increases, led five hundred thousand coal miners on strike. Over the course of the year, UMW members struck against government wage ceilings four separate times, prompting the government to temporarily nationalize the mines and forcibly return the men to work. In the end, however, the government accepted a face-saving agreement to pay the miners for time traveled from surface to coal face—therefore, not an "official" increase in wage *rates*—to end the turmoil.

These brief but massive mine strikes in defiance of the government proved to be a turning point. Although public opinion polls indicated a clear majority recognized the justice of the miners' demands, an equally evident majority condemned both Lewis and the strikes as unpatriotic. Buoyed by this public sentiment, congressional conservatives quickly passed the War Labor Disputes Act, giving the president the power to seize strike-threatened companies and prosecute anyone who struck such government-held property. These features of the Smith-Connally Act, as it was also called, had little direct impact, since virtually all unions but the UMW still honored the no-strike pledge. Of more lasting import was the act's prohibition against using union dues to support candidates in federal elections.

There was another legacy of these coal strikes, however, that confounded efforts to discipline worker protest. Although most workers supported the no-strike pledge in principle and voted, in the UAW, to keep it in practice, many also found the coal miners' defiance of inequitable regulations infectious, if not admirable. The result was a dramatic rise in the number of strikes already sweeping American industry. The record number of nearly five thousand walkouts that occurred in 1944 was one-third higher than the year before and represented more strikes—and strikers—than even 1937. Most were brief, many were limited to a single department, and the majority had little to do with wages. The retiming of jobs and the accelerating work pace prompted many walkouts, but the most frequent occasion for downing tools was to protest the firing of union militants who refused to accept the company's unilaterally imposed production standards. Occasionally, local union officers openly endorsed the walkouts, though more often they signaled passive support by delaying or giving only halfhearted expression to their obligatory back-to-work order. On other occasions, however, workers struck in open defiance of their union, the company, and the government, and the leaders of these "wildcat" strikes were often severely punished—removed from local office by their union, fired by the company, and sometimes drafted by the army. Discipline was equally harsh for wildcat strikers protesting the integration of previously whites-only workplaces, though more of these "hate strikes" had occurred in the early years of the war, when labor shortages and public pressure forced companies to desegregate production jobs. Most union leaders supported strict penalties and even military intervention to end walkouts by racially prejudiced workers, and the hate strikes had abated dramatically by 1944.

As the war drew to a close in 1945, these unsettled conditions were cause for apprehension by both business and labor leadership. Businessmen saw wartime strikes as symptomatic of conditions that threatened their future control of peacetime enterprise and the workplace. The full employment of the war years and the emphasis on continuous production at all costs had eroded shop floor discipline; workers knew they were obligated to work long hours under arduous conditions, but they also knew that jobs were plentiful and the penalties, therefore, diminished for absenteeism, dilatory work, even insubordination. Equally troubling to business leaders was the fact that foremen, caught in the cross fire between worker insurgency and management resistance, were turning to unionization as a matter of self-protection under the newly organized Foreman's Association of America—a prospect that led C. C. Carlton, president of the Automotive Manufacturers Association, to speculate that American industry might degenerate "from mass production into just sheer mob production, with no boss and no leadership there to run it."[15] The entire experience of wartime mobilization was a dangerous precedent in the eyes of many business leaders, since the full employment and unprecedented prosperity of the war years had created a popular constituency for massive government intervention in the economy. Above all else, in the worst-case speculations of American businessmen there loomed the newly empowered labor movement, protected by government policy and ever-more vocal in calling for postwar expansion of social security, public healthcare, and public planning for full employment.

The labor movement's apprehensions were the mirror opposite of management's. Where the latter conjured an expanding movement emboldened by government protection, the former saw itself imperiled by the government's evident shift from the New Deal welfare state to the wartime garrison state. Union leaders worried that government withdrawal from the peacetime economy might lead to the same strikebreaking and union decline that had followed World War I. With the winding down of war production, overtime pay and piece rate premiums were already disappearing and straight-time wages no longer kept pace with inflation. Layoffs had already begun, and with them fears that economic depression would return once the artificial stimulus of war production was removed.

POSTWAR CONFRONTATION

Within weeks of Japan's surrender in August 1945, labor and management squared off in their single most important confrontation of the twentieth century. Over the next two years, first in strike action and then in political action, the two sides would contest the future course of labor, social, and economic relations in the United States. "The whole style of the post-war economy is being set now," as one UAW broadside declared in 1945. Few doubted the truth of this prophesy.

At stake were two differing conceptions of labor's role in a capitalist economy. For unionists, that role began with modest claims to a voice in the workplace. "All we desire," said Van Bittner of the Steelworkers, "is to bargain collectively for wages, hours, and working conditions. The responsibility for controlling industry as such rests with industry."[16] Most industrial union leaders (if not all craft unionists) had also long reconciled themselves to the principles of "scientific management" and time study in regulating work practices, though many agreed with CIO president Philip Murray's quip that many such practices "were less scientific than extortionate," seeking "to get more out of labor without a proportionate return."[17] To fully realize the potential productivity of American industry, argued Murray, employers should accept "organized labor [as] an active participant in determining production procedures and administrative policies designed to increase output."[18] Even at this level, Murray cautioned, "labor-management cooperation under a single employer is too limited a field," because the "interdependence of all industry"[19] required labor participation in determining industry-wide practices, as exemplified by the Amalgamated Clothing Workers. Murray and other labor liberals saw a reformed government as the final guarantor of industrial democracy, sustaining full employment in peacetime with social welfare programs, public investment, and progressive tax policies that would redistribute income and boost consumer demand.

Business leaders who would have rejected this entire labor agenda in years past now demonstrated a measured pragmatism in 1945–1947, born of necessity. The labor movement was far stronger at wars' end than had been the case in 1919–1920, and public opinion less supportive of outright union busting. Rather than oppose all unions and all social reform, business could only "capture the leadership of public opinion," as Walter Weisenburger put it in his address to the Congress of American Industry, "if it makes, and dramatizes, a conscientious and determined effort to solve the nation's legitimate economic problems."[20] This meant, for example, that many business leaders, instead of calling for total repeal of the National Labor Relations Act, called instead for amendments that would regulate union practices and restrict future growth. Further, the wartime experience under the no-strike pledge had persuaded managers like James Towsen of West Virginia Pulp and Paper Co. that "the international and local [union] officials are often less radical in their demands than the rank and file who roll the snowballs for them to throw."[21] Companies like Ford, where young Henry II took control during the war and finally purged Harry Bennett and his thugs, were therefore prepared to accept the modest formulation of Van Bittner—"to bargain collectively for wages, hours, and working conditions"[22]—while rejecting Philip Murray's more expansive industrial democracy.

No company was more diligent in drawing this distinction than General Motors. No company, on the other hand, faced a greater challenge. Far more so than Murray, UAW vice president Walter Reuther was willing to put the claims of industrial democracy on the bargaining agenda in 1945, demanding not only that GM pay substantial wage increases, but also that the company pay for these from its record profits rather than marking up the price of its automobiles. Reuther, who also called on management "to open their books" to prove they could not afford a 30 percent wage increase without price increases, staked his claim to the high ground. "Labor is not fighting for a larger slice of the national pie," he wrote in the *New Republic*. "Labor is fighting for a larger pie," protecting the public against inflationary price increases while redistributing profits to working people. Rather than being "a narrow economic pressure group," the UAW, said Reuther, was fighting "to make progress with the community and not at the expense of the community."[23] GM chairman Alfred Sloan thought otherwise. "General Motors . . . will not bargain for wages with an operating statement in one hand,"[24] he wrote to a colleague. Publicly, GM condemned Reuther's demands as a usurpation of management's right to manage the business. "America is at the crossroads!" one company advertisement proclaimed. "It must preserve the freedom of each unit of American business to determine its own destiny."[25]

In November 1945, after voting by a 6–1 margin in favor of striking, 175,000 UAW members downed tools and began nationwide picketing of GM's eighty factories and warehouses. Their walkout marked the beginning of the biggest strike wave in American history, topping the previous record of 1919. By the end of January 1946, industry-wide strikes by steelworkers, packinghouse workers, and electrical equipment workers had raised the number of strikers nationwide to 1.6 million; throughout 1946, coal miners, railroad workers, teachers, utility workers, municipal workers, and many others also walked off the job, demanding hefty wage increases to compensate for wartime sacrifices and inflation. All told, 4.6 million workers went on strike that year, some of them in citywide general strikes that shut down much of Oakland (California), Rochester (New York), Stamford (Connecticut), and Lancaster (Pennsylvania).

This massive confrontation marked several turning points in American history. First, no major corporation attempted to bring strikebreakers into their plants, and—consequently—there was little of the bloodshed that characterized previous labor upheavals between 1877 and 1937.

Corporations were less inclined to risk public condemnation for strike-breaking, and there was less opportunity in any case; strikers' ranks remained solid throughout, with none of the racial or ethnic fragmentation that previously allowed employers to pit worker against worker. Second, strike issues were not dominated by the overriding question of whether unions should exist at all—with that matter settled between 1933 and 1945, the focus in 1946 turned to the actual bargaining relationship between capital and labor. Finally, the outcome of these strikes established a pattern that prevailed for decades thereafter: Management could be forced to pay higher wages, but not so easily compelled to share governance of the firm with union negotiators or government regulators. This was especially evident at the end of the 113-day GM strike. Like U.S. Steel, General Electric, Chrysler, and other major corporations, GM agreed to substantial wage increases of nearly 17 percent; on the other hand, it categorically rejected government mediation, refused to open its books, and, in response to Reuther's unique demand for codetermination of the firm, compelled the UAW to abandon any claim to joint negotiation of corporate pricing and profits.

Inevitably, the very size and breadth of the strike wave politicized this first round of peacetime bargaining, making the federal government a crucial player in deciding its outcome. In most cases, the government weighed in on management's side, using the War Labor Disputes Act to throttle union militancy. President Harry Truman, only recently installed in office following FDR's death in 1945, temporarily nationalized packinghouses, railroads, and coal mines in an effort to head off or forcibly end the walkouts. When striking railroad workers defied the government, Truman threatened to draft them and call in the army; when the coal miners refused the president's back-to-work order, the government secured a court injunction and $3.5 million in fines against the union, ending the strike. In these same months, the labor movement also suffered major legislative defeats in Congress as Republicans and conservative Democrats dismantled federal price controls, cut corporate taxes, and, with countless amendments, made the 1946 Employment Act an empty promise of full employment.

These setbacks gave a special urgency to the efforts of the CIO's Political Action Committee (PAC), formed in 1943 after passage of the War Labor Disputes Act. Under the leadership of Sidney Hillman, PAC had mobilized stewards and local officers to register union voters, raise voluntary contributions for pro-labor candidates, and get out the vote in

1944 to reelect FDR. "Wages, hours, and working conditions have become increasingly dependent upon policies adopted by Congress and the national administration," Hillman observed at PAC's founding. "Labor must bring its full influence to bear in shaping these decisions."[26] Some left-wingers hoped that PAC could serve as the nucleus for an eventual Labor Party, modeled on the British example. In practice, however, Hillman made PAC an auxiliary to the liberal wing of the Democratic Party, and in 1946 even this limited role was beyond the CIO's reach after Hillman died and PAC's efforts faltered. With daily headlines dominated by massive strikes and federal seizure of whole industries, conservatives mobilized public fears of a "CIO takeover" and won a resounding victory in the November congressional elections. For the first time since 1932, the Republican Party would control both the House and Senate, foreclosing any hope of reviving the New Deal.

Ten years before, the sweeping victories of New Deal liberals and FDR in the 1936 elections had heralded the sit-down strikes and union triumphs of 1937. The 1946 ascendancy of the Republican Party now heralded a different kind of turning point. In the new Congress, work immediately began on a major overhaul of the National Labor Relations Act, following much of the reform agenda specified by the National Association of Manufacturers and other business lobbyists. Passed by overwhelming majorities in May 1947—including a majority of Democrats in both the House and Senate—the Labor-Management Relations Act (LMRA), or Taft-Hartley Act as it was popularly known, recast the legal context for labor relations in the United States. When Congress overrode President Truman's veto the following month, Taft-Hartley officially amended the Wagner Act with a multitude of provisions designed to constrain unions:

- Whereas the Wagner Act had only specified management unfair labor practices, Taft-Hartley added union ULPs for which management or individual workers could seek redress through the NLRB. Mass picketing was one such ULP, deemed to be coercive in its impact on workers choosing not to support the union. Other union ULPs included secondary boycotts of stores carrying nonunion or struck goods, and refusal to handle or transport such "hot cargo" goods—a tactic previously used by union warehousemen to force nonunion trucking companies to recognize the Teamsters.

- Foremen were denied the protections of federal labor law, meaning their unions were now vulnerable to the kinds of management retaliation otherwise prohibited under the Wagner Act. Immediately following passage of Taft-Hartley, Ford fired striking members of the Foreman's Association of America at its Dearborn, Michigan, plant and canceled recognition of the FAA.

- Union dues could not be used to support candidates for federal office, resurrecting provisions of the now lapsed War Labor Disputes Act. Corporations were likewise barred from backing candidates, limiting support to individual and voluntary contributions.

- Under Section 14(b) of the act, states were given the option of passing a so-called right-to-work law prohibiting mandatory membership under union shop provisions. Within six years, seventeen states in the South and West had passed such laws. Because unions were legally obligated to represent the entire workforce, 14(b) permitted individual workers to opt out of the union while still enjoying the benefits of collective bargaining—making them "free riders" in the eyes of union advocates. Another part of the act required that in states still permitting union shop contracts, the NLRB would conduct a special vote to determine if workers favored such a provision requiring union membership as a condition of employment. This portion of Taft-Hartley was dropped in 1951, however, when the consistently heavy majorities in favor of mandatory membership (supported in 97 percent of the forty-six thousand elections conducted) proved embarrassing to those who had predicted the opposite outcome.

- In cases where a strike was deemed to be against the national interest, the president could now seek a court injunction requiring an eighty-day "cooling-off" period, government mediation, and an NLRB vote on the employer's last offer before a walkout could legally occur. Business leaders preferred this approach to the previous method of seizing private property under the War Labor Disputes Act, since these temporary "nationalizations" could, they feared, become customary and perhaps permanent.

- The Taft-Hartley Act designated grievance arbitration as a primary mechanism of dispute resolution in labor-management conflicts. "Final adjustment by a method agreed upon by the parties," read Section 302(d), "is hereby declared to be the desirable method for settlement of grievance disputes." The Taft-Hartley Act thereby made the War Labor Board's emphasis on stability a matter of peacetime law rather than wartime emergency. Strikes were still legally protected, but the courts would hereafter favor arbitration and stability, no matter how prolonged the process, over strike action and economic disruption.

- Finally, unions could be sued (and could also bring suit) for breach of contract, including unauthorized strikes during the agreement.

CIO and AFL leaders alike condemned Taft-Hartley as a "Slave-Labor Act," some linking it to a rightward drift in U.S. politics that portended the potential for fascism and complete annihilation of the labor movement. Scattered strikes, mass rallies, and caravans of protesting workers demonstrated against the law's imminent passage, but most union leaders, fearful that disruptive tactics would only accelerate the drift to the right, focused instead on electing liberal congressmen committed to Taft-Hartley's repeal. The CIO, said Philip Murray, "has disapproved in most cases of mass demonstrations, caravans, and the like,"[27] a statement that—contrasted with CIO rhetoric and tactics in 1937—marked how far the labor movement had traveled in substituting respectable conduct for raucous confrontation.

Predictions of the labor movement's imminent collapse and the arrival of fascism proved to be exaggerated in any case. With one crucial exception, Taft-Hartley's emphasis on preserving a stable status quo had less impact on collective bargaining where it already existed than it did on slowing union organization in regions and industries where it was weak. The exception was a provision in the Act that had little to do with collective bargaining and much to do with the emerging Cold War. By requiring every union officer to sign an affidavit swearing that "he is not a member of the Communist Party nor affiliated with such party," and by excluding any union whose officers failed to do so from the protections of the law, Taft-Hartley helped set in motion events that would split the labor movement and dramatically change the prospects for union growth.

COLD WAR IN THE LABOR MOVEMENT

In the immediate aftermath of Taft-Hartley's passage, CIO president Murray refused to sign the noncommunist affidavit. Murray was a devout Catholic and lifelong Democrat, but like many others in the labor movement, he resented the law's implication that union leaders were *automatically* tainted as subversive and, therefore, compelled to pledge their loyalty or lose the protection of U.S. law. No "nonfascist" affidavit, for example, was demanded of businessmen, despite the fact that a vocal minority—William Randolph Hearst and the senior Henry Ford among them—had openly sympathized with Hitler's Germany in the 1930s. Since 1935, Murray, John L. Lewis, and other moderate labor leaders had submerged their personal antipathy to communism and pursued a united front with labor radicals. In 1947, Murray still supported this "Popular Front" and would refuse to sign the noncommunist affidavit so long as two conditions prevailed: first, that the Communist minority continued to subordinate their political agenda to labor's united front, and second, that the political climate still favored such a coalition.

Both conditions, however, were already changing as the nation shifted from its wartime alliance with the Soviet Union, to postwar confrontation. As a renewed Red scare came to dominate national politics, labor unity dissolved between 1947 and 1950, leading eventually to near universal compliance with the Taft-Hartley oath and the CIO's expulsion of eleven left-wing unions.

The hysteria surrounding this postwar Red scare had much in common with the Red scare of 1919–1920, particularly the manner in which conservatives and antiunion employers exploited fears of a revolutionary minority as a pretext for suppressing a larger left-liberal labor movement. Yet, the Red scare that began to gain momentum after 1945 was also different. In contrast to the beleaguered and impoverished regime that barely survived World War I, the Soviet Union was now a powerful totalitarian state, its armies spread across Asia and east Europe. The revolutionary aftershocks of World War II were also far more extensive, bringing Europe's colonial regimes to an end and creating the prospect (realized in 1949) of Communist victory in China. Capitalism was momentarily on the defensive, and Soviet power was growing, symbolized by the U.S.S.R.'s success in developing atomic weapons to match the U.S. arsenal. In this context, the revelation that confessed spies had passed scientific information to the Soviets created a sensation in the press, prompting exaggerated fears of a larger conspiracy to undermine the United States. An escalating search for "Red agents" soon spread across the country as Democrats and Republicans competed for headlines, the latter through the House Un-American Activities Committee (HUAC), revived in 1945, and the former through President Truman's "Loyalty Oath" program of 1947, directed at millions of workers in defense-related industries and the federal government.

The grounds for political suspicion grew ever broader as Truman, HUAC, and later Senator Joseph McCarthy stoked the flames of this modern-day witch hunt, with McCarthy finally accusing even the U.S. Army and President Dwight Eisenhower of "coddling Communists." Thousands of defense workers, public employees, union leaders, teachers, and filmmakers were fired, suspended, or blacklisted because they had joined the Communist Party, or had participated in left-wing protests during the Great Depression, or had signed a petition opposing the Taft-Hartley Act—all legal activities that now implicated millions of Americans as possible "security risks." In the federal civil service alone, more than fifteen thousand employees resigned or were fired between 1947 and 1956, most of them because they or someone in their family held politically tabooed beliefs. HUAC meanwhile compelled witnesses to take the stand and divulge the names of suspected communists they had known or worked with; witnesses who refused to cooperate risked being cited for contempt of Congress and sent to prison. State and local governments gave further impetus to the Red Hunt, in some cases casting a wider net than even the federal government—Detroit's police Red Squad, for one, was collecting political files on Detroit citizens that eventually included more than one hundred thousand "suspected" subversives.

Communists in the labor movement would have had a tough time surviving this anti-Red crusade even if their party had been able to fall back on a mass base of support. By 1947, however, this was no longer even conceivable. The CP had grown during World War II to a peak of sixty-five thousand members, many of them intellectuals and professionals who admired the Soviet Union for its struggle against Nazi Germany, but who little understood or concerned themselves with the Soviet regime's one-party dictatorship. Unlike its European counterparts, the U.S. CP had only a small following in the industrial working class and no heroic legacy of underground resistance to fascism. Individual Communists had played important roles in organizing unions and, after 1935, mobilizing support for the New Deal, but most had downplayed or even concealed their CP membership, adding credence to the charge that "they must have something to hide." When communists won election to top union office, as they did in roughly a quarter of the CIO's national unions, it was because members appreciated their hard work, or courage, or leadership—not, in most cases, their Communist ideology. The latter was probably a liability, particularly as the CP parroted Soviet policy changes and forced party members to zigzag erratically across the political landscape. When the Soviet Union had called for a military alliance in the 1930s against the Nazis, U.S. Communists had enthusiastically urged the same; when Soviet leader Joseph Stalin suddenly signed a treaty with Nazi Germany in 1939, U.S. Communists had just as suddenly (though not so enthusiastically) reversed field and denounced U.S. military preparations; when Hitler suddenly launched a surprise attack on the Soviets in 1941, U.S. Communists had reversed direction yet again and called for U.S. workers to support military preparedness. After the United States entered World War II as an ally of the Soviets, U.S. Communists had even abandoned their previous militancy and became zealous supporters of any measure that maximized war production, with little apparent regard for the unequal sacrifices demanded of U.S. workers. "We can't dilly-dally around," said CP ally and leader of the west coast longshoremen, Harry Bridges, speaking to the CIO executive board in 1942; in his union, Bridges boasted, business agents (as local union representatives were called) "are business agents second, they are speedup men first."[28]

When World War II ended and the Soviet Union declared its opposition to the U.S. "Marshall Plan" for rebuilding and rearming western Europe, U.S. Communists fell in line once again with Soviet policy and broke with the CIO majority. The split between liberal-moderate labor on the one hand and the left-CP minority widened all the further in 1948, when U.S. Communists refused to endorse Democratic President Harry Truman for reelection and instead helped form an independent "Progressive Party" led by former Vice President Henry Wallace. Labor's united front was irrevocably breached, since most CIO and AFL unions were convinced that only Truman—whose antistrike measures in 1945–1946 were forgiven after his unsuccessful veto of the Taft-Hartley Act—could beat Republican candidate Thomas Dewey. Most unions mobilized their members in an all-out effort for the president, and when Truman won a surprising come-from-behind victory, he publicly declared that "Labor did it." CIO leader Murray and other labor liberals were triumphant. The CP and its remaining labor allies, on the other hand, were exposed and demoralized by Wallace's paltry showing—barely one million votes, representing less than 3 percent of the total.

Labor unity, such as it was before 1947, collapsed under the combined pressures of Cold War, Red scare, and revived competition between rival unions. Under Taft-Hartley, NLRB elections between competing unions would exclude from the ballot any organization whose leaders had refused to sign the noncommunist affidavits. Philip Murray's policy of noncompliance was therefore a risky business for CIO unions, since NLRB election procedures often decided the outcome when AFL rivals tried to "raid" members. Consequently, most CIO unions had signed the Taft-Hartley affidavit by the fall of 1947, and many, in turn, had launched their own raids on the remaining CIO unions that still refused to comply. The largest of these, the United Electrical Workers (UE), counted five hundred raids by CIO and AFL rivals between 1947 and 1949. In the latter year, after the union withheld its dues from the CIO to protest the raiding, the CIO expelled the UE (as well as a second left-wing union, the Farm Equipment Workers), and chartered the International Union of Electrical Workers (IUE) as a replacement. In 1950, the CIO expelled nine more left-wing unions, including Harry Bridges's west coast longshoremen, the Fur and Leather Workers, the Food and Tobacco Workers, and the Mine, Mill, and Smelters union. These unions had a better-than-average record of representing their members' interests, but in the midst of a Cold War with Russia and a shooting war (in 1950) with North Korea, political conformity with government policy was the benchmark. The dissident unions had opposed the Marshall Plan, rejected President Truman, and refused the noncommunist oath, and it was on these political grounds that CIO leaders denounced them as subversives working "toward the achievement of the program or purposes of the Communist Party."[29]

The amputation of the CIO's left wing was a key turning point in the postwar history of the labor movement. Thereafter, compliance with the demands of political conformity would exact a heavy toll, measured in ever-tightening strictures on internal dissent and a diminishing capacity—or willingness—to mobilize workers for social reform. This was not because the expelled unions had always been models of internal democracy or crusading zeal. Many did have exemplary records for organizing, political mobilization, and support for civil rights, but left-wing union leaders could be just as heavy-handed as their liberal and conservative rivals, and sometimes (particularly during World War II) they could be decidedly unmilitant. More telling was the government's decisive intervention in the labor movement's internal affairs, reinforcing a narrow orthodoxy and superficial patriotism that defined all nonconformity as un-American. Factional rivals inside any union could now attack their left-of-center opponents as communist "fellow travelers" and thereby win headlines, credibility, and government backers. Walter Reuther, who won election as UAW president in 1946 on a platform opposing the CP's role in the auto union, condemned Michigan's governor for launching "a Red Hunt whose ultimate victims are intended to be *not* Communists, but all effective labor leaders and labor unions."[30] Yet even Reuther's brand of liberal anticommunism included the firing of seventy-five staff members after he won control of the UAW executive board in 1947, followed by the forced removal of elected local leaders who refused to sign noncommunist affidavits.

This relatively mild purge paled in comparison to the inquisition-like atmosphere that hounded UE for the decade following its expulsion from the CIO. Marked as fair game for any CIO or AFL union that wished to poach its membership, even UE's left-wing leaders felt compelled to sign noncommunist affidavits or risk total dismemberment. Their belated compliance improved the union's chances of survival but still exposed it to the kind of campaign that overwhelmed Westinghouse Local 601 in East Pittsburgh, one of the union's oldest strongholds. Because the company had asked the NLRB to clarify which union represented the workforce—the CIO's IUE or the now independent UE—an election was scheduled for April 1950 with both unions on the ballot. UE was denied access to local radio stations and the print media and had little vocal support outside the plant. The IUE labored under no such disabilities. FBI agents and local judges spoke at IUE rallies; the state commander of the Veterans of Foreign Wars denounced the UE; HUAC held special hearings on UE Local 601 that hinted darkly of possible Communist sabotage at the plant; Pittsburgh's daily press reported these unfounded allegations in banner headlines; Catholic priests denounced UE from the pulpit, linking the union with Soviet oppression of east European Catholics; and finally, the day of the balloting, IUE sound trucks circled the plants warning that a UE victory would lead to cancellation of the plant's defense contracts. Given this floodtide of anti-UE propaganda, the IUE's victory was surprisingly narrow; in voting that brought 90 percent of the workforce to the polls, the IUE garnered 5,763 votes to the UE's 5,663—a margin of just one hundred votes.

Elsewhere, UE won some of the hundreds of challenges brought against its locals, and lost many more. Its strong showing in many of these contests was a measure of how deeply some workers valued a union that, however controversial the positions taken by some of its leaders, never-theless delivered substantial improvement and "fought the good fight" against hostile employers. IUE, by comparison, would prove to be far more accepting of concessionary agreements, signing contracts that weakened seniority rights and granted management wider discretion in timing jobs. Over time, some would come to rue their allegiance to IUE and its erratic leader, James Carey—the same man who had first led UE before being voted out of office in 1941. In 1963, IUE vice president James Click resigned, charging that Carey had made the IUE a "hopeless mess of dishonesties, confusion, and ineffectiveness in which all sem-blance of democracy . . . had disappeared."[31] Two years later, Carey was removed from office after the U.S. Labor Department found evidence that the IUE president had resorted to massive vote stealing to win reelection.

Unlike most of the other expelled CIO unions, UE would survive the Red scare, but only as a shadow of its former self. By 1962, mem-bership had fallen from its 1946 total of 365,000 to a committed rear-guard of just fifty-five thousand. Some of the difference was accounted for by the membership raids of the IUE, UAW, USW, and AFL crafts, but overall union membership in the electrical workers' jurisdiction was 30 percent lower by 1955 and corporations were substantially stronger. Where once there had been a single, predominant, industry-wide union presenting a united front to employers, there were fourteen separate unions in the 1960s with no coordinated bargaining agenda. Companies like GE could compel the weakest union to accept its conditions and then force the same terms on each remaining union as a take-it-or-leave alternative. Here, the Red scare meant fragmentation and defeat for labor until the late 1960s, when Carey's opponent and successor, Paul Jen-nings, steered IUE toward a bargaining alliance and "no raiding" pact with UE.

For the Communist Party, these years also marked the end of its con-troversial role in the labor movement. Many CP members abandoned the party in fear, particularly after government prosecution sent twenty-eight leaders to prison after 1951 for their advocacy (however rhetorical) of violent revolution. Thousands more deserted the CP in shock after the Soviet invasion of Hungary in 1956 and Premier Khrushchev's revelations of Stalinist tyranny. Evidence of the Soviet government's brutal suppres-sion of political opponents, often ignored in the 1930s, was now irrefutable. By 1957, forty years after the Russian revolution and the his-toric split in the U.S. left between socialists and communists, little more than five thousand members remained in the Communist Party, and only a handful of these remained in the labor movement. Even the CP's socialist rivals dwindled to insignificance, leaving the Socialist Party—once the pride of Eugene Debs and nearly 120,000 members in 1912—counting just one thousand aging followers by the end of the 1950s.

SOLIDARITY DIVIDED

"If someone insists there is discrimination against Negroes in this country," warned Albert Canwell, chairman of Washington State's Fact Finding Committee on Un-American Activities in 1947, "there is every reason to believe that person is a Communist."[32]

With any challenge to the status quo now branded as un-American, unions were targeted not only for their advocacy of economic justice but also for their espousal of racial equality. Because the Communist Party promoted both these causes, the paranoid logic of the Red scare tarred millions of noncommunist left-wingers and liberals with the same broad brush. "Of course the fact that a person believes in racial equality doesn't *prove* that he's a Communist," as the chairman of one federal loyalty board put it, "but it certainly makes you look twice, doesn't it."[33]

Conservatives "looked twice" at the labor movement and claimed to see Red, for it was unions, more so than any other institution in U.S. life, that championed interracial solidarity in the 1930s and 1940s. At a time when the prevailing racism of the white majority favored an apartheid-like separation of races throughout society, it was only in the CIO and some AFL unions that blacks and whites claimed equal status and commingled on a routine basis. Not every union matched the movement's high ideals in their daily practice, but the mere fact that black workers were organized under these principles gave black union members—particularly in the CIO—an unprecedented power and assertiveness. Desegregation of military production during World War II was a case in point. When President Roosevelt first refused to issue an executive order desegregating war plants, it was A. Philip Randolph and the Brotherhood of Sleeping Car Porters (AFL) that threatened to bring twenty-five thousand black protesters to Washington, D.C., forcing the president's hand; when auto companies then balked at upgrading blacks to defense jobs, it was black foundry workers and custodians at Chrysler, Dodge, Ford, and Packard who went on strike in protest;

when white workers in these plants and elsewhere responded to the arrival of black workers with hate strikes, it was union leaders from the UAW and other CIO affiliates that denounced the walkouts and quickly brought them to an end.

Black membership in CIO unions grew to three hundred thousand by the end of World War II, with many locals in the UAW, Packinghouse Workers, and other unions electing black leaders to their bargaining committees and executive boards. Some of these locals also pushed outward into surrounding neighborhoods, desegregating the whites-only bars and restaurants near the factories. "We cannot effectively unite our members inside the plant," declared the Fair Employment Practices Committee of UAW Local 212 in Detroit, "and permit bigoted, narrow-minded, cockroach businessmen to flagrantly practice discrimination right outside the plant."[34] Integrated committees from Local 212 visited restaurants near the factory, requesting, then demanding service for black members. Thousands of black workers from Local 212, Ford Local 600, and other CIO unions swelled the ranks of Detroit's NAACP, making it the largest chapter in the nation and infusing it with direct action tactics—picket lines and mass rallies—that contrasted sharply with the organization's traditional emphasis on court challenges. "The CIO," observed Horace White, an NAACP board member and one of Detroit's first black ministers to support the UAW, "has usurped moral leadership in the [Negro] community."[35] Similar conclusions were drawn in those few regions of the South where CIO unions had gained a foothold under the wartime protection of the federal government. "One cannot visit Winston-Salem [North Carolina]," observed a reporter for the *Pittsburgh Courier* in 1944, speaking of left-wing unions like the Food, Tobacco, and Agricultural workers (FTA), "without sensing a revolution in thought and action. If there is a 'New' Negro, he is to be found in the ranks of the labor movement."[36]

It was these growing ties between labor and civil rights activists that alarmed many conservatives, particularly in southern states where white supremacy and antiunion violence were twin fixtures of public policy. The fact that the FTA, like many other unions actively promoting black-white solidarity, had left-wing leaders with ties to the Communist Party further inflamed southern segregationists. It was in the South, therefore, that the postwar mobilization against labor took an especially savage turn in 1946, when the CIO launched "Operation Dixie" to organize the region. With 250 organizers committed to the campaign, CIO leaders hoped to transform the South's social and political landscape, ending the low-wage conditions that drew industry southward, and toppling conservative Democrats with the votes of union workers.

These high hopes, however, died quickly. With the end of wartime restraints on employer antiunionism, southern mill owners felt free to oppose Operation Dixie with mass firings, evictions from company housing, denial of credit, open surveillance, and frequent beatings. Union organizers who protested these illegal tactics to the NLRB had to endure a seemingly endless round of appeals until, in the words of one, "by the time we won, we had no members."[37] Organizers arrested for "trespassing" were sentenced to chain gangs, and others were driven out of town at gunpoint. Even when a particularly determined group of workers overcame these obstacles and won an NLRB election, they were often greeted by a lockout or permanent plant closing.

None of these employer tactics, however, were nearly so debilitating as the outright refusal of many white workers to join the union. In the textile industry, which the CIO targeted because the workforce was white and the issue of race less salient, the refusal to join was born of fearful memories of mass firings after the 1934 strike. "Their brains were soaked in the Depression mentality of the 1930s," recalled union sympathizer Palmer Weber. "When they saw a union organizer, the union organizer was a threat to their jobs." In other industries where there was a significant number of black workers, whites refused to join because the CIO was seen as a threat to white supremacy. Many would refuse to even participate in interracial meetings. "I've had it all fall apart right there," organizer Woody Biggs said of his experience trying to bring black and white union supporters together in Mississippi. "Whites just wouldn't do it." When a few dared to participate, it was virtually impossible to find a meeting place that would allow such open defiance of southern apartheid. "We met in the woods, under railroad bridges, and just anywhere," recalled organizer B. T. Judd. "You could not do anything about race relations, because that's the way politicians got elected."[38] Even in the few enclaves of CIO organization in the South, race relations were often sharply polarized. In one steelworker local in Alabama where the races were evenly divided, most blacks joined the NAACP and most whites joined the Ku Klux Klan. In FTA's Local 22 in Winston-Salem, blacks supported the union and consistently reelected black leadership, but only a handful of the five thousand white workers at R. J. Reynolds ever joined the local. The AFL, meanwhile, generally organized segregated locals in the South, or ignored blacks altogether.

After a year of demoralizing defeats, the CIO withdrew half its organizers and unofficially abandoned Operation Dixie. Defeat became an ugly rout in many cases as CIO and AFL unions joined the Red hunt and began raiding left-wing locals in the South. In Alabama, the USW attacked the Mine, Mill, and Smelters union in 1949 by promising white workers they could divide the membership into segregated locals; in a campaign featuring robed Klansman denouncing Mine Mill as "the nigger union," the voting split along racial lines, with the USW winning 2,696 to 2,233. In Winston-Salem, a six-week strike in 1947 by FTA Local 22 revealed a host of similar vulnerabilities. At the start of the walkout, most white workers sided with R. J. Reynolds and crossed the picket line, making it a "race strike"; in the middle of the confrontation, HUAC subpoenaed three FTA leaders to give testimony on why they refused to sign non-communist affidavits; by the end of the strike, the AFL's Tobacco Workers Union was openly recruiting white workers. The CIO soon after targeted Local 22 for raiding and eventually expelled the FTA in its purge of left-wing unions. Even so, in the 1950 NLRB elections where Local 22 faced the combined opposition of the AFL, the CIO, and "No Union," the FTA appeared to win the run-off election by forty-five votes among nine thousand ballots—until the NLRB counted the disputed ballots of white supervisors, giving the sixty-six-vote victory to "No Union."

Although these and other reversals hastened the decline of labor-left activism at the forefront of the civil rights movement, the larger struggle for black emancipation would survive and return with new vigor in the 1950s. It would, in fact, be the first social movement to overcome the repressive logic of the Red scare. The compelling force behind this renewed mobilization was the same that had previously given rise to the CIO's interracial solidarity: the migration of African-Americans from southern farms to southern cities, and from South to North that continued through the 1940s and into the 1950s. Fleeing a declining cotton culture, black migrants were drawn to urban life by wartime labor shortages and a postwar economy that—contrary to widespread fears of renewed depression—grew with the stimulus of pent-up consumer demand, government support for housing and defense, and the global dominance of U. S. corporations. Black veterans of World War II and the Korean War returned to these growing urban centers of African-American life with a heightened sense of entitlement and a heightened awareness of newly independent countries where people of color had overturned colonial rule. Expectations were growing, and so was the potential to act on them—with more union jobs, more NAACP branches, more church congregations, and more urban voters prepared to support a revived movement for black equality.

On December 1, 1955, a singular act of courage would galvanize this potential when Rosa Parks, a black seamstress in Montgomery, Alabama, refused to surrender her "whites-only" seat on a bus. Her arrest, followed by a nine-month boycott of the city bus system by Montgomery's black citizens, would elevate the Reverend Martin Luther King to national prominence and inspire many more campaigns of civil disobedience to desegregate public facilities in the North and South. It would also reveal a deeply divided labor movement. Union activists could rightfully claim an important role in organizing and sustaining the Montgomery movement, for it was E. D. Nixon of the Brotherhood of Sleeping Car Porters who organized the boycott, A. Philip Randolph and the UAW who helped finance it, and the Montgomery locals of the Packinghouse Workers who helped support it. But there were labor activists on the opposing side as well, with the whites-only union of Montgomery bus drivers not only denouncing the boycott, but refusing to contemplate any settlement that didn't restore segregated seating. The Montgomery Carpenters hall meanwhile served as a meeting place for the Klan, and union carpenters built a public gallows to hang the NAACP in effigy—above the inscription "Built by Organized Labor."

Just days after Rosa Parks's arrest exposed these divisions within the labor movement, the same conflicts were evident at the historic "unity convention" that created the newly merged AFL-CIO. Meeting in New York City the first week of December 1955, George Meany of the AFL and Walter Reuther of the CIO had pledged the AFL-CIO's 135 affiliated unions to a constitution encouraging "all workers without regard to race, creed, color, national origin or ancestry to share equally in the full benefits of union organization." To this end, many AFL affiliates had already opened their ranks to unskilled workers and deleted "whites-only" language from their constitutions. At the very moment of the AFL-CIO's founding, however, its executive council voted to admit two unions—the Locomotive Firemen and the Railroad Trainmen—that barred black members. A. Philip Randolph, the only council member to oppose their admission on racial grounds, also condemned the AFL-CIO for failing to discipline affiliates that discriminated against black members. When defenders of federation policy argued that the AFL-CIO was obligated to respect the autonomy and voluntary compliance of its affiliated unions,

Randolph and others noted that the AFL-CIO felt no such obligation when it disciplined, even expelled, unions for corrupt practices or Communist politics.

From its founding, the AFL-CIO was riven by this contradiction between its official rhetoric on racial equality and its actual practice, particularly as the latter was carried out by affiliated unions. The national AFL-CIO was generally progressive, supporting implementation of the Supreme Court's desegregation orders, contributing money to voter registration and civil rights groups in the South, and inviting Martin Luther King to speak at its national meetings. But the AFL-CIO made little effort to mobilize its membership or align its affiliated unions with the civil rights movement, and it refused to even endorse the 1963 March on Washington for Jobs and Freedom. AFL-CIO president George Meany publicly supported the aims of the march, but said he was "fearful that there would be disorder, that people would get hurt, and that it would build up resentment in Congress"[39] against pending civil rights legislation.

It was left to individual unions, state councils, and locals to take actions that would advance—or oppose—racial equality, making the AFL-CIO a study in contrasts. In the South, some white leaders like Claude Ramsey, president of the Mississippi AFL-CIO after 1959, built alliances with the NAACP and worked closely with voter-registration drives targeting African-Americans. Ramsey's actions put himself and other labor-liberals at considerable risk in a state where right-wing opposition to desegregation was deep and violent. In 1963, Medgar Evers, a prominent civil rights leader and a friend of Ramsey, was gunned down by white supremacists; in 1964, Mississippi segregationists murdered six civil rights workers and bombed thirty-seven black churches during the "Freedom Summer" campaign to register voters; in December of that year, Otis Mathews, an official of Woodworkers Local 5443 who had just signed an agreement abolishing discriminatory practices at the Masonite Corporation, was held at gunpoint and whipped by Klansmen who poured liquid corrosives on his flesh. Despite repeated death threats, Ramsey remained defiant. "I understand the Klan has really given me hell in their last few rallies. Instead of one shotgun loaded, I am now keeping two."[40] His defiance, although inspiring to some, antagonized many white union members who joined the Klan and supported white supremacy. In the first six years of Ramsey's tenure, the Mississippi AFL-CIO Council lost one-third of its members as segregated locals disaffiliated from the state body. Similar trends were evident across the South, with AFL-CIO state councils generally supporting the mobilization of black voters against conservative antilabor Democrats, while many local unions openly defended continued segregation. "The labor boys played a big part in the [pro] segregation fight," recalled right-wing leader Samuel Englehart, head of the white Citizens Councils in Alabama. "The business people would give lip service, but the labor people would get out and work."[41]

In the North, there was considerably more labor support for civil rights activism, especially in unions with large black memberships and a legacy of black-white unity in the organizing drives of the 1930s and 1940s. The UAW played an especially visible role, with Walter Reuther joining A. Philip Randolph and Martin Luther King in the front ranks of the 1963 March on Washington. The UAW's national leaders funneled financial support to civil rights organizations and publicly urged union members to support equal voting rights and desegregation of public accommodations. Yet Reuther's highly visible initiatives failed to address the underlying institutional barriers to black advancement. "Walter Reuther's rhetoric did not comport with reality," observed William Gould, a former UAW attorney and future chairman of the NLRB. "At the very time of the 1963 March on Washington, of which Reuther was a leader . . . , and at the very time when the construction unions were being pilloried for their exclusionary tactics, hardly any black UAW members were to be found in the high-paying and prestigious skilled trades jobs."[42] Indeed, African-Americans were only 3 percent of the skilled trades at Ford and less than 1 percent at GM and Chrysler, making auto's skilled workforce as segregated as the more notorious construction crafts. In the Steelworkers, an even more pervasive institutional racism was codified in collective bargaining agreements that ghettoized black workers in the worst departments, usually the coke ovens, blast furnaces, and general labor pool. Instead of "whites-only" policies, segregation was maintained with apparently race-neutral provisions. Promotional openings in the better, higher-paid, or skilled categories were advertised to the white incumbents of those departments, while black applicants, if they learned of the openings and passed the discriminatory evaluations, lost all the seniority they had accumulated in their previous department and took significant pay cuts in transferring to "entry-level" positions in better departments. Few could surmount these barriers, and few of the complaints that blacks directed against departmental seniority and discriminatory job postings were pursued by the union or considered by the company.

These practices contrasted sharply with the exceptional activism of the United Packinghouse Workers (UPW). In the mid-1940s, decades before the UAW, USW, and other majority-white unions integrated their top leadership, the UPW had already elected African-Americans to its national executive board. The union's comprehensive antidiscrimination policy of 1950 was not merely a matter of convention rhetoric, but an imperative that every local was expected to implement, including not only desegregation of locker rooms and cafeterias, but also of skilled jobs and all-white departments. "Discrimination lowers the wages, not only of Negro and all women workers," a UPW pamphlet argued in 1953, "but it robs all white men, too,"[43] undercutting the best-paid workers with the competition of exploited minorities. White UPW members in the South still opposed desegregation as a threat to their status and their jobs, but the opposition of some was no doubt muted by the UPW's simultaneous campaign to end regional discrimination in pay rates. Between 1941 and 1953, the UPW raised the pay of southern packinghouse workers from just 55 percent of northern rates to 95 percent—and was only able to do so, the union reminded its southern members, because of the support of majority-black locals in the stockyards of Chicago and Kansas City. In return for this act of solidarity, the union argued, white workers in the South should accept elimination of the racial division of labor.

There was no comparable assault, however, on the sexual division of labor, not in the UPW or any other union. Unlike the experience of African-American men, who gained a permanent foothold during World War II in production jobs throughout heavy industry, the five million women who entered the workforce during the war did not hold place at the end of the fighting. They were not expected to, since the prevailing ideology of "the wife at home" had only been suspended during the wartime emergency, not repealed. "Now the women are going back into the home and the children are back in school where they belong,"[44] a UPW leaflet observed with obvious satisfaction in 1946. There was no place in this agenda for women as primary breadwinners, and this preju- dice was widely reinforced by "expert" opinion and the mass media. Women "would do well to recapture those functions in which they have demonstrated superior capacity," advised authors Marynia Farnham and Ferdinand Lundberg in 1947. "Those are, in general, the nurturing func- tions around the home."[45] Acting on this stereotype, employers in virtu- ally every industry, union or nonunion, either terminated their women employees or transferred them back to traditional female jobs where wages were lower and promotion nonexistent.

Not all women accepted these dogmatic prescriptions. "The catch phrase, 'a woman's place is in the kitchen' is a silly slander," the UAW's Fair Practices Department declared in 1946, "a cover slogan for tricky attacks on everyone's standard of living and everyone's political rights."[46] UAW women protested their discriminatory treatment with grievances and the occasional picket line, but their complaints had little impact on local unions that denied seniority or transfer rights to women. In the postwar UPW, women also protested the union's failure to address their grievances, particularly lower base wages for women in entry-level jobs. "It is very nice to sit here convention after convention and agree with us women," complained delegate Gazelle Koubsky at the UPW's 1953 convention, "but yet you sit back and you don't do a darn thing when you get back into the plant."[47] By 1956, the UPW had at least negotiated an end to lower base pay for women's jobs, but little was done to eliminate separate seniority lists, nor was there significant progress in eliminating the hiring and transfer procedures that locked women into narrowly specified job ghettos.

One dilemma for women seeking change in these areas was the all-too-obvious fact that, compared with the movement for black civil rights, there was no unity among women over the desirability of eliminating discriminatory job barriers. "I will not do a man's job," as UPW steward Goldie Lamb recalled of her attitude in the 1950s. "A man is supposed to be the breadwinner. He deserves that job."[48]

That many women could internalize their subordinate status and deny their own place in the economy meant there was little likelihood that employers or unions would be pressured to address women's needs or even acknowledge their presence. Even in the 1930s, when women's wages buoyed family survival and women's activism invigorated community-based unions, the labor movement's self-image had been overwhelmingly masculine. In garment unions where the majority of members were women, "Labor" was still most often symbolized in union newspapers and leaflets as a brawny man, a heroic soldier, or an embattled boxer, all fighting labor's battles in a masculine world. Yet year by year, even after the postwar shakeout had supposedly returned women to the home, the proportion of women wage earners slowly grew, from 25 percent of the labor force in 1940, to 29 percent by 1950, to 32 percent by 1960. The number of women union members grew as well, reaching 15 percent of total membership by 1960, but there was no matching increase in their leadership role. Union activism demanded a huge commitment of time and energy—for meetings, bargaining, organizing, and travel to and fro— and it was these demands that clashed head-on with the competing claims of women's maternal, homebound role. Because employers provided no maternity leave or day care, and because unions rarely even raised these issues in bargaining, most women were inevitably marginalized in the workplace and the union.

The exceptions led solitary and often difficult lives. Rose Pesotta, a successful organizer in the International Ladies Garment Workers Union (ILGWU) and the only woman on its national executive board between 1934 and 1942, felt the voice of a solitary woman was "a voice lost in the wilderness."[49] Constantly traveling across the United States in her role as union vice president, Pesotta never married, had no children, and confided in her diary that "everybody has a private life. I have none." In 1942, despite the fact that she was the only woman in the national leadership of a union with 85 percent women members, she refused to run for reelection and returned to her former occupation as a sewing machine operator.

TENUOUS ACCOMMODATION

AFL-CIO leader George Meany was exultant in 1964. "To a greater degree than ever before in the history of this country," he said after President Lyndon Johnson's reelection that fall, "the stated goals of the Administration and of Congress, on the one hand, and of the labor movement, on the other, are identical."[50] Not only had Johnson defeated Republican Barry Goldwater by the largest margin in U.S. history, and done so with strong labor backing, but AFL-CIO endorsed candidates had also dramatically boosted the Democratic Party's congressional majority, making it the most pro-labor Congress since 1936 according to AFL-CIO leaders.

Labor was at its political zenith in 1964–1965, with an almost unbroken string of legislative victories. Chief among these was the successful campaign to include fair employment practices in the Civil Rights Act of 1964. When first proposed by President Kennedy, this landmark legislation would have prohibited racial discrimination in restaurants, hotels, theaters, and other public accommodations, but would have done little to address employment discrimination. Meany joined the efforts of A. Philip

Randolph and NAACP leader Roy Wilkens to include equal employment opportunity in the law, both because "it is morally right," and perhaps more so because it would shift the burden of desegregating jobs from the AFL-CIO to the government. "We need a federal law," as Meany put it, "to help us do what we want to do: mop up those areas of discrimination which still persist in our own ranks."[51] After Kennedy's assassination, Congress passed and President Johnson signed a revised version of the bill that included prohibitions against employment discrimination by race or gender. "We are the only major [nonchurch] institution in America that supported fair employment practices legislation," Meany later boasted. "No national employer organization, to my knowledge, supported [it]."[52] Meany was less forthcoming about the AFL-CIO's efforts to exempt union-negotiated seniority provisions from the law's application, and he consistently understated the real extent of racial discrimination within union ranks. These shortcomings would later be highlighted as many unions (as well as employers) resisted the application of the law, but on balance, labor had done more in 1964 than any other majority-white institution to ensure passage of the bill.

Enactment of other labor-endorsed legislation soon followed, including bills that created Medicare, provided federal aid for education, raised Social Security benefits, increased the minimum wage, and expanded programs to wage a "War on Poverty." The major setback for the AFL-CIO was failure to repeal Section 14(b) of the Taft-Hartley Act, despite the support of President Johnson and congressional Democrats. A repeal measure passed the House in 1965 but was killed in the Senate by the Republican minority's prolonged filibuster.

Labor's legislative lobbying and its well-established alliance with the Democratic Party were now the principal focus of union activism, marking a fundamental shift in the way that most unions defined their mission. "Thirty years ago," as garment union leader David Dubinsky had observed in 1958, "the important thing was for a union leader to know how to organize economic strength. Organize! Strike! Settle! That was labor-management relations. But today, with laws and labor boards, almost all of our problems are settled at the conference table through negotiations. This requires new skills, a different kind of intelligence. Now it is diplomacy instead of the big stick."[53] Peaceful coexistence between capital and labor might still be punctuated by conflict, such as the four-month national steel strike of 1959, fought over crew sizes and work rules. The number of hours lost to strikes in that year was second only to 1946, and throughout the 1950s and early 1960s, strike activity remained high at between three thousand and four thousand walkouts in most years. But even the more prolonged of these battles, like the steel strike, now generally followed a predictable pattern of ritualized combat, with token picketing and no serious effort at strikebreaking. Most negotiations reached a settlement without a strike, and even in 1959, the hours lost represented only one-half of 1 percent of total work time.

For the most part, union officers groomed themselves as "responsible leaders," George Meany even boasting to a reporter that "I . . . never went on strike in my life, never . . . ordered anyone else to go on strike, and never had anything to do with a picket line."[54] Dubinsky's garment union, the ILGWU, was also loath to strike or even organize new members in an industry where the union's aging white-male leadership was increasingly out of touch with a workforce that was majority female and increasingly multiracial. Dubinsky and Meany preferred to represent workers before Congress, labor boards, arbitration panels, and national negotiations, where they often found corporate leaders who shared their emphasis on stability and bureaucratic procedure. As early as 1946, Henry Ford II had envisioned such an approach in terms that stood in sharp contrast with the antiunionism of his grandfather. "We of the Ford Motor Company have no desire to 'break the Unions,' to turn back the clock," he said in his keynote speech to the Society of Automotive Engineers. "We must look to an improved and increasingly responsible Union leadership for help in solving the human equation in mass production." Negotiating such solutions, he added, should be done "with the same efficiency and good temper that marks the negotiation of a commercial contract between two companies."[55] Like any commercial contract, a labor contract was valuable to business leaders to the degree it delivered predictable results, and the "business unionism" of the AFL-CIO was certainly more predictable and less threatening than the class-conscious "social unionism" of the early CIO. Liberal business leaders hoped to keep it that way. "Cooperation with responsible labor leadership," as the Rockefeller Brothers Report put it in 1958, "should serve to . . . eliminate the forces which might take root in a strained and troubled environment."[56] Pattern bargaining conducted at the national level could achieve this end by addressing problems in a uniform way and preempting local conflict or deviation from centralized procedures.

That these trends encouraged passivity and demobilization at the grass roots was lamented by critics and opposed by wildcat strikers in the many unauthorized walkouts that flared throughout the 1950s. Among the Big Three automakers alone there were an estimated 270 local wild-cat strikes during the decade, most of them over disputed shop rules regulating work intensity, seniority rights, and discipline. Even so, many union members and most academic observers welcomed the labor movement's apparent incorporation into a permanent system of industrial jurisprudence. "Almost all the articulate members of the community," George Brooks observed during a 1961 meeting of labor relations specialists, "now accept the same objectives in industrial relations, variously called maturity, industrial stability, responsibility, or statesmanship."[57] A few "labor statesmen" even went so far as to disavow any concern for the rank-and-file members they represented in this "mature" process. "Unions are big business," as Teamsters president Dave Beck put it. "Why should truck drivers and bottle washers be allowed to make big decisions affecting union policy? Would any corporation allow it?"[58]

Most union leaders condemned Beck and the Teamsters for the corrupt practices and flagrant racketeering that characterized the union's top leaders in these years, and in 1957 the AFL-CIO expelled the Teamsters on these grounds. Yet in every major union—the overwhelming majority of them free of Teamster-style collusion with employers and gangsters—there was a discernible narrowing of grassroots initiative and participatory democracy. In part, this was the inevitable downside of national contracts with industry-wide norms for wages, benefits, and working conditions. Although "pattern" agreements eliminated the opportunity for employers to seek competitive advantage by exploiting labor, the elevation of key issues to these national forums also made the process more remote to local members. Some unions countered this tendency with bargaining conferences that gave local delegates a chance to shape the national union's negotiating priorities, but the result was sometimes more symbolic than substantive when union staff controlled the proceedings and preempted debate. National contracts were also growing longer, from the usual one-year agreements of the 1930s to terms of three, even five, years in the 1950s and 1960s. In the lengthening stretch between contract negotiations, decisions were increasingly a matter of prolonged adjudication through grievance and arbitration systems, with workers in the meantime either obligated to accept management-imposed initiatives, or held "guilty until proven innocent" if they contested disciplinary procedures. Consequently, the union steward who worked on the job while collecting dues and leading workplace actions had less to do: dues were now automatically deducted from paychecks, and contractual no-strike clauses prohibited job actions during the term of most agreements.

There was, however, little sustained protest of these bureaucratic trends, especially among white workers. Protests over working conditions and the slow pace of grievance adjudication did sometimes boil into unauthorized wildcat strikes, but these did not usually cohere into dissident movements. The Red scare had muted workplace radicalism, and the general prosperity muted dissent in any case. Most unions were able to deliver good wages and dramatically improved benefits, including pension plans and medical insurance that put some workers on a par with the "middle-class" aspirations of the American dream. The culture of mass consumption, briefly previewed in the 1920s, returned in the postwar era on a floodtide of television and radio advertising, relentlessly promoting a lifestyle of acquisitive individualism that contrasted sharply with the countercultural claims of worker solidarity and collective action. Now, the quest for material goods—the latest car model, the suburban ranch home, the new washer-dryer—and the improved standard of living that they brought served many workers as compensation for alienated toil in repetitive and often dead-end jobs. "We're all working for one purpose, to get ahead," as one autoworker told researcher Eli Chinoy. "I don't think a person should be satisfied. My next step is a nice little modern house of my own." Chinoy, noting that U.S. culture encouraged men to "get ahead" in both their jobs and their material acquisitions, concluded that "workers who respond to both these admonitions use the second to rationalize their failure to achieve the first. As long as possessions continue to pile up, the worker can feel that he is moving forward."[59]

There were, of course, troubling signs that even as it acquired the trappings of respectability and political success, the labor movement was nevertheless perched on precarious foundations. Technological change was accelerating in industries like coal mining, where mechanization replaced pick and shovel methods, and in longshoring, where bulk loading and containerization winnowed the dock gangs. Many manufacturers were also dismantling the urban production centers where they had originally concentrated production, decentralizing their operations to smaller, rural factories connected by the expanding highway system. Automation and decentralization undermined the strongholds of union power that had led the organizational drives of the UAW, URW, and UPW, and because employers were locating a growing number of their new plants in the nonunion South, the union's bargaining leverage was all the more diluted. In the economy generally, manufacturing employment (where unionization was high) was falling behind the rapidly expanding white-collar sectors (where unionization was low) as corporate bureaucracies and government agencies hired more clerical workers, sales clerks, and technicians. Although the number of dues-paying union members rose through the 1950s and into the 1960s, reaching seventeen million in 1965, their proportional weight in the labor force had declined from the 1953 peak of 32 percent to a more modest 26 percent in 1965.

For African-Americans, these trends were especially ominous. The relative decline of manufacturing, combined with automation and decen-tralization, eliminated many of the lower rungs of upward mobility pre-viously used by white immigrants, leaving blacks trapped in inner city ghettos, their hopes for advancement blocked. Employers who closed aging plants in the inner city were opening new operations in distant sub-urbs, far removed from African-American workers (who often lacked pri-vate or public transportation), and inaccessible to minority homebuyers (who often confronted segregated housing). Even the long-esteemed job of Pullman Porter was in decline as railroads were surpassed by highway and air travel. President Johnson's "War on Poverty" was too small to make a durable impact on these trends, but it was large enough to draw the attention of conservative critics, who stigmatized welfare as a social-istic giveaway to an "undeserving" minority.

The New Deal model of universal benefits available to all, exempli-fied by Social Security, was also eroding as benefits fell behind inflation, to be supplanted by a new regime of private pension and healthcare plans conferred upon those with "good" jobs, or a strong union. The result was a diminished form of welfare state that differed in key respects from the political economy of western European capitalism. In the latter, unions were a dominant force in left-wing or "Social Democratic" labor parties that won a measure of legislative power and pushed for national policies protecting workers: laws that established national healthcare sys-tems, as in Britain; laws that give employees a voice on corporate boards and plant-level "Works Councils," as in Germany; laws that committed the government to genuine full-employment, as in Sweden; and laws that required all companies to provide for paid vacations and uniform pen-sions, as in France. In the United States, by contrast, public welfare ben-efits were far lower and far more restricted to the very poor, leaving the majority of workers dependent on either a "privatized" welfare system of company-specific benefits, or no benefits at all. Unlike the comparatively uniform and universal programs supported by European Social Democracy, America's hybrid system of public-private welfare contributed to a more polarized working class, characterized at one extreme by the inner-city poor subsisting on low-wage jobs and meager welfare benefits, and at the other extreme by the working "middle class" earning the highest wages in the world. Solidarity between the two was especially difficult when these divisions were demarcated by segregated housing and aggravated by racial tension.

Unique to this U.S. system was the absence of independent labor politics. Past efforts to form a Labor Party or build a Progressive alternative had failed, and the combined impact of Cold War and Red scare made any such initiative seem quixotic in the postwar decades. In this hostile climate, the U.S. labor movement had drawn all the closer to the Democratic Party; the principle exception was the Teamsters union, which endorsed Republicans for national office after being expelled from the AFL-CIO for corrupt practices. Dependence on the Democrats would inevitably dilute labor's voice, since the party platform had to serve southern segregationists, urban-machine politicians, civil rights activists, corporate liberals, and military-industrial technocrats, in addition to labor. In fact, there was little that unified this fragile coalition besides a generally pro-business perspective and a fading commitment to the New Deal. Democrats were more receptive to labor than Republicans, but only by degree, and only as the labor movement purged itself of dissenting opinion. Party distinctions hardly mattered, in any case, when it came to foreign affairs, where Democrats and Republicans, Labor and Business, together endorsed a bipartisan strategy of anticommunism and free trade. As a junior partner in this bipartisan coalition, the AFL-CIO not only gave its endorsement to anticommunist regimes that were sometimes dictatorial and antilabor but also worked covertly as a conduit for CIA moneys funneled to anticommunist unions around the world.

The depth of the labor movement's collaboration with official foreign policy was demonstrated during the 1965 crisis in the Dominican Republic. Three years previous, the country's elected president, Juan Bosch, had won office on promises to nationalize U.S. and other foreign-owned corporations and redistribute land to impoverished peasants. A military coup sent Bosch into exile, but in 1965 a popular uprising was on the verge of restoring him to power when President Johnson sent twenty-five thousand troops to ensure support for a pro-U.S. junta. The Dominican labor movement gave its overwhelming support to Bosch and the rebels, with only one exception: a pro-U.S. labor federation founded, funded, and led by AFL-CIO organizers. George Meany heartily endorsed President Johnson's unfounded claim that fifty-three "known Communists" had taken control of the rebellion in Santo Domingo, thereby justifying military intervention in the capital city. The pro-U.S. regime elected in 1966 subsequently suppressed the independent labor movement and banned all unions from free-trade zones established for the factories of Gulf & Western, Colgate-Palmolive, and Philip Morris, among others. George Meany little doubted that U.S. workers benefited by such accommodation with, and support for, the international status quo. For him and other AFL-CIO leaders long-schooled in the anticommunist crusade of the 1940s and 1950s, it was enough that U.S. troops had prevented "another Cuba." As yet, they saw little reason to question the assumption that free trade and the global extension of U.S. military and economic power were the foundations of continued domestic prosperity.

There were, however, straws in the wind: an urban "disturbance" in Harlem; an escalating civil war in Vietnam; the first Japanese imports. In the social and political whirlwind that followed 1965, the labor movement would discover the tenuous nature of its accommodation with corporate America.

5

AT THE CROSSROADS

On August 5, 1981, U.S. Secretary of Transportation Drew Lewis announced the firing of 11,300 federal air traffic controllers for conducting an illegal strike. "None of these people will ever be permitted to come back,"[1] Lewis promised on the third day of the nationwide walkout. The firings and the subsequent collapse of the strike would mark the end of the Professional Air Traffic Controllers Association (PATCO). It would also mark a turning point for the U.S. labor movement. Confronted by the federal government's decisive act of strikebreaking, the first in many decades to actually destroy a union, the AFL-CIO's response was limited to a national boycott and symbolic acts of solidarity.

This was not because there was any lack of sympathy among AFL-CIO leaders and activists for the underlying grievances that motivated PATCO members. In labor circles, these white-collar professionals were widely regarded as deserving better treatment at the hands of the Federal Aviation Administration (FAA), the government agency responsible for running the nation's five hundred control towers. Particularly in big-city airports where air traffic was most crowded during peak travel hours, controllers who guided as many as ten to twenty airplanes at a time had to contend with obsolete radar, balky computers, chronic understaffing, mandatory overtime, rotating shift schedules, and a bureaucratic and inflexible management. Whereas governments in Europe and Canada

155

recognized the uniquely stressful aspects of the job and limited the work-week for air traffic controllers to between thirty-two and thirty-eight hours, the FAA required a forty-hour week plus overtime—a burden that might have been acceptable at smaller, less-crowded airports, but which controllers at big-city air towers considered unsafe. PATCO members complained bitterly of the conditions under which they worked and the resentment they felt toward the FAA, which dismissed complaints about controller burnout by claiming the job was no more stressful than that of a city bus driver. Many controllers saw it differently. "We were always running scared," recalled one PATCO member, referring to fears that a single mistake would kill hundreds of people. "After an incident [near miss], you were never any good afterwards. You worked traffic, you stayed cool, and you puked your guts out in the bathroom afterwards."[2] Although FAA studies alleged otherwise, PATCO members claimed that these conditions caused high levels of hypertension and heart disease that felled many controllers before they reached retirement.

Issues of stress, safety, and autocratic management were not, how-ever, the issues PATCO first took to the public or emphasized at the bar-gaining table. In one of several strategic mistakes that weakened PATCO's public support, the union instead put wages at the top of its list, demand-ing a $10,000 annual increase as well as early retirement and a shortened workweek. At a time when the average PATCO member was earning $31,000 a year—nearly double the national median of $16,563—it was unlikely that the traveling public would support the deliberate disruption of airline service to win a 33 percent wage increase. An early Gallup poll indicated that two out of three people surveyed believed that PATCO members, as federal employees, should not have violated their solemn oath to forego strike action, and 60 percent supported President Ronald Reagan's decision to fire them for violating that promise.

In fact, PATCO had not only failed to win public support, it had also distanced itself from the rest of the labor movement, adopting a go-it-alone strategy that assumed the FAA could not manage air traffic without the skilled and experienced PATCO workforce. In the 1980 presidential elections, when virtually all of the AFL-CIO's 110 unions had opposed Ronald Reagan for his antiunion views, PATCO had endorsed the Repub-lican candidate in return for his written promise to "work very closely with you to bring about a spirit of cooperation."[3] Even after Reagan, once in office, ordered the mass firing of strikers, PATCO's president clung to the naive belief that the president of the United States had been "tragically ill-advised and fed false information."[4] Only at the last minute did PATCO seek the support of private-sector airline unions—Pilots, Machinists, Flight Attendants—and other AFL-CIO affiliates who might have been able to shut down the air transport system with sympathy strikes and civil disobedience, forcing a political solution. Airline unions, however, harbored a long-standing resentment of PATCO's previous aloofness and failure to support their (legal) walkouts. Moreover, sympathy action now would violate legally binding no-strike contracts, bringing court injunctions and massive fines against participating unions—a prospect few union leaders relished, especially in defense of PATCO's wayward strategy. The Pilot's union, the key to shutting down the system, refused to cooperate and went so far as to issue public statements supporting the government's claim that replacement controllers were keeping the airways safe.

President Reagan's determination to break the strike, even if it meant a temporary disruption of airline travel and a heightened risk of accidents, proved decisive. With labor's strike support limited to fund-raising and an ineffective boycott, PATCO died a slow death. By 1982, the union was decertified and bankrupt, and the nation's air traffic system was nonunion. (Though only temporarily: the striker replacements found conditions bad enough that they too formed a union and pressed for collective bargaining with the FAA.)

PATCO's demise was disheartening enough, but there was worse to come as this high-profile defeat exposed fatal weaknesses in the labor movement's capacity to articulate common goals and mobilize public support. PATCO's militancy had been narrowly based and elitist, premised on go-it-alone strategies and political deal making that left the union isolated and vulnerable. In turn, the larger labor movement, unwilling to risk its respectability and its bankable assets in an all-out campaign to save PATCO from itself, had demonstrated an uninspired caution that did not go unnoticed. Among private-sector employers with a unionized workforce, a growing minority of managers were already thinking the unthinkable—to break the union rather than bargain with it. Reagan's defeat of PATCO now put a presidential seal of approval on the hard-line strategy for doing so. The key lesson that militant managers drew from PATCO was to turn the labor movement's traditional strike weapon against itself; by taking a strike or provoking one, the well-prepared employer could win half the battle—removing union members from the workplace. To keep them out required a complex legal strategy, for unlike federal employees who had no legal protection for striking, private-sector workers were protected by the National Labor Relations Act, which prohibited employers from firing workers for strike activity. There was, however, an obscure loophole contained in a 1938 Supreme Court decision, *Mackay Radio,* that permitted employers to continue operations by "permanently replacing," rather than firing, striking workers. Nominally, the strikers were only replaced in their particular positions and were not severed from the company, meaning the employer would legally have to return them to the first new positions that became available. But unless and until there were such openings—and in an era of "downsizing" there were virtually none—the effect was the same as firing.

Mackay Radio was little known and little used before 1981, but it soon became the bane of the labor movement as a growing number of employers dusted off their law books and mobilized "permanent replacements" to displace striking workers, or drive them back to work under the threat of being replaced. The lengthening list of companies joining the strikebreaking trend included some of the country's largest corporations: Browne and Sharpe in 1981; Maytag and Greyhound Bus in 1983; Phelps Dodge and Continental Airlines in 1984; BASF, Hormel, and *The Chicago Tribune* in 1985; Colt, TWA, and Boise Cascade in 1986; John Morrell and International Paper in 1987; Eastern Airlines, Pittston Coal and Greyhound (again) in 1989; the *New York Daily News* in 1990; Ravenswood Aluminum in 1991; Caterpillar in 1992; Bridgestone-Firestone and the Detroit newspapers in 1995. Unions were able in some of these cases (Colt, Pittston, and most of those that followed) to salvage some kind of return to work, but only after years of struggle and significant concessions to employer demands. By the estimate of U.S. Congressman William Clay, in the 1980s alone some three hundred thousand strikers lost their jobs to permanent replacements, sending a profound chill through union ranks. Strike activity plummeted accordingly, with the number of major walkouts of one thousand or more workers falling from an average of 290 a year in the 1970s to just thirty-five a year by the 1990s. The fall in union representation accelerated as well, spurred by strikebreaking, intensifying import competition, and an epidemic of plant closings following the economic recession of the early 1980s. By the end of the century, just 14 percent of all civilian workers were union members, down from 23 percent in 1980.

President Reagan's defeat of PATCO was the symbolic turning point for this downward slide in union representation. As union membership fell, there was a corresponding drop in pay, marking an end to the decades-long ascent that began after World War II. Real hourly wages (measured against the rising cost of living) had grown by 80 percent between 1947 and 1978, but fell thereafter as deunionization, recession, and the shift to low-wage service jobs drove earnings downward. When they finally bottomed out in the mid-1990s, real wages had fallen back to the levels of the late 1960s. Family income did rise slightly after the mid-1980s, but only because the average married couple with children worked three hundred more hours a year outside the home in 1996 than in 1979—most of the added burden falling on the wife. By the mid-1990s, only 42 percent of all full-time workers had an employer-provided pension plan with a guaranteed retirement benefit, and 43 million Americans had no health insurance of any kind at the end of the twentieth century. The very rich, on the other hand, were prospering. In 1980, the income of the average chief executive officer (CEO) of America's largest corporations was forty-two times greater than that of a typical factory worker according to *Business Week*; by 1997, average CEO pay had ballooned to $7.8 million, 326 times the average factory worker's earnings. In that year, the richest 5 percent of families feasted on 21 percent of the nation's total aggregate income according to the U.S. Bureau of the Census—more than the combined income of the bottom half of the population and dramatically higher than the 15 percent share the very rich had taken in 1980.

THE ROAD DOWNWARD

This dramatic shift in the balance of power between employers and workers had many causes, most falling under two headings: labor had become more vulnerable since 1965, and employers had become more aggressive. The PATCO firings and the strikebreaking that followed put these two trends in sharper relief.

Labor's vulnerability was in part a legacy of the late 1960s and early 1970s, when U.S. military intervention in Vietnam provoked a widening protest, polarizing the nation and fragmenting the labor movement. Antiwar activists refused military service and demonstrated against the war, and minority workers and women challenged discriminatory practices in society and the workplace. Fueling these dissenting movements was an underlying cultural protest, marked by the rejection of traditional gender roles and sexual mores, widespread experimentation with drugs, and an impatience with established leaders and bureaucratic procedures. The spirit of dissent left no group or institution untouched, but it was only in the labor movement that all of these varied protests found a forum. While management could insulate the boardroom from street-level conflict, unions were, by their nature, closer to the ground, with a diversity of membership and opinion found in few other arenas. Any leadership would have been hard pressed to accommodate the explosive conflicts of the era, but AFL-CIO president George Meany, rather than accommodate the spirit of rebellion, aligned the labor movement with the status quo. Although still proclaiming his support for the civil rights movement, Meany defended many of the institutionalized practices that trapped women and minorities in low-wage job ghettos; his support for Presidents Johnson and Nixon in their anticommunist crusade in Vietnam likewise put him on the conservative end of the political spectrum. These positions won the approval of some workers, particularly older white males who had served in earlier wars and accumulated seniority in jobs now targeted for affirmative action. Yet this same defense of the status quo alienated a growing number of dissidents, eventually splitting the labor movement into antagonistic camps of antiwar "doves" and pro-war "hawks."

Dissent was evident as early as 1965, when the Negro American Labor Council, led by A. Philip Randolph, issued a convention resolution that "military action is no remedy for the settlement of the problem in Southeast Asia or Santo Domingo."[5] Labor opposition to Meany's policies thereafter grew dramatically in numbers and rhetoric. In 1968, after several years straddling the fence, UAW president Walter Reuther took the autoworkers union out of the AFL-CIO, condemning the federation as "too fat, too complacent, too far out of touch with changing times."[6] The following year, the UAW joined with the Teamsters to form the Alliance for Labor Action (ALA), an improbable coalition of the nation's two largest unions that, however short-lived, gave antiwar sentiments considerably greater visibility in the labor movement. Meany condemned the ALA's antiwar pronouncements as giving aid to the enemy, and Joseph Bierne of the Communication Workers warned that "millions would be laid off"[7] if the Pentagon's war expenditures were cut back. Antiwar unionists countered by dubbing Vietnam "A Rich Man's War and a Poor Man's Fight," as stated in a 1970 declaration signed by leaders of twenty-two unions. "During the last 10 fiscal years," the declaration continued, "the Vietnam war has cost ten times more than Medicare, 16 times more than Aid to Education, 33 times more than Housing and Community Development, [and] 18 times more than the War on Poverty." The cost in lives was mounting as well, eventually totaling over fifty thousand U.S. soldiers and a million Vietnamese killed in the fighting.

Numbers like these had already turned the Reverend Martin Luther King against the war. "We must combine the fervor of the civil rights movement with the peace movement"[8] the Nobel Peace laureate told demonstrators at the first antiwar march he led in 1967. The following year King linked both these movements with labor by traveling to Memphis, Tennessee, and picketing with striking sanitation workers, members of the American Federation of State, County, and Municipal Employees (AFSCME). With his assassination during that strike, some of the nation's largest cities—Chicago and Washington, D.C., among them—erupted in rebellion, reproducing scenes of urban rioting already previewed the previous summer in Detroit, Newark, and elsewhere. National Guard and U.S. Army troops were called upon to suppress many of these disorders, which left more than 150 dead and thousands injured in the summers of 1967 and 1968. Among the casualties was the Democratic Party. Ruptured by antiwar politics and racial polarization, the Democratic coalition splintered into its constituent parts: Cold-War liberals and AFL-CIO unions, who fell just short of electing Hubert Humphrey president in 1968; antiwar liberals and their labor allies, who fell far short of electing George McGovern president in 1972; and southern segregationists and their northern allies—many of them white union members—who fell behind Alabama Governor George Wallace in both elections.

Polarization within the labor movement was also evident at the grass roots as radicals and younger workers challenged the authority of corporate managers and union leaders alike. With the anticommunist obsessions of the Cold War increasingly discredited, and with the Taft-Hartley Act's noncommunist affidavits already nullified by the Supreme Court in 1965, the acceptable range of political debate opened to the left. Even so, labor dissidents who came of age in the 1960s and 1970s, some of them linked with campus radicals and the antiwar movement, were as scornful of "Old Left" Communists as they were of George Meany. Their impatience with bureaucratic procedures and autocratic leaders was evident in a growing and varied range of protest movements: the League of Revolutionary Black Workers, an alliance of locally based militants concentrated in Detroit's auto plants; Miners for Democracy, a movement in the coalfields of West Virginia, Ohio, and Pennsylvania that won control of the

UMW in 1973 and restored democratic procedures to the union; Teamsters for a Decent Contract, organized by over-the-road freight drivers in 1975 and merging the following year with car haulers and UPS workers to form Teamsters for a Democratic Union; and a similar movement in the United Steel Workers, where Ed Sadlowski won election as district director in 1974 and subsequently lost his bid for president in 1977.

The widespread ferment in the labor movement was especially visible among public employees. President Kennedy's 1962 executive order had established the right to bargain collectively (but not to strike) over non-wage issues in the federal sector, and most states subsequently provided comparable or greater rights to state and local government workers. With these enabling changes in the law, public-employee unions began to enroll thousands of teachers, sanitation workers, police, and firemen, boosting the level of unionization among government workers from 13 percent in 1960 to 39 percent in 1976. Emblematic of the changing sentiment among public-sector workers was the massive wildcat strike of postal workers that began in New York City in March 1970, spreading within a week to two hundred cities and towns across fifteen states. Unlike PATCO eleven years later, the postal strikers had two critical factors favoring their illegal walkout against the federal government and their own national leaders. "If practically everybody strikes, then nobody is going to get hurt," as one federal worker told the *Washington Star*. "After all, they can't fire everybody"[9]—not when two hundred thousand strikers made it the biggest wildcat in U.S. history. A second source of strength was the public perception that postal employees, although breaking the law, were also uniquely deserving of more pay. Senior postal workers in New York City earned 25 percent less than the U.S. government's own threshold for a "moderate" standard of living, and the lowest-paid among them actually qualified for the city's supplemental welfare benefits. After President Nixon's mobilization of thirty thousand unarmed soldiers to move the mail in New York proved ineffective, the strikers settled for the promise—largely kept—of congressional action to speed promotions and boost wages 14 percent.

In the private sector, as Vietnam spending simultaneously drove unemployment down and prices up, workers with less to fear from job loss and more to gain from strike action also took to picket lines in record numbers. Among them were hospital workers and migrant farm laborers protesting low wages and heavy workloads in industries that were not yet protected by federal labor law, but where Hospital Workers 1199 and the

United Farm Workers of Cesar Chavez still gained support among African-American and Latino workers. Their militancy helped drive the number of strikes upward, from thirty-five hundred a year in the early 1960s to fifty-five hundred a year between 1968 and 1974. Of special significance were two successful company-wide strikes: a 101-day walkout against General Electric in the winter of 1969–1970, led by a coalition of fourteen unions that included the UE and IUE for the first time since the Cold War; and a sixty-seven-day strike by UAW members against GM in 1970 that won cost-of-living protection for wages and early retirement for workers with thirty years' seniority. Wildcat strikes also figured in the rising militancy of 1970, as fifty thousand Teamsters launched a national wildcat against long-haul trucking firms. With the mobilization of the Ohio National Guard to protect trucking terminals, the state's 145th Infantry soon achieved the dubious distinction of serving in every form of civil disturbance that marked these years: having previously intervened against ghetto riots, the 145th would soon be rushed from strike duty to the campus of Kent State University, where guardsmen killed four student antiwar protesters.

Taken together, these events conveyed both the strengths and the weaknesses of a labor movement facing dramatic change. On the one hand, even as Vietnam War spending drove prices upward, unionized workers were able to defend their standard of living against an inflation rate that rose from less than 2 percent in 1965 to over 12 percent in 1974. Collective bargaining and, when necessary, strike action kept many union members ahead of rising prices, widening the gap between union and nonunion pay from 19 percent in the late 1960s to 30 percent in the late 1970s. Workers widely regarded unions as effective in this and other realms, with heavy majorities of those polled (including managerial employees) agreeing in the 1977 "Quality of Employment Survey" that unions improved wages (87 percent), protected against unfair practices (84 percent), and increased job security (80 percent).

On the other hand, 66 percent of workers surveyed also agreed that union leaders "do what's best for themselves," tracking previous surveys that consistently ranked union officials below their counterparts in business, religion, government, and academia. Some of this negative image stemmed from the antilabor bias of corporate-owned media, and the high-profile prosecution and imprisonment of corrupt leaders like James Hoffa of the Teamsters. There was a larger blemish on labor's image, however, and much of this was self-inflicted. Although most union leaders could rightfully draw a distinction between themselves and a small minority of mob-dominated "bosses," many took home salaries that were double or triple those of their members, and some enjoyed incomes that rivaled those of low-end corporate executives. The bureaucratic procedures and factional politics that characterized many unions stifled dissent and widened still further the gulf between leaders and members. This growing distance was symbolized by the lavish settings at AFL-CIO leadership meetings, held in beach-side resorts in Florida and the Caribbean, where the media found—and pictured—Meany and his colleagues in sleepy repose at poolside. "Do you really want to wallow in luxury like a bunch of capitalists?" Walter Reuther once scolded the assembled leaders at such a Miami meeting. "Yeah," replied the president of the Bricklayers, Harry Bates, with no hesitation or apparent concern.[10]

MILITANT MANAGEMENT

In these same years, a growing number of corporate managers began to rethink their post–World War II accommodation with organized labor. This fundamental reevaluation was driven by three considerations. First, the widening gap between union and nonunion wages put organized employers at a growing competitive disadvantage. Second, with most unions devoting only 3 percent of their budgets to organizing new members, the nonunion sector was growing rather than shrinking, making the threat—and for employers, the attraction—of low-cost labor all the more compelling. Finally, in virtually every realm of economic activity, the long and comfortable dominance of U.S. corporations was coming to an end, putting additional pressure on management to find low-cost alternatives to long-accepted practices.

Evidence of the suddenly shifting terrain of global competition was inescapable from the late 1960s onward, as the U.S. economy lurched from one crisis to the next and profits bounced downward. Oil prices shot upward following war and revolution in the Middle East, dampening demand for the gas-guzzling cars of U.S. automakers and contributing to steep recessions in 1974 and 1979–1981—the worst downturns since the Depression decade of the 1930s. Germany and Japan had recovered from the devastation of World War II, building factories, steel mills, and shipyards that were newer and often more technologically advanced than the aging capital stock of U.S. corporations. Japanese imports were especially successful in consumer electronics and automobiles, contributing to a doubling of foreign trade in the 1970s, from little more than 10 to more than 20 percent of gross domestic product. Imports were not altogether "foreign," however, as many U.S. companies chose to revive flagging profits by moving operations to low-wage economies in Asia, Latin America, and the Caribbean. Movement of capital was evident within the United States as well, as companies disinvested from older unionized operations in the Northeast and Midwest and directed new investment to the South and West. With the corresponding growth of service-sector and white-collar occupations where unions were historically weak—in banking, insurance, legal services, clerical, fast food, retail, and healthcare—the remaining union strongholds in manufacturing shrank all the faster as a share of total employment.

Employers were committed to keeping it that way by adopting more aggressive tactics in opposing union organization. In the 1950s, the NLRB had to reinstate workers illegally fired for pro-union activity in just 4 percent of the elections held to determine whether workers wanted union representation; by the early 1980s, that percentage had soared to 32 percent of all such elections. In 1985, an average of one of every thirty-eight workers who voted for the union would be illegally fired (and later reinstated by NLRB order), compared with a ratio of just one in six hundred during the late 1950s. Much of this growth in illegal firings occurred in the healthcare industry, where overworked nurses and low-wage workers in housekeeping and food service began to join Hospital Workers 1199, AFSCME, and the Service Employees International Union (SEIU) in the 1970s. When a 1974 amendment to the National Labor Relations Act extended the law's protections to workers in nonprofit hospitals, managers fearful of union success turned to a new breed of "union avoidance" firms like Modern Management Methods (3M's); whose one hundred consultants reportedly managed five hundred campaigns countering union organizing drives in healthcare during 1978–1979. Saint Elizabeth's Hospital in Boston was one of 3M's clients and a beneficiary of its hardball tactics. After 3M turned back an organizing drive in 1978, the NLRB cited the hospital for a long list of unfair labor practices, from threatening, interrogating, and spying on workers, to illegally suspending and firing them for their legal union activities. In the face of this intimidation, the union lost the original election as well as the following rerun ordered by the NLRB.

Union avoidance was the catchword in management circles by the end of the 1970s, expanding from healthcare into construction, where the

Associated Builders and Contractors took the lead, and manufacturing, where the National Association of Manufacturers created the "Council on a Union Free Environment" in 1977. Spurred by the PATCO defeat and the strikebreaking that followed, the union-avoidance industry boomed in the 1980s, with an estimated seven thousand consultants and attorneys specializing in the new science by the end of the decade. Unlike the physical intimidation and fatal violence so often practiced against unions between 1877 and 1937, the late twentieth-century variant relied on psychological stroking and repeated warnings of the negative outcomes attributed to union organization—that unions meant possible conflict, possible strikes, possible plant closings, and probably all of these things. "The enemy was the collective spirit," as confessed union-buster Martin Levitt described his tactics while consulting at 3M and later managing his own union-avoidance firm. "I got hold of that spirit while it was still a seedling; I poisoned it, choked it, bludgeoned it if I had to, anything to be sure it didn't blossom into a united workforce."[11]

In this, ironically, Levitt found that the NLRA could be "a union buster's best friend." In its complexity, as he described it, "the . . . law presents endless possibilities for delays, roadblocks, and maneuvers that can undermine a union's efforts,"[12] allowing wide latitude to employers willing to pay small fines in the future while intimidating workers in the present. In the 1980s, the NLRB ordered companies to reinstate an average of six thousand workers each year who had been illegally fired for union activity, and estimates of the total number illegally fired, including those who did not seek reinstatement, ranged as high as ten thousand a year. For most of these workers, justice would be delayed if not denied outright. At the end of the decade, the Government Accounting Office found that the median time for the NLRB to decide an unfair labor practice case was three hundred days, and for workers seeking reinstatement for illegal firings, even longer: an average of three years to complete the prolonged appeals process. As a result, workers who did finally win reinstatement to their jobs often returned to workplaces where the organizing drive had long since collapsed as a result of the employer's ULPs. With legal remedies postponed to an uncertain future, fewer workers were willing to risk the consequences of joining a union drive; in a 1991 Fingerhut-Powers poll, 79 percent of those surveyed agreed with the statement that "nonunion workers will get fired if they try to organize a union." Many unions were also reluctant to risk more than a few percentage points of their overall budgets to campaigns that ended in failure at least half the time. Between

1975 and 1990, the union win rate in NLRB elections held steady at around 50 percent, but the number of elections fell by half, from 7,700 to 3,600.

Unions turned to political action to reverse these trends, focusing on reform measures that would strengthen workers' rights and expedite NLRB procedures. Yet even when union-endorsed Democrats controlled the White House, the labor movement could not win passage of its reform agenda. Presidents Jimmy Carter and Bill Clinton both endorsed labor law reform, Carter backing a 1978 bill to streamline and strengthen NLRB protections, and Clinton backing a 1994 bill to prohibit permanent replacement of strikers. Their endorsements were weak, however, and Democratic leaders abandoned both bills when confronted by corporate pressure and Republican filibusters. The prevailing trend in these years was a bipartisan consensus opposing government intervention in the economy, with most Democrats disputing only the degree, rather than the direction, of Republican policy. Although President Ronald Reagan gave special priority to dismantling what remained of the New Deal welfare state, it was actually President Carter who backed the first measures deregulating the economy. The result in both trucking and airlines was the sudden appearance of low-wage, nonunion competitors and bitter struggles to protect the wages and working conditions of unionized workers.

President Clinton could still present himself as a friend of labor, particularly with his appointment to the National Labor Relations Board of William Gould, a strong advocate for the use of court injunctions against companies that violated labor rights. Clinton's opposition to further tax cuts for the wealthy won labor's support, and in the early years of his presidency he also championed healthcare reform—though his unsuccessful effort to regulate private insurance companies fell short of the tax-supported national healthcare system (modeled after Canada) that most unions favored. Otherwise, Clinton generally heeded the counsel of media advisors and corporate executives, many of them serving in his cabinet and staff. In 1993, he gave vigorous support to the North American Free Trade Agreement (NAFTA), a measure designed to protect and expand the already significant investment by U.S. corporations in Mexico. In 1996, he favored replacing federal welfare programs for thirteen million people (two-thirds of them children) with state programs requiring "workfare," often at poverty-level wages. Passage of these bills embittered many of Clinton's labor supporters, in part because both measures increased the threat of low-wage competition, and in part because Democratic support for these Republican-endorsed bills underscored the declining political influence of the labor movement. In the eyes of many, the Democratic Party—the party of Franklin Roosevelt and the New Deal—now answered primarily to corporate donors who outspent labor 9–1 in 1995–1996 (according to Common Cause) in soft-money donations to the Democratic National Committee.

THE ROAD AHEAD

"I am a product of the social compact that lifted America out of the Great Depression and working Americans into the middle class." Speaking in 1996 at Columbia University's "Teach-In with the Labor Movement," AFL-CIO president John Sweeney was recalling the post–World War II accommodation of labor as "a formula for the strongest economy, the largest middle class, and the most successful society this world has ever known."

"But now, those days are gone," Sweeney told the standing-room-only crowd of students, unionists, and teachers in Low Library. The surroundings alone signified something new, since most of the AFL-CIO's top leaders had shunned university campuses since the Vietnam era. Sweeney's candor was also unusual. Barely a year in office after his "New Voice" slate defeated the federation's incumbent officers, he went beyond the expected denunciation of corporate greed and government duplicity and called attention to labor's own failings. "American labor must also change. That is why I ran for President of the AFL-CIO, and that is why I won. Here's the truth: the weakness of labor encouraged employers to take the low road. And only by rebuilding our strength can we bring American business back to the high road of high wages."[13]

Many saw in Sweeney the best hope for such a turnaround. Just as John L. Lewis and the United Mine Workers had shown the way for the labor movement of the 1930s, so it was hoped that Sweeney's leadership of the Service Employees International Union would serve as a model for organizing in the 1990s and 2000s. As SEIU president between 1980 and 1995, Sweeney had made his union the AFL-CIO's fastest-growing affiliate, growing from 550,000 to nearly one million members at a time when most unions were shrinking. Although some of this growth came from merger with smaller independent unions, much of it was the fruit of Sweeney's new approach: raising dues (previously among the lowest in the AFL-CIO) and devoting 25 percent of the expanded budget to organizing at a time when other unions earmarked less than 5 percent of their budgets for recruiting new members. Sweeney increased the union's national staff from twenty to more than two hundred and targeted their work on organizing whole industries and regions, using direct action and community-wide mobilizations to organize janitors, healthcare workers, and clerical workers. SEIU locals were now expected to concentrate their resources on organizing, and local leaders who failed to implement this mandate found themselves temporarily removed from office as the national union placed their local under trusteeship.

Although Sweeney would not be able to wield the same top-down pressure on AFL-CIO affiliates as he had exercised at SEIU, his high-profile commitment to organizing marked a possible turning point. Previous AFL-CIO leaders had focused on reforming labor law first, and only then devoting resources to organizing. Sweeney argued against this policy of perpetual postponement. "We'll organize now without the law, so that we can later organize under the law."[14] In many cases, SEIU organizers had avoided the snares and delays of NLRB elections, persuading employers—with demonstrations and community pressure—to accept third-party monitoring of alternative, expedited procedures for confirming the union's majority support. Sweeney proposed more of the same for the AFL-CIO as a whole, and in this he also followed in the footsteps of Lewis and early CIO organizers, who had plunged ahead with organizing long before the Supreme Court validated the Wagner Act.

Sweeney's sense of urgency was well placed, for not only was the percentage of union members at its lowest level since the early 1930s, but management was now reorganizing the workplace on new principles that challenged the union's very claim to speak for workers. In a wide range of industries, from manufacturing to communications and services, employers in the 1980s and 1990s were preaching the virtues of "employee involvement" and teamwork in fashioning a new, more responsive workplace. Unions might once have been a necessary counterweight to dictatorial managers schooled in the style of Frederick Taylor, but this would no longer be the case according to industry leaders. Instead of the narrowly specialized jobs, repetitive tasks, and top-down bureaucracy of old-style mass production, the new principles of "lean production" promised to empower workers who participated in quality circles and work teams, giving them the latitude to rotate jobs, improve the work process, and take responsibility for quality. According to managers and consultants who promoted the new approach, workers who enjoyed such control over their work environment would hardly need a union, or if already unionized, would not need an adversarial union. Modern managers, so the argument went, now had compelling reasons to pursue a cooperative approach, since heightened competition, quality-conscious customers, and new computer-based technologies all demanded a workforce that was more flexible, better trained, and more committed.

This "empowerment" strategy for business success found many advocates in government and academic circles, and some support among business leaders in industries where new products and new technologies required innovation and experimental thinking. Even here, union advocates claimed a positive role for collective bargaining, since companies that solicited worker participation in decision making often found that union members were more forthcoming. A union worker could criticize supervisory abuse or poor planning and still be protected by the collective bargaining agreement, whereas nonunion workers were more vulnerable to reprisal if a supervisor resented their "meddling." The case for union protection also rested on the claim that once innovation settled into volume production, the previous latitude given technicians and workers often gave way to hard-nosed cost cutting and work standardization. Where managers still favored cooperative approaches, there remained the inevitable conflicts over wages, benefits, and other conditions of work that divided owners and workers. From this perspective, companies trying to maximize profitability would—sooner or later—begin cutting training budgets, downsizing work teams, and intensifying the work pace, forcing the remaining workers to "self-manage" their own speedup. Without a union, employee involvement meant responsibility without authority—a formula for stress rather than empowerment in the eyes of union advocates.

Even so, the very promise of empowerment could be a potent antidote to union organizing, and nonunion companies that installed "action committees" or quality circles often found they could use these management-created forums to counter the union's appeal. Union organizers, on the other hand, saw such committees as little different from the company unions of the 1930s, imposing a top-down agenda on how workers represented their needs to the employer. In 1992–1993, NLRB members (the majority Republican appointees) supported the union position in two landmark cases against Electromation Corporation and Dupont, ruling that employee involvement committees that addressed the terms and conditions of employment were lawful if such programs were negotiated with a union, but were violations of the Wagner Act if imposed by management and used to circumvent genuine worker representation. In the case of Electromation, the NLRB found that the company's Action Committees were management dominated because "employees were not given any real choice in the committee's formation" and because "the employer . . . defined and limited the subject matter to be covered . . . , determined the committees' composition, and appointed management representatives to the committees." The ruling prompted bitter denunciations by business leaders and eventually led to proposed legislation, "The Team Act," that would amend the NLRA to permit such management initiatives. Vetoed by President Clinton in 1996, the proposal highlighted the dramatically shifting terrain of labor-management relations at the end of the twentieth century. The very definition of a "worker" was in dispute, with managers claiming that a growing proportion of employees were exercising sufficient discretion and responsibility in their work to qualify as management personnel—and therefore exempt (under Taft-Hartley) from the protections of the National Labor Relations Act.

Unions would have to fashion entirely new legal and organizational strategies to counter these arguments and win the support of white-collar professionals and technicians. Although doctors, lawyers, engineers, and scientists generally aspired to a professional autonomy that appeared incompatible with union solidarity, a growing number found themselves working for healthcare bureaucracies, corporations, or public agencies that constrained both their professional latitude and their income. If they were to follow the lead of teachers, nurses, reporters, actors, and other professionals that had turned to unions for protection, there would have to be a variety of organizational forms to accommodate their unique circumstances. Particularly in professions where individual performance determined pay, collective bargaining would not likely focus on fixed salaries but on minimum standards that would raise the starting point for individual negotiations, as in unions for actors, professional athletes, and university professors. In turn, altogether different union structures and bargaining agendas would have to be developed for the rapidly growing number of temporary workers and contingent employees, since they lacked even a stable workplace around which to organize.

TURNING POINTS

Considering the many challenges confronting unions—from the competition of low-wage imports to the ever-widening frontiers of technological and occupational change—there were ample grounds for predicting the labor movement's final dissolution. As with previous downturns in the history of labor, there were also grounds for hope that a new movement would emerge from the setbacks of the late twentieth century. Each of these contending claims, of labor's demise or resurgence, could find supporting evidence in "turning points" that seemed to augur doom or salvation.

Sometimes the same events offered evidence for both predictions. At Firestone tire, for example, pessimism and hope alternated in rapid succession in the 1980s and 1990s as the company went through a series of wrenching transformations. When Japan's Bridgestone tire company bought Firestone's U.S. plants in 1988, the change in ownership seemed to herald a welcome turnaround from the adversarial relations that had long prevailed between Firestone and the United Rubber Workers (URW). Bridgestone managers signaled a new approach with a dramatic restructuring of the company's production system and labor relations, centered on the use of cross-trained workers, "self-managed" work teams, reduced supervision, and a "Partnership for Involvement" with the URW. Higher productivity, better quality, and improved labor relations were the first reported fruits of these changes. A major academic study with the evocative title *Beyond Mass Production* highlighted Bridgestone-Firestone in 1993 as a company moving toward a new system of "innovation-mediated production," in which "the factory itself becomes a laboratory like setting" for the "synthesis of intellectual and manual labor."[15]

These optimistic claims were rudely deflated, however, when the government leveled record fines in 1994 of $7.4 million against Bridgestone's Oklahoma plant for "willful" safety violations that produced amputated fingers, mangled arms, and at least one preventable death. The same year, Bridgestone management demanded that URW workers accept mandatory twelve-hour shifts, 30 percent lower pay for new hires, cuts in healthcare benefits, fewer holidays, elimination of seniority rights for job and shift assignments, and other concessions. Rather than accept these harsh terms, the URW called a strike in July 1994 at five Bridgestone-Firestone plants; ten months later, however, the union called off the strike when the company began to permanently replace its former "Partners for Involvement." Bankrupted by the failed strike and unable to mount further resistance, the URW's remaining members voted to merge with the United Steel Workers (USW) in 1995, ending the rubber union's sixty-year history with a demoralizing defeat.

In yet another turnaround, however, the USW managed to salvage a partial victory from this apparently irreversible failure. Unable to risk further strike action, the USW launched a simultaneous campaign of workplace mobilizations and public demonstrations. Inside the plants, union members—many wearing buttons saying, "Working under Protest"— refused to work overtime, boycotted employee involvement programs, and followed safety and work rules to the letter, avoiding the shortcuts some managers had previously urged workers to take. Outside the plant, USW members and supporters leafleted customers at hundreds of Bridgestone-Firestone tire stores, urging a consumer boycott. Demonstrations at the Democratic National convention and the Indianapolis 500 drew public attention to the dispute, and international support widened the struggle to twenty-six countries where demonstrations, work stoppages, and slowdowns harried Bridgestone's worldwide operations. After eighteen months, the combined effect of these militant tactics and the prospect of NLRB fines for the company's unfair labor practices persuaded company managers to accept a compromise settlement. Most of the concession demands were withdrawn, though twelve-hour shifts remained in force.

The USW's moral victory at Bridgestone-Firestone seemed to validate the emphasis that many reformers put on new grassroots strategies for mobilizing union members and organizing nonunion workers. Many took the SEIU's "Justice for Janitors" campaign in the late 1980s and early 1990s as the exemplar of these new approaches. After office-building owners had replaced unionized janitors with low-wage, nonunion contractors, SEIU countered with frequent demonstrations, political outreach, and civil disobedience to revitalize a declining membership and regain much of the lost ground. Instead of reorganizing building-by-building, SEIU built citywide movements that targeted big contractors and office complexes, overcoming the isolation and fear of reprisal that hindered single-site organizing drives. The first contracts the union won also gave incentive for both employers and workers to support continued organizing by postponing the move to union standards until 50 percent of the market was organized. The union's innovative and combative tactics proved effective in a variety of circumstances, including Chicago, with an older workforce and a more traditional local; Milwaukee, where the workforce was predominantly African-American; and Los Angeles, where Mexican and Central American immigrants conducted a spirited campaign in the face of police attacks. Victory in the Los Angeles campaign seemed to demonstrate once again the lessons of Lawrence in

1912: that immigrant workers exploited for their poverty and their vulnerability could still organize on their own behalf when given the opportunity and the support of union organization.

If SEIU's Justice-for-Janitors campaign was a turning point for labor, foretelling a renewed capacity to mobilize low-wage service workers and immigrants, it was also an uneven and equivocal marker of labor's capacity for change. While SEIU was organizing thousands of janitors in Los Angeles, the same union was losing members in New York City, where SEIU's local 32B-32J fell from seventy thousand to fifty-five thousand building-service workers in the late 1990s. Even as the local signed a new collective bargaining agreement in 1996 creating a lower second-tier wage for new hires, the local's president was busy amassing a small fortune—$500,000 from multiple union salaries, a Manhattan penthouse, a Long Island estate, and a $1.5 million retirement bonus. After charging that local staff were colluding with building superintendents in a job-selling racket, dissident union members reported being trailed and harassed by private detectives hired by the union. In 1999, SEIU's national leaders finally stepped in and suspended the local's top thirty-eight officers, vowing to clean up the local and commit its resources to organizing. Shortly afterward, the local president announced his resignation. Although these changes were widely applauded, it was also evident that the SEIU's top leaders had long tolerated the brazen corruption of union principles in Local 32B-32J.

For every turning point that promised renewal, there seemed to be contrary evidence of the labor movement's continued malaise. In 1997, the Teamsters won widespread public support—by 2–1 margins in opinion surveys—for a national strike of United Parcel Service, ultimately forcing the company to agree that thousands of part-time workers would eventually be promoted to full-time positions. The union had no money in its strike fund to support a national walkout, but after months of pre-strike mobilizations through job-site surveys, petitions, and parking-lot rallies, little more than 1 percent of the Teamster's 185,000 UPS members crossed the picket lines—a notable achievement in its own right. Immediately on the heels of this victory, however, it was revealed that Teamster president Ron Carey, a reformer who had reduced his own salary and purged corrupt local leaders after his election in 1991, had allowed outside consultants to illegally divert union money to his 1996 reelection campaign. Carey's removal from office cast doubt on how thoroughly a once corrupt union could shed its old ways and democratize its internal affairs.

THE NEXT CENTURY

At the close of the 1990s it was hard to know which events augured gen-uine turning points—marking union renewal or quickening decline—and which were false starts. With the labor movement at a historic crossroads, it remained for future generations to assess, with the aid of hindsight, which events at the close of the twentieth century heralded the dominant trends of the twenty-first.

Whatever the outcome, it was evident that labor's revival or demise would be decided on an international scale. In this regard, the history of the 1930s was only a partial guide. In that decade of union revival and growth, worker solidarity had widened to include the less skilled as well as skilled, black as well as white, women as well as men, ethnic as well as Anglo-American. But this revival occurred in an era when immigration was declining and the economy was still predominantly national in scope. Seventy years later neither of those conditions still held. Employ-ers in the year 2000 were operating on a world stage, moving manufac-turing jobs across borders and around the globe: to Indonesia, where Nike made footwear; to China, where Wal-Mart made clothing; to Mex-ico, where General Motors made cars, trucks, and auto parts. In these and other countries where government policy weakened or suppressed unions, workers labored long hours for $12.00 a day, or less. Although their underpaid toil produced goods that few of these workers could afford to buy, the same products were fetching top dollar as exports to the United States. Even data processing and engineering work could be sent around the world, beamed by satellite to low-cost workers in the Philippines or India. For service jobs that could not be moved—in health-care, food service, hotel and janitorial services—low-wage labor could be drawn from an ever-widening stream of global job seekers, many of them undocumented immigrants desperate for work and vulnerable to depor-tation.

For U.S. unions, this global labor market posed a difficult dilemma. By condemning corporate globetrotting in search of the lowest possible wages and working conditions, unions could win significant public sup-port. The labor movement's grassroots campaign to defeat NAFTA in 1993 was a case in point. By drawing attention to the exploitation of Mexican workers and the prospect of job losses for U.S. workers, unions had nearly derailed the once-certain passage of this program for eliminating tariffs and protecting corporate investment. A growing constituency now saw free trade as a "race to the bottom," pitting U.S. workers against underpaid competitors, and it was the mobilization of this widely shared sentiment that later blocked extension of NAFTA to South America in the late 1990s. On the other hand, conservatives could also tap into this sentiment by calling for protective tariffs or the summary expulsion of undocumented immigrants. Either measure vilified the victims—the foreign and immigrant workers who took these jobs out of desperation—and precluded a wider solidarity with workers confronting the same transnational corporations. Union advocacy of cross-border solidarity was more convincing when posed in terms of fair trade rather than free trade, with the emphasis on labor standards that would restrict imports in cases where employers used child labor or denied workers the right to organize. Such a program of international solidarity was difficult to implement, however, given the wide disparities in living conditions, the diverse cultures, and the different languages that separated workers in North America, much less the world.

Yet some of these differences could produce unexpected strengths. Among Latino immigrants taking low-wage service jobs in the United States, union organizers often reported a high level of class consciousness, particularly among those with experience in political and union struggles in their own land. "There, you were in a union, they killed you," said one SEIU organizer of Central American workers who had come to Los Angeles. That experience made these workers all the bolder when it came to the risks of being fired for union organizing in the United States—because "here, you [only] lost a job at $4.25."[16]

On the other side of the border, U.S. trade unionists also found they could pursue new alliances if, rather than calling for the "return of U.S. jobs," they called instead for U.S. corporations to respect worker rights and pay wages that allowed people to buy what they made—instead of exporting it to the United States. Steps toward such an approach quickened in 1998, when AFL-CIO president John Sweeney traveled to Mexico (the first visit by a U.S. labor leader since John L. Lewis in 1938) and spoke with unionists from a wide range of organizations. "We want to work with our brothers and sisters in all parts of the Mexican labor movement and with freedom lovers throughout Mexican society," Sweeney said in his speech at the National Autonomous University of Mexico. The immediate need, Sweeney stressed, was to "find practical ways to work together by seeking and developing coordinated cross-border organizing and bargaining strategies."[17]

If developing these strategies was a paramount challenge for the labor movement at the start of the new century, it was equally evident that implementing such approaches would depend on a new generation of activists and leaders. It was in this respect that the prospects for union renewal appeared more promising in the 1990s than at any time since the 1970s. University and college teach-ins organized by the AFL-CIO and sympathetic professors on a wide range of campuses in 1996–1997 exposed students, intellectuals, and union activists to debate about the future of work and workers and what was to be done about both. In the closing years of the decade, this emerging student activism blossomed into campus Anti-Sweat Shop campaigns, often in alliance with "UNITE"—the Union of Needletrades, Industrial and Textile Employees, formed by the merger of the Amalgamated Clothing Workers and the ILGWU. Thousands of student activists also found a direct link to the labor movement through organizing drives among graduate teaching assistants, or in "Union Summer" projects assisting off-campus organizing drives, consumer boycotts, or voter registration.

If unions were to enlist the next generation of activists for the long haul, these beginnings would have to be followed by a fundamental reorientation of goals and vision, one that matched the evident changes in the workplace. "The new faces of the workforce belong mainly to people of color and women," as Kamu Marcharia, deputy director of the AFL-CIO's Union Summer project, observed in a 1998 forum. These young people "feel a spiritual drain and are on a quest for a sense of self-worth and a place to make a fight to uplift humanity. Unions could be the place to meet those needs, but not unless they take on issues of concern to communities of color."[18] Youthful activism also needed a year-round outlet, not just a summer fling. "Let's face it, we've got a problem!" Amy Newell, former secretary treasurer of the United Electrical workers, warned at the same forum. "Decades of business unionism, when members weren't expected, or even allowed, to do much except pay their dues, have taken a toll. A culture of passivity developed that few at the top were interested in upsetting."[19]

Here, perhaps, was the crucial issue facing the labor movement at the start of the new millennium. Herman Benson, a former union organizer and director over many years of the Association for Union Democracy, framed it succinctly in remarks welcoming the initiatives of John Sweeney and the AFL-CIO's new leaders, but calling for further reforms to democratize the federation's unions. "Before the labor movement can effectively spread the message of freedom and social justice to the nation," he observed in the closing year of the twentieth century, "it must renew that same spirit within its own ranks and convince its own members that this great movement belongs to them."[20]

In this, the unfinished struggle for workplace justice has always presented the same challenge, now as in 1877 and 1937. With the ever-widening reach of market competition and corporate organization, individual striving invariably confronts repression as well as opportunity, disappointment as well as fulfillment. On this uncertain terrain, union renewal will depend on the degree to which workers see the labor movement as *their* means for securing prosperity on a socially equitable basis.

SUGGESTED READING

American Social History Project. *Who Built America? Working People and the Nation's Economy, Politics, Culture & Society.* Vol. 2, *From the Gilded Age to the Present.* New York: Pantheon, 1992.

Auerbach, Jerold. *Labor and Liberty: The La Follette Committee and the New Deal.* New York: Bobbs-Merrill, 1966.

Babson, Steve. *Building the Union: Skilled Workers and Anglo-Gaelic Immigrants in the Rise of the UAW.* New Brunswick, N.J.: Rutgers University Press, 1991.

Bernstein, Irving. *The Turbulent Years: A History of the American Worker, 1933–1941.* Boston: Houghton Mifflin, 1970.

Brecher, Jeremy. *Strike!* San Francisco: Straight Arrow Books, 1972.

Brody, David. *Labor in Crisis: The Steel Strike of 1919.* Urbana: University of Illinois Press, 1987.

Caute, David. *The Great Fear: The Anti-Communist Purge under Truman and Eisenhower.* New York: Simon and Schuster, 1978.

Clark, Paul F., Peter Gottlieb, and Donald Kennedy, editors. *Forging a Union of Steel: Philip Murray, SWOC, and the United Steelworkers.* Ithaca, N.Y.: ILR Press, 1987.

Draper, Alan. *Conflict of Interests: Organized Labor and the Civil Rights Movement in the South, 1954–1968.* Ithaca, N.Y.: ILR Press, 1994.

Dubofsky, Melvyn, and Warren Van Tine. *John L. Lewis: A Biography.* Urbana: University of Illinois Press, 1986.

Fantasia, Rick. *Cultures of Solidarity: Consciousness, Action, and Contemporary American Workers.* Berkeley: University of California Press, 1988.

Faue, Elizabeth. *Community of Suffering & Struggle: Women, Men, and the Labor Movement in Minneapolis, 1915–1945.* Chapel Hill: University of North Carolina Press, 1991.

Filipelli, Ronald L., and Mark D. McColloch. *Cold War in the Working Class: The Rise and Decline of the United Electrical Workers*. Albany: The State University of New York Press, 1995.

Fine, Sidney. *Sit-Down: The General Motors Strike of 1936–1937*. Ann Arbor: The University of Michigan Press, 1969.

Foner, Philip. *The Great Labor Uprising of 1877*. New York: Monad Press, 1977.

Fraser, Steven. *Labor Will Rule: Sidney Hillman and the Rise of American Labor*. New York: The Free Press, 1991.

Freeman, Joshua B. *In Transit: The Transport Workers Union in New York City, 1933–1966*. New York: Oxford University Press, 1989.

Goldfield, Michael. *The Color of Politics: Race and the Mainsprings of American Politics*. New York: The New Press, 1997.

Gould, William B. *Black Workers and White Unions: Job Discrimination in the Unites States*. Ithaca, N.Y.: Cornell University Press, 1977.

Griffith, Barbara S. *The Crisis of Organized Labor: Operation Dixie and the Defeat of the CIO*. Philadelphia: Temple University Press, 1988.

Gutman, Herbert G. *Work, Culture, and Society in Industrializing America*. New York: Vintage Books, 1977 (1966).

Harris, H. William. *Keeping the Faith: A. Philip Randolph, Milton P. Webster, and the Brotherhood of Sleeping Car Porters, 1925–37*. Urbana: University of Illinois Press, 1991 (1977).

Harris, Howell John. *The Right to Manage: Industrial Relations Policies of American Business in the 1940s*. Madison: University of Wisconsin Press, 1982.

Horowitz, Roger. *"Negro and White, Unite and Fight!" A Social History of Industrial Unionism in Meatpacking*. Urbana: University of Illinois Press, 1997.

Jacoby, Sanford M. *Employing Bureaucracy: Managers, Unions, and the Transformation of Work in American Industry, 1900–1945*. New York: Columbia University Press, 1985.

Kessler-Harris, Alice. *Out to Work: A History of Wage-Earning Women in the United States*. Oxford: Oxford University Press, 1982.

Kochan, Thomas, Harry Katz, and Robert McKersie. *The Transformation of American Industrial Relations*. Ithaca, N.Y.: ILR Press, 1994.

Larrowe, Charles. *Harry Bridges: The Rise and Fall of Radical Labor in the U.S.* New York: Lawrence Hill and Co., 1972.

Leab, Daniel J. *The Labor History Reader*. Urbana: University of Illinois Press, 1985.

Levitt, Martin J., with Terry Conrow. *Confessions of a Union Buster*. New York: Crown Publishers, 1993.

Lichtenstein, Nelson. *The Most Dangerous Man in Detroit: Walter Reuther and the Fate of American Labor*. New York: Basic Books, 1995.

Lynd, Staughton, editor. *"We Are All Leaders." The Alternative Unionism of the Early 1930s.* Urbana: University of Illinois Press, 1996.

Milkman, Ruth. *Farewell to the Factory: Autoworkers in the Late Twentieth Century.* Berkeley: University of California Press, 1997.

Montgomery, David. *The Fall of the House of Labor: The Workplace, the State, and American Labor Activism, 1865–1925.* Cambridge: Cambridge University Press, 1987.

Mort, Jo-Ann, editor. *Not Your Father's Union Movement: Inside the AFL-CIO.* New York: Verso Books, 1998.

Nadworny, Milton J. *Scientific Management and the Unions, 1900–1932. A Historical Analysis.* Cambridge, Mass.: Harvard University Press, 1955.

Salvatore, Nick. *Eugene V. Debs: Citizen and Socialist.* Urbana: University of Illinois Press, 1982.

Santino, Jack. *Miles of Smiles, Years of Struggle. Stories of Black Pullman Porters.* Urbana: University of Illinois Press, 1989.

Schatz, Ronald W. *The Electrical Workers: A History of Labor at General Electric and Westinghouse, 1923–60.* Urbana: University of Illinois Press, 1983.

Sexton, Patricia Cayo. *The War on Labor and the Left: Understanding America's Unique Conservatism.* Boulder, Colo.: Westview Press, 1991.

Strum, Philippa. *Louis D. Brandeis, Justice for the People.* New York: Schocken Books, 1984.

Tentler, Leslie. *Wage Earning Women: Industrial Work and Family Life in the United States, 1900–1930.* New York: Oxford University Press, 1978.

Tillman, Ray M., and Michael S. Cummings, editors. *The Transformation of U.S. Unions: Voices, Visions, and Strategies from the Grassroots.* Boulder, Colo.: Lynne Rienner Publishers, 1999.

Tomlins, Christopher L. *The State and the Unions: Labor Relations, Law, and the Organized Labor Movement in America, 1880–1960.* London: Cambridge University Press, 1985.

Watkins, T. H. *The Great Depression: America in the 1930s.* Boston: Little, Brown & Company, 1993.

Weinstein, James. *The Decline of Socialism in America, 1912–1925.* New York: Vintage Books, 1967.

Zieger, Robert H. *The CIO, 1935–1955.* Chapel Hill: University of North Carolina Press, 1995.

NOTES

INTRODUCTION

1. George Barnett, *Presidential Address,* American Economics Association, December 29, 1932.

CHAPTER 1

1. *Pittsburgh Sunday Globe,* quoted in Philip Foner, *The Great Labor Uprising of 1877* (New York: Monad Press, 1977), 63.

2. Robert Bruce, *1877: Year of Violence* (Chicago: Ivan R. Dee, 1989 [1959]), 161.

3. Bruce, *1877,* 160.

4. Foner, *The Great Labor Uprising,* 230.

5. Matthew Josephson, *The Robber Barons: The Great American Capitalists, 1861-1901* (New York: Harcourt Brace Jovanovich, 1964 [1934]), 316.

6. *Pittsburgh Critic,* quoted in Foner, *The Great Labor Uprising,* 103.

7. American Social History Project, *Who Built America? Working People and the Nation's Economy, Politics, Culture & Society,* Vol. 1 (New York: Pantheon Books, 1989), 530.

8. Josephson, The Robber Barons, 325.

9. Josephson, *The Robber Barons*, 374.

10. John Garraty, *The American Nation: A History of the United States since 1865*, Vol. 2 (New York: Harper & Row, 1966), 460.

11. Garraty, *The American Nation*, 482.

12. Josephson, *The Robber Barons*, 364–365.

13. David Montgomery, *The Fall of the House of Labor: The Workplace, the State, and American Labor Activism, 1865–1925* (Cambridge: Cambridge University Press, 1987), 60.

14. Nick Salvatore, *Eugene V. Debs: Citizen and Socialist* (Urbana: University of Illinois, 1982), 103–104.

15. Salvatore, *Eugene V. Debs*, 137.

16. Charles Beard and Mary Beard, *New Basic History of the United States* (Garden City, N.J.: Doubleday and Company, 1960 [1944]), 379.

17. Steven Fraser, *Labor Will Rule: Sidney Hillman and the Rise of American Labor* (New York: The Free Press, 1991), 42.

18. Norman Ware, *The Labor Movement in the United States, 1860–1890* (New York: Vintage Books, 1964 [1929]), xv–xvi.

19. Richard Oestreicher, *Solidarity and Fragmentation: Working People and Class Consciousness in Detroit, 1875–1900* (Urbana: University of Illinois Press, 1986), 228.

20. Herbert Gutman, *Work, Culture, and Society in Industrializing America* (New York: Vintage Books, 1977 [1966]), 135.

21. Garraty, *The American Nation*, 427.

22. Gutman, *Work, Culture, and Society*, 132.

23. Gutman, *Work, Culture, and Society*, 198.

CHAPTER 2

1. Steven Fraser, *Labor Will Rule: Sidney Hillman and the Rise of American Labor* (New York: The Free Press, 1991), 50.

2. Fraser, *Labor Will Rule*, 46.

3. *Chicago Daily Socialist*, in Fraser, *Labor Will Rule*, 52.

4. Fraser, *Labor Will Rule*, 47.

5. Fraser, *Labor Will Rule*, 61.

6. James Weinstein, *The Corporate Ideal in the Liberal State: 1900–1918* (Boston: Beacon Press, 1968), 17.

7. James Weinstein, *The Decline of Socialism in America, 1912–1925* (New York: Vintage, 1967), 20–21.

8. Weinstein, *The Decline of Socialism,* 71.

9. Weinstein, *The Corporate Ideal,* 17.

10. Weinstein, *The Corporate Ideal,* 17.

11. Weinstein, *The Corporate Ideal,* 11.

12. Weinstein, *The Corporate Ideal,* 87.

13. Weinstein, *The Corporate Ideal,* 9.

14. Harry Braverman, *Labor and Monopoly Capital: The Degradation of Work in the Twentieth Century* (New York: Monthly Review, 1974), 102, 113, 118.

15. David Gartman, *Auto Slavery: The Labor Process in the American Automobile Industry, 1897–1950* (New Brunswick, N.J.: Rutgers University Press, 1986), 148–149.

16. Steve Babson, *Building the Union: Skilled Workers and Anglo-Gaelic Immigrants in the Rise of the UAW* (New Brunswick, N.J.: Rutgers University Press, 1991), 25.

17. David Hounshell, *From the American System to Mass Production, 1800–1932* (Baltimore: The Johns Hopkins University Press, 1984), 6.

18. David Montgomery, *The Fall of the House of Labor: The Workplace, the State, and American Labor Activism, 1865–1925* (Cambridge: Cambridge University Press, 1987), 251.

19. Philippa Strum, *Louis D. Brandeis, Justice for the People* (New York: Schocken Books, 1984), 162.

20. Strum, *Louis D. Brandeis,* 162.

21. Milton Nadworny, *Scientific Management and the Unions, 1900–1932. A Historical Analysis* (Cambridge: Harvard University Press, 1955), 21–22, 76–79.

22. Alfred Chandler, "Mass Production and the Beginnings of Scientific Management," Harvard Business School, Case Study 9-377-223, 1977, 12.

23. Strum, *Louis D. Brandeis,* 167.

24. Gartman, *Auto Slavery,* 94.

25. U.S. Commissioner of Labor, "Regulation and Restriction of Output," *Eleventh Special Report* (Washington, D.C.: U.S. Government Printing Office, 1904), 108.

26. Nadworny, *Scientific Management and the Unions,* 70–71.

27. Steve Babson, with Ron Alpern, David Elsila, and John Revitte, *Working Detroit: The Making of a Union Town* (Detroit: Wayne State University Press, 1986), 32.

28. *Iron Age* in Montgomery, *The Fall of the House of Labor*, 240.

29. William Cahn, *Lawrence 1912: The Bread and Roses Strike* (New York: The Pilgrim Press, 1977), 76.

30. Montgomery, *The Fall of the House of Labor*, 311.

31. Cahn, *Lawrence 1912*, 114.

32. Cahn, *Lawrence 1912*, 216.

33. Cahn, *Lawrence 1912*, 132.

34. Philip Foner, *History of the Labor Movement in the United States*, Vol. IV (New York: International Publishers, 1965), 350.

35. Montgomery, *The Fall of the House of Labor*, 358.

36. Montgomery, *The Fall of the House of Labor*, 358.

37. David Brody, *Labor in Crisis: The Steel Strike of 1919* (Urbana: University of Illinois Press, 1987), 86.

38. Brody, *Labor in Crisis*, 112.

39. Brody, *Labor in Crisis*, 123.

40. Brody, *Labor in Crisis*, 122.

41. Brody, *Labor in Crisis*, 174.

42. Brody, *Labor in Crisis*, 149.

43. Robert Murray, *Red Scare: A Study in National Hysteria, 1919–1920* (New York: McGraw-Hill, 1964 [1955]), 219.

44. Weinstein, *The Decline of Socialism*, 235.

45. Murray, *Red Scare*, 265.

46. John Garraty, *The American Nation: A History of the United States since 1865*, Vol. 2 (New York: Harper & Row, 1966), 640.

47. Brody, *Labor in Crisis*, 79.

48. Brody, *Labor in Crisis*, 79.

49. Stuart Ewen, *Captains of Consciousness: Advertising and the Social Roots of Consumer Culture* (New York: McGraw Hill, 1976), 64.

50. Jack Santino, *Miles of Smiles, Years of Struggle. Stories of Black Pullman Porters* (Urbana: University of Illinois Press, 1989), 8, 30.

51. Santino, *Miles of Smiles*, 48.

52. Santino, *Miles of Smiles*, 43.

53. Santino, *Miles of Smiles*, 35.

54. *Nation's Business* in David Brody, *Workers in Industrial America: Essays on the Twentieth Century Struggle* (New York: Oxford University Press, 1980), 48.

55. Brody, *Workers in Industrial America*, 61.

CHAPTER 3

1. Irving Bernstein, *The Lean Years: A History of the American Worker, 1920–1933* (Boston: Houghton Mifflin, 1960), 435.

2. John Kenneth Galbraith, *The Great Crash, 1929* (Boston: Houghton Mifflin, 1988 [1954]), 145.

3. Bernstein, *The Lean Years,* 294.

4. Bernstein, *The Lean Years,* 294.

5. Maurice Sugar, *The Ford Hunger March* (Berkeley: Meiklejohn Civil Liberties Union, 1980), 25.

6. Studs Terkel, *Hard Times: An Oral History of the Great Depression* (New York: Pantheon Books, 1986 [1970]), 5.

7. Bernstein, *The Lean Years,* 257.

8. Sugar, *The Ford Hunger March,* 102.

9. David Brody, *Workers in Industrial America: Essays on the Twentieth Century Struggle* (New York: Oxford University Press, 1980), 73.

10. Sugar, *The Ford Hunger March,* 102.

11. American Social History Project, *Who Built America? Working People and the Nation's Economy, Politics, Culture & Society,* Vol. 2 (New York: Pantheon Books, 1992), 335.

12. Sugar, *The Ford Hunger March,* 30.

13. Elizabeth Faue, *Community of Suffering & Struggle: Women, Men, and the Labor Movement in Minneapolis, 1915–1945* (Chapel Hill: University of North Carolina Press, 1991), 65.

14. Steve Babson, *Building the Union: Skilled Workers and Anglo-Gaelic Immigrants in the Rise of the UAW* (New Brunswick, N.J.: Rutgers University Press, 1991), 103–104.

15. T. H. Watkins, *The Great Depression: America in the 1930s* (Boston: Little, Brown & Company, 1993), 123.

16. Ronald Schatz, *The Electrical Workers: A History of Labor at General Electric and Westinghouse, 1923–60* (Urbana: University of Illinois Press, 1983), 60–61.

17. Brody, *Workers in Industrial America,* 77.

18. Thomas Klug, "Labor Market Politics in Detroit: The Curious Case of the 'Spolansky Act' of 1932," *Michigan Historical Review* 14 (Spring 1988), 5.

19. Bernstein, *The Lean Years,* 349.

20. American Social History Project, *Who Built America?,* 340.

21. *United Action* in Faue, *Community of Suffering & Struggle,* 63.

22. Steve Babson, with Ron Alpern, David Elsila, and John Revitte, *Working Detroit: The Making of a Union Town* (Detroit: Wayne State University Press, 1986), 57.

23. Babson et al., *Working Detroit,* 57.

24. *Detroit Times* in Babson et al., *Working Detroit,* 54–55.

25. *New York Times* in American Social History Project, *Who Built America?* 340.

26. Bernstein, *The Lean Years,* 378.

27. Roy Rosenzweig, "'Socialism in Our Time': The Socialist Party and the Unemployed," *Labor History* 20 (Fall 1979), 494.

28. Rosemary Feurer, "The Nutpickers' Union, 1933–34," in Staughton Lynd, ed., *"We Are All Leaders." The Alternative Unionism of the Early 1930s* (Urbana: University of Illnois Press, 1996), 30.

29. Judith Stearn-Norris and Maurice Zeitlin, *Talking Union* (Urbana: University of Illinois Press, 1996), 45.

30. Wyndham Mortimer, *Organize! My Life as a Union Man* (Boston: Beacon Press, 1971), 52.

31. Mark Naison, *Communists in Harlem during the Depression* (New York: Grove Press, 1983), 78.

32. Naison, *Communists in Harlem,* 36–37.

33. Naison, *Communists in Harlem,* 36, 38.

34. *Amsterdam News* in Naison, *Communists in Harlem,* 64–65.

35. Rosenzweig, "'Socialism in Our Time,'" 497–498.

36. American Social History Project, *Who Built America?* 345.

37. Watkins, *The Great Depression,* 106.

38. Babson et al., *Working Detroit,* 60.

39. American Social History Project, *Who Built America?,* 345.

40. Arthur Schlesinger Jr., *The Coming of the New Deal* (Boston: Houghton Mifflin, 1958), 5.

41. Bernstein, *The Lean Years,* 263.

42. Christopher Tomlins, *The State and the Unions: Labor Relations, Law, and the Organized Labor Movement in America, 1880–1960* (London: Cambridge University Press, 1985), 100.

43. Steven Fraser, *Labor Will Rule: Sidney Hillman and the Rise of American Labor* (New York: The Free Press, 1991), 261.

44. Schlesinger, *The Coming of the New Deal,* 97.

45. Irving Bernstein, *The Turbulent Years: A History of the Amercan Worker, 1933–1941* (Boston: Houghton Mifflin, 1970), 35.

46. Fraser, *Labor Will Rule,* 290.

47. Melvyn Dubofsky and Warren Van Tine, *John L. Lewis: A Biography* (Urbana: University of Illinois Press, 1986), 143.

48. Bernstein, *The Turbulent Years,* 37.

49. Dubofsky and Van Tine, *John L. Lewis,* 138.

50. Robert Zieger, *Rebuilding the Pulp and Paper Workers' Union, 1933–1941* (Knoxville: University of Tennessee Press, 1984), 69.

51. Zieger, *Rebuilding the Pulp and Paper Workers' Union,* 69.

52. Bernstein, *The Turbulent Years,* 98.

53. Bernstein, *The Turbulent Years,* 93.

54. Winifred Wandersee, "'I'd Rather Pass a Law than Organize a Union': Francis Perkins and the Reformist Approach to Organized Labor," *Labor History* 34 (Spring 1993), 21.

55. Jerold Auerbach, *Labor and Liberty: The La Follette Committee and the New Deal* (New York: Bobbs-Merrill, 1966), 51.

56. Brody, *Workers in Industrial America,* 90.

57. Brody, *Workers in Industrial America,* 92.

58. Babson et al., *Working Detroit,* 65.

59. Warren Hinckle, *The Big Strike: A Pictorial History of the 1934 San Francisco General Strike* (Virginia City, Nev.: Silver Dollar Books, 1985), 16.

60. Bernstein, *The Turbulent Years,* 221.

61. Charles Walker, *American City: A Rank-and-File History* (New York: Arno, 1971), 109.

62. Walker, *American City,* 208.

63. Babson, *Building the Union,* 168.

64. Babson, *Building the Union,* 134.

65. Joshua Freeman, *In Transit: The Transport Workers Union in New York City, 1933–1966* (New York: Oxford University Press, 1989), 54.

66. Michael Kozura, "We Stood Our Ground: Anthracite Miners and the Expropriation of Corporate Property, 1930–1941," in Lynd, *"We Are All Leaders,"* 213.

67. Watkins, *The Great Depression,* 211.

68. Bernstein, *The Turbulent Years,* 299.

69. Janet Irons, "The Challenge of National Coordination: Southern Textile Workers and the General Textile Strike of 1934," in Lynd, *"We Are All Leaders,"* 78–79.

70. *New York Times* in Jeremy Brecher, *Strike!* (San Francisco: Straight Arrow Books, 1972), 169.

71. Irons, "The Challenge of National Coordination," 91–92.

72. Wandersee, "'I'd Rather Pass a Law,'" 21.

73. Barton Bernstein, "The New Deal: The Conservative Achievements of Liberal Reform," in Barton Bernstein, ed., *Towards a New Past: Dissenting Essays in American History* (New York: Pantheon Books, 1968), 274.

74. Auerbach, *Labor and Liberty*, 55.

75. Auerbach, *Labor and Liberty*, 56.

76. Bert Cochran, *Labor and Communism: The Conflict That Shaped American Unions* (Princeton: Princeton University Press, 1977), 104.

77. Cochran, *Labor and Communism*, 97.

78. Cochran, *Labor and Communism*, 75.

79. Babson, *Building the Union*, 116.

80. Auerbach, *Labor and Liberty*, 65.

81. Steve Jeffreys, *Management and Managed: Fifty Years of Crisis at Chrysler* (Cambridge: Cambridge University Press, 1986), 61.

82. James Matles and James Higgins, *Them and Us: Struggles of a Rank-and-File Union* (Englewood Cliffs, N.J.: Prentice-Hall, 1974), 64.

83. Matles and Higgins, *Them and Us*, 67.

84. Arthur Schlesinger Jr., *The Politics of Upheaval* (Boston: Houghton Mifflin, 1966), 329.

85. Schlesinger, *Politics of Upheaval*, 518.

86. Schlesinger, *Politics of Upheaval*, 502.

87. Schlesinger, *Politics of Upheaval*, 325–326.

88. James McGregor Burns, *Roosevelt: The Lion and the Fox* (New York: Harcourt, Brace & World, 1956), 235.

89. John Borsos, "Solidarity Unionism in Barberton, Ohio, 1933–41," in Lynd, *"We Are All Leaders,"* 274.

90. Cochran, *Labor and Communism*, 83.

91. Schlesinger, *The Politics of Upheaval*, 639.

92. Charles Larrowe, *Harry Bridges: The Rise and Fall of Radical Labor in the U.S.* (New York: Lawrence Hill and Co., 1972), 25–26.

93. Schlesinger, *The Politics of Upheaval*, 562.

94. Eric Leif Davin, "The Very Last Hurrah? The Defeat of the Labor Party Idea, 1934–1936," in Lynd, *"We Are All Leaders,"* 141.

95. Schlesinger, *Politics of Upheaval*, 593.

96. Davin, "The Very Last Hurrah?" 126.

97. Davin, "The Very Last Hurrah?" 131.

98. Barton Bernstein, "The New Deal," 279.

99. Sidney Fine, *Sit-Down: The General Motors Strike of 1936–1937* (Ann Arbor: The University of Michigan Press, 1969), 155.

100. Davin, "The Very Last Hurrah?" 139.

101. Fine, *Sit-Down*, 96.

102. Fine, *Sit-Down*, 57.

103. Fine, *Sit-Down*, 56, 59–61.

104. Brody, *Workers in Industrial America*, 105.

105. Fine, *Sit-Down*, 306.

106. Babson et al., *Working Detroit*, 76.

107. Babson et al., *Working Detroit*, 80.

108. Babson et al., *Working Detroit*, 82.

109. Babson et al., *Working Detroit*, 82.

110. H. William Harris, *Keeping the Faith: A. Philip Randolph, Milton P. Webster, and the Brotherhood of Sleeping Car Porters, 1925–37* (Urbana: University of Illinois Press, 1991 [1977]), 201.

111. Roger Horowitz *"Negro and White, Unite and Fight!" A Social History of Industrial Unionism in Meatpacking* (Urbana: University of Illinois Press, 1997), 33.

112. Brody, *Workers in Industrial America*, 97.

113. Horowitz, *"Negro and White,"* 75.

114. Fine, *Sit-Down*, 328.

115. *New York Times, Chicago Tribune, St. Louis Post-Dispatch* in Auerbach, *Labor and Liberty*, 122–123.

116. Babson, *Building the Union*, 223.

117. *Business Week* in Melvyn Dubofsky, *The State and Labor in Modern America* (Chapel Hill: University of North Carolina Press, 1994), 160.

118. Robert Zieger, *The CIO, 1935–1955* (Chapel Hill: University of North Carolina Press, 1995), 131.

119. Lynd, *"We Are All Leaders,"* 10.

120. Auerbach, *Labor and Liberty*, 27–28.

CHAPTER 4

1. Howell John Harris, *The Right to Manage: Industrial Relations Policies of American Business in the 1940s* (Madison: University of Wisconsin Press, 1982), 111.

2. Harris, *The Right to Manage*, 64–65.

3. Harris, *The Right to Manage*, 69.

4. Harris, *The Right to Manage*, 111.

5. Nelson Lichtenstein, *Labor's War at Home: The CIO in World War II* (New York: Cambridge University Press, 1982), 23.

6. Nelson Lichtenstein, *The Most Dangerous Man in Detroit: Walter Reuther and the Fate of American Labor* (New York: Basic Books, 1995), 149.

7. Lichtenstein, *The Most Dangerous Man*, 148.

8. Robert Zieger, *The CIO, 1935–1955* (Chapel Hill: University of North Carolina Press, 1995), 143.

9. Lichtenstein, *Labor's War at Home*, 78.

10. Harris, *The Right to Manage*, 53.

11. Joshua Freeman, "Delivering the Goods: Industrial Unionism during World War II," in Daniel Leab, ed., *The Labor History Reader* (Urbana: University of Illinois Press, 1985), 402–403.

12. Harris, *The Right to Manage*, 55.

13. Ronald Schatz, "Battling over Government's Role," in Paul Clark, Peter Gottleib, and Donald Kennedy, eds., *Forging a Union of Steel: Philip Murray, SWOC, and the United Steelworkers* (Ithaca, N.Y.: ILR Press, 1987), 93.

14. Melvyn Dubofsky, *The State and Labor in Modern America* (Chapel Hill: University of North Carolina Press, 1994), 188.

15. Harris, *The Right to Manage*, 87.

16. Harris, *The Right to Manage*, 71.

17. Morris Cooke and Philip Murray, *Organized Labor and Production: Next Steps in Industrial Democracy* (New York: Harper & Brothers, 1940), 261.

18. Cooke and Murray, *Organized Labor*, 261.

19. Cooke and Murray, *Organized Labor*, 221.

20. Harris, *The Right to Manage*, 182.

21. Harris, *The Right to Manage*, 51.

22. Harris, *The Right to Manage*, 71.

23. Lichtenstein, *The Most Dangerous Man*, 235.

24. Lichtenstein, *The Most Dangerous Man*, 230.

25. Lichtenstein, *The Most Dangerous Man*, 230.

26. Steven Fraser, *Labor Will Rule: Sidney Hillman and the Rise of American Labor* (New York: The Free Press, 1991), 503.

27. Zieger, *The CIO*, 250.

28. Zieger, *The CIO*, 179.

29. Zieger, *The CIO*, 286.

30. Roger Keeran, *The Communist Party and the Auto Workers Unions* (Bloomington: Indiana University Press, 1980), 263.

31. Ronald Filipelli and Mark D. McColloch, *Cold War in the Working Class: The Rise and Decline of the United Electrical Workers*. (Albany: The State University of New York Press, 1995), 168.

32. David Caute, *The Great Fear: The Anti-Communist Purge under Truman and Eisenhower* (New York: Simon and Schuster, 1978), 168.

33. Caute, *The Great Fear,* 168.

34. Steve Babson, with Ron Alpern, David Elsila, and John Revitte, *Working Detroit: The Making of a Union Town* (Detroit: Wayne State University Press, 1986), 160.

35. Robert Korstad and Nelson Lichtenstein, "Opportunities Found and Lost: Labor, Radicals, and the Early Civil Rights Movement," *Journal of American History* 75 (December 1988), 798.

36. *Pittsburgh Courier* in Korstad and Lichtenstein, "Opportunities Found and Lost," 793.

37. Barbara Griffith, *The Crisis of Organized Labor: Operation Dixie and the Defeat of the CIO* (Philadelphia: Temple University Press, 1988), 95.

38. Griffith, *The Crisis of Organized Labor,* 38, 79, 72.

39. Alan Draper, *Conflict of Interests: Organized Labor and the Civil Rights Movement in the South 1954–1968* (Ithaca: ILR Press, 1994), 4.

40. Draper, *Conflict of Interests,* 154.

41. Draper, *Conflict of Interests,* 24.

42. William Gould, *Black Workers and White Unions: Job Discrimination in the United States* (Ithaca, N.Y.: Cornell University Press, 1977), 371–372.

43. Roger Horowitz, *"Negro and White, Unite and Fight!" A Social History of Industrial Unionism in Meatpacking* (Urbana: University of Illinois Press, 1997), 226.

44. Horowitz, *"Negro and White,"* 227.

45. Alice Kessler-Harris, *Out to Work: A History of Wage-Earning Women in the United States* (Oxford: Oxford University Press, 1982), 297.

46. Nancy Gabin, "Women Workers and the UAW in the Post–World War II Period: 1945–1954," in Leab, ed., *The Labor History Reader,* 413.

47. Horowitz, *"Negro and White,"* 229–230.

48. Horowitz, *"Negro and White,"* 239.

49. Alice Kessler-Harris, "Organizing the Unorganizable: Three Jewish Women and their Union," in Leab, ed., *The Labor History Reader,* 284–286.

50. Archie Robinson, *George Meany and His Times: A Biography* (New York: Simon and Schuster, 1981), 241.

51. Robinson, *George Meany,* 236.

52. Robinson, *George Meany,* 235.

53. Bert Cochran, *Labor and Communism: The Conflict That Shaped American Unions* (Princeton: Princeton University Press, 1977), 334.

54. Robert Zieger, *American Workers, American Unions* (Baltimore: The Johns Hopkins University Press, 1994 [1986]), 158–159.

55. Harris, *The Right to Manage*, 146.

56. Cochran, *Labor and Communism*, 321.

57. David Brody, "Workplace Contractualism in America: An Historical/Comparative Analysis," Conference on Industrial Democracy, Wilson Center, Washington, D.C., March 1988, 1.

58. Cochran, *Labor and Communism*, 339.

59. Eli Chinoy, *Automobile Workers and the American Dream* (Urbana: University of Illinois Press, 1992 [1955]), 126.

CHAPTER 5

1. Arthur Shostak and David Skocik, *The Air Controllers' Controversy: Lessons from the PATCO Strike* (New York: Human Sciences Press, 1986), 12.

2. Shostak and Skocik, *The Air Controllers' Controversy*, 22.

3. Shostak and Skocik, *The Air Controllers' Controversy*, 79.

4. Shostak and Skocik, *The Air Controllers' Controversy*, 80.

5. Philip Foner, *American Labor and the Indo-China War* (New York: International Publishers, 1971), 25–26.

6. Foner, *American Labor and the Indo-China War*, 62.

7. Foner, *American Labor and the Indo-China War*, 84.

8. Foner, *American Labor and the Indo-China War*, 46.

9. *Washington Star*, in Jeremy Brecher, *Strike!* (San Francisco: Straight Arrow Books, 1972), 273.

10. Harold Meyerson, "Labor Gets Organized," *Los Angeles Weekly* (February 14–20, 1997).

11. Martin Levitt, with Terry Conrow, *Confessions of a Union Buster* (New York: Crown Publishers, 1993), 2.

12. Levitt, with Conrow, *Confessions*, 13.

13. John Sweeney, "Time for a New Contract," *Dissent* (Winter 1997), 35–36.

14. Nelson Lichtenstein, "A Man for Our Season? The Sweeney-Lewis Parallels," *Democratic Left* XXIV (September-October 1996), 5.

15. Martin Kenney and Richard Florida, *Beyond Mass Production: The Japanese System and Its Transfer to the U.S.* (New York: Oxford University Press, 1993), 192–201, 4, 9.

16. Roger Waldinger, Chris Erickson, Ruth Milkman, Daniel J. B. Mitchell, Abel Valenzuela, Kent Wong, and Maurice Zeitlin, "Justice for Janitors," *Dissent* (Winter 1997), 43.

17. Dan LaBotz, ed., *Mexican Labor News,* February 2, 1998, 4.

18. "No More Mourning in America: A Forum," in *The Nation* 267 (September 21, 1998), 20.

19. "No More Mourning in America: A Forum," in *The Nation* 18.

20. Ray Tillman and Michael Cummings, eds., *The Transformation of U.S. Unions: Voices, Visions, and Strategies from the Grassroots* (Boulder, Colo.: Lynne Rienner Publishers, 1999).

INDEX

Abbott, Edith, 8
Adamic, Louis, 52
Adamson Act, 37
AFL-CIO: business unionism, 146–49, 160; civil rights movement, 141–43, 146–47; organizing drives, 168–69; student-labor unity, 177; U.S. foreign policy, 152–53, unity convention, 141
African-American workers, 151: conflict with white workers, 16; Great Depression, 56–57; skilled trades, 143; strike-breakers, 42; union membership, 138; *See also* Pullman porters
AFSCME, 161
air traffic controllers. *See* Professional Air Traffic Controllers Associations (PATCO)
Alifas, N. P., 29
Alliance for Labor Actin (ALA), 160
Amalgamated Association of Iron and Steel Workers, 41
Amalgamated Clothing Workers (ACW), 30, 43, 59, 72Amalgamated Meat Cutters, 107, 109
American Association of Foreign Language Newspapers (AAFLN), 47
American Federation of Labor (AFL): early years, 12–13; factionalism, 107–108; federal locals, 75–76; membership levels, 58–59; organization structure, early, 41; organized crime, 59
American Industrial Union, 30
American Labor Party. *See* labor parties
American Liberty League, 91
American Railway Union (ARU), 8–9
American Woolen Company, 31
American Workers Party, 77
Americanization, 45, 47

Anti-Sweat Shop campaigns, 177
antistrike injunctions, 1920s, 46
arbitration, 22, 117–18, 120, 130
Archibald, Kate, 121
Armour, 103, 107
auto industry, during Great Depression, 53
Auto-Lite, 77–78

Baer, George, 7
Baldwin, Roger, 111
Banking Act. *See* New Deal legislation
bargaining, productivity, 43
Barnett, George, xiii–xiv
Battle of the Overpass, 104
Beck, Dave, 149
Beecher, Henry Ward, 7
Bennett, Harry, 104
Benson, Herman, 177
Beyond Mass Production, 172
Bierne, Joseph, 160
Biggs, Woody, 139
binding arbitration. *See* arbitration
Bittner, Van, 124–25
Black, Hugo, 69
black-white unity. *See* integration, union
bootleg mining, 82
Bosch, Juan. *See* Dominican Republic
boycotts, secondary, 128
Brandeis, Louis, 25, 28–29
Bridges, Harry, 80, 133
Bridgestone tire company, 172
Brooks, George, 149
Brophy, John, 71, 81
Brotherhood of Sleeping Car Porters (BSCP), 48–49, 101–102, 141
Browder, Earl, 88
Brubaker, Howard, 72
building trades, 42–43, 53

building trades, 42–43, 53
Bulcke, Gerry, 77
business unionism, 148
Butler, J. R., 82

Campbell, Harvey, 53
Canwell, albert, 137
capitalism: corporate power, rise of, 4–8;
    labor's role in, 124–25; and the New
    Deal, 92; reform of, 22–23, 100
Carey, James, 81, 136
Carey, Ron, 174
Carlton, C. C., 124
Carnegie, Andrew, 6, 7
Carnegie, Steel, 4
Carpenters Union, 17
Carter, Jimmy, 167
Cassily, Estelle Gornie, 99
Central Labor Union, 79
Chicago police, 4
Chinoy, Eli, 150
Chrysler Corporation, 89–90, 99
Cigar Makers Union, 12
cigar workers strike, 99
Civil Rights Act of 1964, 146–47
civil rights movement, and labor,
    141–144
Clay, William, 158
Clayton Act, 37, 46
Clinton, Bill, 167
closed shop, 119
clothing workers. *See* Amalgamated
    Clothing Workers (ACW)
coal miners. *See* United Mine Workers
Cold War, 131–37
collective bargaining, 70–71, 114–15,
    127
Colorado Coal and Iron Company, 4
Committee for Industrial Organization
    (CIO): 1937 elections, 106; 1944
    elections, 127–28; factionalism,
    107–108; formation of, 86–87;
    integration of, 102, 137–40; Labor's
    Non-Partisan League, 93; Operation
    Dixie, 138–40; United Electrical
    workers, purge of, 135–36
Committee of Industrial Organization
    (CIO): union recognition, at U.S. Steel,
    100–101
Communist Part: ideology, 133;
    membership loss, 136–37; organizing

efforts, 1930s, 60–64; Popular Front, 88;
    racial unity, struggle for, 64; Scotsboro
    Boys, support for, 64; Unemployed
    Councils, 62–64
company spies. *See* espionage, corporate
company unions. *See* employee
    Represented Plans (ERPs)
Confederación de Uniones de Compesinos
    y Obreros Mexicanos, 79. *See also*
    Mexican-American workers
Congress of Industrial Organizations
    (CIO), 3
Conklin, E. G., 54
construction workers. *See* building trades
consumerism, 47, 150
Coolidge, Calvin, 45
corporate paternalism. *See* paternalism,
    corporate
corruption, union, 174
Cotton Code, 82–83
cotton pickers. *See* Southern Tenant
    Farmers' Union (STFU)
Cotton Textile Board, 83
craft unions, 12–13. *See also* skilled labor
Cutting, Bronson, 66

Davis, Richard 17
Debs, Eugene, 8–9, 23, 33, 45
Dellums, C. L., 48–49
Democratic Party: African-American
    support, 94–95; labor alliance with, 93,
    94, 146–47; losses, 1960s, 161
desegregation. *See* civil rights movement
Dies, Martin, 106
dissident union. *See* unions, dissident
dock workers. *See* International
    Longshoreman's Association
Dominican Republic, 152–53
Dubinsky, David, 87, 93, 95, 108, 147
Dunne, Ray, 80–81
Dupont, 170–71

Earle, George, Governor, 95
Easley, Ralph, 25
economy: 1936–1937, 88; 1937 recession,
    105; globalization of, 164–65, 175,
    xiv–xv; mass markets, 26; national, 5.
    See also North American Free Trade
    Agreement (NAFTA)
Edgar Thompson steel strike, 31
Eisenhower, Dwight D., 132

elections: 1936, 90–95; 1937, 106–7;
Franklin D. Roosevelt, 67–68; left-wing
candidates, 45
electoral politics, 35–38, 127–28, 152
Electromation Corporation, 170–71
Ellis, Frank, 80
Emerson, Thomas, 74
employee representation plans (ERPs):
beginnings of, 39–40; Chrysler
Corporation, 89–90; Colorado Fuel and
Iron, 41; General Electric, 90; 1930s, 74;
Roosevelt's support of, 92; U.S. Steel,
89, 101; under Wagner Act, 89–90
Employment Act of 1946, 127
Englehart, Samuel, 143
espionage, corporate, 89
Espionage and Sedition Acts, 39
Ettor, Joe, 32, 33
Evers, Medgar, 142

factionalism, labor, 107–8
factories, automation of. *See* labor,
mechanization of
factory reorganization, turn-of-century, 26
Fahy, Charles, 86
Fair Labor Standards Act, 106
Fair Practices Department (UAW), 145
Farm Equipment Workers, 134
Farnham, Marynia, 144
fatalities, workplace. *See* injuries,
workplace
Federal Aviation Administration (FAA),
155–56
Federal Emergency Relief Act. *See* New
Deal legislation
federal locals (AFL), 75–76
Felski, Marie, 21
Firestone Tire, 172
firings, illegal, 165, 166
Fish, Frederick, 41
Fitzgerald, Frank, 106
flying squadrons. *See* picketing, flying
squadrons
Flynn, Elizabeth Gurley, 32
Food, Tobacco, and Agricultural workers
(FTA), 140
Food Workers Industrial Union, 79
Ford, Ernest, 48
Ford, Henry, 27–28, 52
Ford, Henry, II, 148

Ford Motor Company, 46, 104
foreign-born workers. *See* immigrant
workers
foreign policy, 152-53
Foreman's Association of America, 123–24,
129
Foss, Eugene, 32–33
Foster, William Z., 64
Fountain, Clayton, 60
free trade. *See* North American Free Trade
Agreement (NAFTA)
Freedom Summer campaign, 142
French, V. C., 58
Fruehauf Trailer, 89
Funsten Nut Company strike, 65

garment workers. *See* Amalgamated
Clothing Workers (ACW); Hart,
Schaffner & Marx; International Ladies
Garment Workers Union (ILGWU);
Kuppenhimer company
Gary, Elbert, 46
Gellhorn, Martha, 92
General Cigar strike, 99
General Electric, 58, 74, 90, 105–6, 163
General Motors, 126, 127, 163
Giovaniti, Arturo, 32
global economy. *See* economy,
globalization of
Goldberg, Fannie, 62
Gompers, Samuel, 12, 17, 34, 38
Goodyear Tire, 74
Gorman, Patrick, 84–85, 94
Gould, Jay, 5
Gould, William, 143
government, federal, growth of, 91
Government regulation. *See* legislation,
labor
government workers. *See* public
employees
Graham, Frank, 119
Great Depression, the 52–58: causes of,
68–69; company benefits, cutbacks of,
58; employment, 53; mass
demonstrations, 61, 65; minority
workers, impact on, 55–58; production,
53; psychological impact of, 59–60;
union gains, 71–73; wages, 53. *See also*
New Deal legislation
Great Uprising of 1877, 1–3

Green, William, 65, 102, 107
grievance arbitration. *See* arbitration
Harding, Warren, 45
Hart, Schaffner & Marx, 20–22, 73
Harvard Economic Society, 52
Haymarket protect, 3–4
Haywood, "Big" Bill, 32
Hearst, William Randolph, 91
Hickock, Lorena, 65–66
Hillman, Sidney, 20, 22, 69, 71, 81, 87, 93
Hinckley, Ted, 57–58
Homestead Steel, 14
Hoover, Herbert, 45, 52, 53
Hospital Workers, 11–99, 162–63
Hotel and Restaurant Employees (HRE), 80
House Un-American Activities Committee
    (HUAC), 106, 107–8, 132
Hutchinson, William, 67, 87

immigrant workers, 31, 176: attacks on,
    43–44, 45, 47; conflict with native-born
    workers, 14–15; of the Great
    Depression, 56; Hart, Schaffner & Marx
    strike, 21
Immigration Acts, 1921, 1924, 45
Independent Union of All Workers
    (IUAW), 79, 80
industrial democracy, 125
industrial revolution, effects of, 13
industrial unionism, 12, 86–87
injuries, workplace, 10, 120
Insull, Samuel, 25
integration, union, 102–3: black-white
    unity, 49; white worker's opposition to,
    139. *See also* solidarity
Intercollegiate Socialist Society. *See* Sanger,
    Margaret
International Ladies Garment Workers
    Union (ILGWU), 30, 72, 148
International Longshoreman's Association,
    77
International Union of Electrical Workers
    (IUE), 134, 135–36
International Workers of the World (IWW),
    32–33, 36

Jennings, Paul, 136
Johnson, Lyndon B., 146
Judd, B. T., 139
Justice for Janitors campaign, 173

Kellor, Francis Alice, 47

Keynes, John Maynard, 69
King, Martin Luther Rev., 141, 161
Knights of Labor, 3, 12. *See also* industrial
    unionism
Koubsky, Gazelle, 145
Ku Klux Klan (KKK), 48, 84, 139, 142
Kuppenhimer company, 21. *See also*
    Amalgamated Clothing Workers (ACW)

La Follette, Robert, 88
La Guardia, Fiorello. *See* New Deal
    legislation, Norris-La Guardia Act
labor: mechanization of, 28, 150
Labor Department, 36–37
labor-management cooperation, 25
Labor-Management Relations Act 9LMRA)
    (Taft-Hartley), 128–30
labor parties, 93–95, 152
Labor Party (Britain), 37
labor relations: at Bridgestone, 172;
    government regulation of, 35, 109,
    121–22; labor accommodation, 147–53;
    management rights, 117; postwar
    (WWII), 124–30; quality circles,
    169–70; war-time (WWII), 118–24. *See
    also* legislation, labor
LaFollette, Robert, 45
Lamb, Goldie, 145
Landon, Alf, 91
Lawrence strike of 1912, 31–34
Le Sueur, Meridel, 57, 59–60
League of Revolutionary Black Workers,
    161
legislation, labor: Adamson Act, 37;
    Clayton Act, 37; Labor-Management
    Relations Act (LMRA) (Taft-Hartley),
    128–30; New Deal (*See* New Deal
    legislation); pro-business, 45–46; pro-
    labor, 1964–65, 146–47; Railroad Labor
    Act of 1926, 70; Sherman Antitrust Act,
    37; War Labor Disputes Act (Smith-
    Connally), 127, 129
Levitt, Martin, 166
Lewis, Drew, 155
Lewis, Garfield, 71
Lewis, John L., 67, 71, 87–88, 93, 118–19,
    122
liberal reform. *See* capitalism, reform of
Lincoln, James, 114
living conditions: Depression era, 52–55;
    early 20th century, 10; during World
    War II, 120–21

Lockhart, Alfred, 103
Locomotive Firemen, 141
Long, Huey, 91
Lovestone, Jay, 108
Loyalty Oath, 132
Lundberg, Ferdinand, 144

Mackay Radio (Supreme Court decision), 158
MacMohn, Douglas, 81
Madden, J. Warren, 89
management rights clauses, 117
March, Herb, 102, 103
Marcharia, Kamu, 177
Martin, Homer, 81, 108
mass picketing. *See* picket lines
Massachusetts Committee for a Labor Party. *See* labor parties
Mathews, Otis, 142
McCarthy, Joseph, 132
McDowell, Mary, 34
McKenney, Ruth, 73, 76
Meany, George, 142, 146, 147, 148, 153
meatpackers, 80
Mechanics Educational Society of America (MESA), 79
Mellon, Andrew, 45, 54
membership, union. *See* union membership
Memorial Day massacre, 105
metalworkers, 40
Mexican-American workers, 57. *See also* Confederación de Uniones de Compesinos y Obreros Mexicanos
middle-class, alliance with garment workers, 22
Mileski, Bill 100
Millis, Harry, 118
Mine, Mill, and Smelters, 140
Miners for Democracy, 161–62
mineworkers. *See* United Mine Workers (UMW)
minimum wage, 70, 106
Mitchell, George, 83
Mitchell, John, 25
Modern Management Methods (3M), 165
Moore, Dave, 62, 66
moral capitalism. *See* capitalism, reform of
Morgan, J. P., 6
Mortimer, Wyndham, 62
Mundale, "Red", 96
Murphy, Frank, 95, 98–99, 100, 106

Murray, Philip, 110, 119, 122, 125, 130

NAACP, 138–39
National Association of Manufacturers, 71. *See also* National Civic Federation
National Automobile Chamber of Commerce, 73–74
National Civic Federation, 45. *See also* National Association of Manufacturers
national contracts, 149
National Guard, 77, 84, 163
National Industrial Conference, 41
National (Industrial) Recovery Act. *See* New Deal legislation
National Labor Board. *See* National Labor Relations Board
National Labor Relations Act. *See* New Deal legislation
National Labor Relations Board, 75, 85–86, 109–11
National Recovery Act. *See* Great Depression, New Deal legislation
National War Labor Board (NWLB) (WWII), 38, 119–22
Negro American Labor Council, 160
New Deal: and 1936 elections, 90; and capitalism, 92; labor support of, 93; opposition to, 91. *See also* New Deal legislation
New Deal legislation: Banking Act, 90; Cotton Code, 82–83; Federal Emergency Relief Act, 69; National (Industrial) Recovery Act (NRA), 70–71, 85; National Labor Relations Act (NLRA) (Wagner Act), 85, 101, 125, 128, 165–66; Norris-LaGuardia Act, 68; Social Security Act, 90–91
Newell, Amy, 177
Nixon, E. D., 141
no-strike pledge (WWII), 119
Non-Partisan League (LNPL). *See* labor parties
Norris, George. *See* New Deal legislation, Norris-La Guardia Act
Norris-La Guardia Act. *See* New Deal legislation, Norris-La Guardia Act
North American Free Trade Agreement (NAFTA), 167, 175–76

open shop, 119–20
Operation Dixie, 138–40
Order of Sleeping Car Conductors, 102

organized crime, in American Federation of Labor, 59
Organizer, The (Teamsters), 78
organizing drives: 1933–37, 79, 86–90; packinghouse workers, 102–3; Pullman porters, 101–102; resistance to, 104–5; in steel industry, 100–101
Orlosky, Stanley, 115
over-production, 69–70. *See also* Great Depression, the
Owen, Chandler, 24

Packinghouse Workers Organizing Committee, 102–3, 109, 141
Palmer, A. Mitchell, 43–44
Palmer raids, 44–45
Parks, Rosa, 141
Parsons, Albert, 4
PATCO, 155–58
paternalism, corporate, 46–47
pattern agreements. *See* national contracts
pattern bargaining. *See* national contracts
Peoples' League. *See* labor parties
Perkins, Francis, 85
permanent replacement workers, 158
Pesotta, Rose, 146
picket lines: illegal, 46: flying squadrons, 78, 83; moving, 33; under Taft-Hartley, 128
Pinkerton, 89
political action committees, 127–28
Popular Front, 88
postal workers, 162
Powderly, Terence, 12
preferential shop, 22
Professional Air Traffic Controllers Association (PATCO), 155–58
profits, corporate, 5–6, 121
public employees, 162
Public Works Administration (PWA), 70
Pullman, George, 9
Pullman porters, 48–49

quality circles, 169–70. *See also* labor relations

racial divisions, 47–48, 137–44
railroad corporations: rise of, 4–6
Railroad Trainmen, 141
Railway Labor Act of 1926, 70
Ramsey, Claude, 142

Randolph, A. Philip, 24, 101–2, 141–42; and Pullman porters, 48–49
Ray, Dale, 114
Red scare: post-World War II, 131–37; Red Squad, Detroit, 132; sedition laws of 1920s, 44
regulations. *See* legislation, labor
Reid, Earl, 86
representation, worker. *See* employee representation plans (ERPs); shop committees
Republican Party, 152
Reuther, Walter, 104, 117, 126, 135, 160, 164
right to work laws, 129
Rockefeller, John D., 6
Roosevelt, Franklin D.: attitudes toward, 91–93; conservative politics of, 66–67; election of, 67–68; on Flint sit-down strike, 97–98

Sadlowski, Ed, 162
Saint Elizabeth's Hospital, 165
Sanger, Margaret, 24
scabs. *See* permanent replacement workers
Schwab, Charles, 49, 52, 53–54
scientific management, 26–30, 125. *See also* speed up
Scotsboro Boys, 64
Scoville, John, 114
segregation, 16–18: labor support of, 142–43. *See also* civil rights movement
Service Employees International Union (SEIU), 173–74
Shapiro, Hannah, 20
Shapleigh, Elizabeth, 31
sharecroppers. *See* Southern Tenant Farmers' Union (STFU)
Sherman Antitrust Act, 37
shipping industry strike of 1934, 76–77
shop committees, 39–40, 117
shop governance, 116–18
Shop Management, 27
Sinclair, Upton, 91
sit-down strikes. *See* strikes, sit-down
skilled labor, 12–13: conflict with unskilled workers, 14–15; craft unions, 13–14; of the Great Depression, 57–58; and shop rules, 13–14; shortage, early 20th century, 26
Skoglund, Karl, 80–81
Sloan, Alfred, 117, 126

Smith, Mat, 57, 59
Smith-Connally Act. *See* War Labor
   Disputes Act
Social Darwinism, 6–7
Social Security Act. *See* New Deal
   legislation
socialist movements. *See* Communist
   Party, Socialist Party
Socialist Party: decline of, 137; early years,
   23–25, 37; split of, 44; Unemployed
   Leagues, 62
solidarity, culture of, 11–12, 63–65
solidarity, international, 176–77
solidarity, union: collapse of, 134–36. *See
   also* integration, union
Southern Tenant Farmers' Union (STFU),
   82
speed up, 29, 96. *See also* scientific
   management
Standard Oil Company, 6
steel industry, 53
Steel Workers Organizing Committee
   (SWOC), 100–101. *See also* United
   Steel Workers (USW)
Steelworkers, 4, 120
Stevenson, Bill, 80
stewards, union, 103, 117, 149–50
stockyard workers. *See* Packinghouse
   Workers Organizing Committee
   (PWOC)
Strasser, Adolf, 12
strike violence. *See* violence, strike-related
strikebreakers, absence of, 126–27
Strikes: Carnegie Steel, 4
strikes: 1910 garment strike, 30; 1914
   Westinghouse, 30; Auto-Lite, 77–78;
   "cooling off" court injunctions, 129;
   cotton pickers, 82; General Electric,
   1969–1970, 163; General Motors, 1970,
   163; "hate", 123; Lawrence strike of
   1912, 31–34; postal workers, 1970, 162;
   "quickie," 103; shipping industry, 1934,
   76–77; sit-down, 90, 95–99; steel, 1919,
   40–42; steel, 1959, 147–48; strike wave:
   of 1919, 40, of 1946, 126–27; Teamsters,
   1934, 78; textile workers, 1935, 83–85;
   United Parcel Service, 1997, 174; UPS,
   174; wildcat, 123, 148–49, 163
Sugar, Maurice, 55
Sumner, William Graham, 6
Sweeney, John, 168–69, 176
Swope, Gerard, 58, 105

Taft, William, 38
Taft-Hartley Act. *See* Labor-Management
   Relations Act
Taylor, Frederick, 27, 29, 39
Taylor, George, 120
Taylor, Myron, 100–101
Teamsters, 78, 174
Teamsters for a Decent Contract, 162
Teamsters for a Democratic Union, 162
Terkel, Studs, 52
textile industry, 53, 82–83
textile workers: Lawrence strike of 1912,
   31–34; strike of 1934, 83–85; United
   Textile Workers, 32
Textile Workers Organizing Committee, 84
Thomas, Norm, 92–93
Tobacco Workers Union, 140
Tobin, Dan, 76
Towsen, James, 125
Transit Workers Union, 81
Truman, Harry, 132
Tucker, Rosina, 49
Turnbull, Bill, 90

Unemployed Councils. *See* Communist
   Party
Unemployed Leagues. *See* Socialist Party
Unemployed Commission, California,
   54–55
unfair labor practices (ULPs), 109, 128
union avoidance, 165–66
union-busting, 155–58
union leaders. *See* union organizers
union membership, 151: decline, 1980s,
   158; growth of, 100, 120; whites-only,
   102
union militancy, 115
Union of Needletrades, Industrial and
   Textile Employees (UNITE), 177
union organizers, 79–82, 163–64
union raiding, 134, 140
union structure, centralized, 115–16
Union Summer, 177
unions: city-wide, 117; dissident, 161–62;
   expulsions, 134–36; opposition to, 114
United Auto Workers (UAW): 1936 GM sit-
   down strike, 95–99; 1945 GM strike, 27,
   126; and AFL, 160; civil rights
   movement, 143; factionalism, 108–9;
   membership growth, 120
United Electrical workers (UE), 105–6, 120,
   134, 135–36

United Farm Workers (UFW), 163
United Mine Workers (UMW): 1943 strike,
122; bootleg mining, 82; Depression-
era gains, 71–72; desegregation,
struggle for, 16–17; formation of, 3;
1920s, 42; union organizers, 80
United Packinghouse Workers (UPW), 116,
1434, 145
United Rubber Workers (URW), 172
United Steel Workers (USW), 115–17,
172–73; 240. *See also* Steel Workers
Organizing Committee (SWOC)
United Textile Workers (UTW). *See* textile
workers
unity, labor: black-white, 82; student-labor,
177. *See* solidarity, culture of; unskilled
labor; organization of, 86–87
U.S. Steel, 89

Vann, Robert, 94–95
Vietnam War, 160–61
violence, strike-related, 3–4, 77–78

wage controls, 120
wages, decline in, 1980s–1990s, 159
Wagner, Robert, 67, 68–69, 70, 75, 111
Wagner Act. *See* New Deal legislation,
National Labor Relations Act
walkouts. *See* strikes
Walsh, Frank, 38
War Labor Disputes Act (WWII), 122, 127,
129
Washington, Booker T., 17

Weber, Palmer, 139
Weir, Ernest. *See* Weirton Steel
Weirton Steel, 74, 75
Weisenburger, Walter, 125
Welborn, J. F., 41
welfare, 151–52
welfare state, European, 151
Westinghouse strike, 191–4, 30
Whirl, J. J., 30
White, Horace, 138
white-collar professionals, 171
whites-only membership. *See* union
membership, whites-only
Wilkens, Roy, 147
Wilson, William, 37
Wilson, Woodrow, 36–38
Wobblies. *See* International Workers of the
World (IWW)
women workers: craft unions, 15–16;
discrimination against, 144–46; Great
Depression, 55–56; union auxiliaries,
78, 98; union membership, 145–46
Women's Emergency Brigade (WEB), 98
Wood, Leonard, 45
Woodcock, Leonard, 76
Woolworth's Department store, 99
work teams. *See* quality circles
workplace accidents. *See* injuries
workplace
Works Projects Administration (WPA),
90–91

Zuk, Mary, 94, 100

ABOUT THE AUTHOR

Steve Babson is a labor program specialist at the Labor Studies Center of Wayne State University in Detroit. His previous books include *Working Detroit: The Making of A Union Town* (Wayne State University Press, 1986) and *Building the Union: Skilled Workers and Anglo-Gaelic Immigrants in the Rise of the UAW* (Rutgers University Press, 1991), the latter based on his dissertation. His current work is focused on new production systems and their impact on work and workers in the global auto industry. With Huberto Juárez Núñez, he has coedited a dual-language collection of studies entitled *Confronting Change: Auto Labor and Lean Production in North America/Enfrentando el Cambio: Obreros del Automóvil y Producción Esbelta en América del Norte* (Autonomous University of Puebla, 1998).

Critical Issues in History

Series Editor: Donald T. Critchlow

Editorial Advisory Board

Paula Baker, University of Pittsburgh; Paul Bushkovitch,
Yale University; Jane DeHart, University of California, Santa Barbara;
William Rorabaugh, University of Washington; James Tracy,
University of Minnesota

The British Imperial Century, 1815–1914: A World History Perspective
by Timothy H. Parsons

The Great Encounter of China and the West, 1500–1800
by D.E. Mungello

Europe's Reformations, 1450–1650
by James D. Tracy

The Idea of Capitalism before the Industrial Revolution
by Richard Grassby

The Unfinished Struggle: Turning Points in American Labor History
1877–Present
by Steven Babson

A Concise History of the Crusades
by Thomas F. Madden